We recently lost our beloved pet "Bear," who was not only our best and dearest friend but also the "Vice President of Sunshine" here at Atlantic Publishing. He did not receive a salary but worked tirelessly 24 hours a day to please his parents. Bear was a rescue dog that turned around and showered myself, my wife, Sherri, his grand-

parents Jean, Bob, and Nancy, and every person and animal he met (maybe not rabbits) with friendship and love. He made a lot of people smile every day.

We wanted you to know that a portion of the profits of this book will be donated to The Humane Society of the United States. *–Douglas & Sherri Brown*

The human-animal bond is as old as human history. We cherish our animal companions for their unconditional affection and acceptance. We feel a thrill when we glimpse wild creatures in their natural habitat or in our own backyard.

Unfortunately, the human-animal bond has at times been weakened. Humans have exploited some animal species to the point of extinction.

The Humane Society of the United States makes a difference in the lives of animals here at home and worldwide. The HSUS is dedicated to creating a world where our relationship with animals is guided by compassion. We seek a truly humane society in which animals are respected for their intrinsic value, and where the human-animal bond is strong.

Want to help animals? We have plenty of suggestions. Adopt a pet from a local shelter, join The Humane Society and be a part of

our work to help companion animals and wildlife. You will be funding our educational, legislative, investigative and outreach projects in the U.S. and across the globe.

Or perhaps you'd like to make a memorial donation in honor of a pet, friend or relative? You can through our Kindred Spirits program. And if you'd like to contribute in a more structured way, our Planned Giving Office has suggestions about estate planning, annuities, and even gifts of stock that avoid capital gains taxes.

Maybe you have land that you would like to preserve as a lasting habitat for wildlife. Our Wildlife Land Trust can help you. Perhaps the land you want to share is a backyard— that's enough. Our Urban Wildlife Sanctuary Program will show you how to create a habitat for your wild neighbors.

So you see, it's easy to help animals. And The HSUS is here to help.

THE HUMANE SOCIETY
OF THE UNITED STATES.

2100 L Street NW • Washington, DC 20037 • 2(

www.hsus.org

D1711637

Table of Contents

  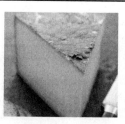 

Chapter 9: Man (and Woman) Cannot Live by Cheese Alone

Chapter 10: Sharing the Bounty: Marketing Your Cheese   305

Chapter 11: Getting Connected   313

Glossary   321

Bibliography   327

Author Biography   330

Index   333

Introduction

Beyond Plastic-Wrapped Slices — Making Cheese at Home

If you are reading this book, you may possess basic kitchen skills or even exceptional culinary abilities. Perhaps you can roast a turkey, bake the perfect loaf of bread, or even turn out four-dozen gingerbread men at 3 a.m., each one with the same number of cinnamon buttons. However, it is likely you have never thought about making cheese. For the average cook, making homemade cheese is something that "Ma" Ingalls did in *Little House on the Prairie* or something organic farmers do somewhere out in Oregon.

Even the bravest of cooks might ask, "Why should I make cheese at home?" After all, even the smallest grocery store has a good selection of favorites, and many gourmet shops, specialty catalogues, and organic markets offer an even wider selection of cheeses for every taste. However, homemade cheese is not just about flavor, although no cheese will ever taste as good as a wedge of home-aged cheddar or a mound of fluffy, hand-crafted cream cheese flavored with fresh herbs. It is also not just about nutrition, even though it is true that with home-produced cheese, you can control the amount of salt, preservatives, and artificial colors in your cheese. It is about achievement — the feeling you get when you conquer a task you believed was impossible. This book will help even the rookie cook see that making cheese is like making any other recipe. With the right ingredients,

equipment, directions, and a bit of patience, a dedicated cook can turn out delicious, nutritious cheese for personal enjoyment or to share with family, friends, and even for the marketplace.

The book is designed to take you on a step-by-step journey into the world of cheese, beginning with its history and most famous flavors. You will then learn all about the various types of milk — cow's, goat's, and sheep's — which make very different, yet equally appealing cheeses. The book includes a mini chemistry lesson in order to understand how rennet, cultures, and other starters give cheese its flavor, aroma, and texture. This book will help you assemble the necessary equipment, much of which can be found in any well-stocked kitchen. Once these preliminary steps are completed, and you understand how the ingredients work with each other, we will begin to create cheese at home.

A selection of simple recipes is included for making fresh cheeses such as cream cheese, cottage cheese, and ricotta, as well as recipes for non-cheese dairy delights such as butter, yogurt, and sour cream. After successfully making soft, fresh cheeses, it is time to move on to slightly more complicated, but still manageable, recipes for firmer cheeses. These include Colby, provolone, Monterey Jack, and mozzarella. Finally, once you master the mystery of basic cheeses, the book provides recipes for the most complex gourmet cheeses like Brie, aged cheddar, Camembert, Muenster, Limburger, and even perfectly ripened blue cheeses. Additional recipes are included that incorporate homemade cheeses into appetizers, soups, entrees, and desserts. The book also provides ideas on how to match cheese with wine and other foods, a list of suppliers for equipment and materials, and information on how to sell cheeses, from tax laws and health codes to packaging and marketing. Throughout the book, you will also read about other cheese makers, both hobbyist and professional, who offer tips and insight for making the perfect cheese.

So come along and explore the wondrous world of homemade cheese. Learn the skills that will bring one of mankind's oldest foods into your kitchen.

Chapter One

It's a Cheese World After All

One spring morning about 3,000 years ago, a merchant got ready for a journey to cross part of the Arabian Desert, packing food and water for both himself and his horse. Just before he was ready to leave, his wife came out and handed him a drinking bag made from the stomach of a lamb. Inside was fresh milk from one of their goats.

The man rode all day in the hot sun, rocking back and forth with his horse's gait. He ate the food and water he brought along, but he forgot about the bag full of milk. When he stopped for the night, the merchant finally noticed the bag looped over the pommel of his horse's saddle, where it had been all day.

The man assumed that the milk would be spoiled, but he opened the bag anyway. Much to his surprise, the bag was full of a thin, sharp-tasting, but refreshing liquid, and floating in this liquid were solid lumps. Out of curiosity, the man speared one of the lumps with his knife and tasted it. The creamy texture and tangy flavor pleased his palate, and he knew he had made a wonderful discovery. When he returned home, he experimented with the ingredients until he could reproduce the recipe. He soon began to sell the product across the region, and others followed suit.

Was this the dawn of the Age of Cheese? It makes a wonderful tale, but there is no evidence this legend has any basis. However, it does contain all of the elements needed to make cheese: milk, **rennet** — a chemical found in the stomach lining of lambs and other animals — heat, and motion to produce the **curds** that become cheese.

The Real History of Cheese

However cheese came to be, it is believed to have been discovered sometime after agriculture was invented. As soon as people began domesticating animals for milk, they started making products such as butter, yogurt, and cheese. Cheese is mentioned several times in the Old Testament, and cheese-filled jars were left in Egyptian tombs so their owners could enjoy cheese in the afterlife. The Greek writer Homer mentioned cheese-production occurring in the mountain caves of ancient Greece from the milk of sheep and goats. Some sources say it was probably feta, which is still crafted and enjoyed today. Roman soldiers relied on cheese as a major part of their diet, while Roman gourmets created and enjoyed a wide variety of cheeses. Cheese and fruit platters were served to Caesar, Augustus, and Nero, while ordinary Romans took a snack of cheese and bread with them on their day trips to the Coliseum. As the Romans conquered much of what is now Europe, they took along their favorite recipes and the science behind making cheese. It is not surprising that areas that saw heavy Roman occupation, such as France and Britain, also became great cheese-producing regions.

As the Roman Empire fell and the Middle Ages began, cheese was still an important commodity. In an agrarian, or farm-based, economy milk from cows, sheep, or goats was fresh and plentiful. While fresh milk goes bad within a day or so, especially without the benefit of modern refrigeration, properly treated cheeses can be stored for months. In addition, cheese making is a skill that does not require excessive muscle or many pairs of hands. While the peasant farmer was out plowing or harvesting, his wife and daughters could tend to and milk the dairy animals and turn the results into cheese. Finally, cheese is both an excellent and renewable source of protein. Once a cow is killed and eaten, the food chain comes to an end. However, most dairy animals give milk for much of the year. Whenever people had extra milk available, they learned to make it into cheese to add important nutrition and delicious variety to their diets.

Christianity was also an agent in the advancement of cheese. Unlike pork and beef, cheese is often a permitted food during Lent and other times of fasting. In addition, many monasteries throughout Europe became famous for their cheeses, as the monks and nuns had the necessary flocks, equipment, knowledge, and time to devote to creating cheese. Even today, some of the world's most famous cheeses, including the French Port du Salut and the Canadian Oka, are still made by monks following centuries-old traditions and recipes. There is even a prize-winning American Gouda being made by nuns in the state of Virginia.

When Europeans came to America, the knowledge of how to make cheese traveled with them. It is not surprising that many of the New World's earliest cheese makers were located in what is now New England. The colonists, mostly English farmers, used the abundant pasturelands to raise dairy herds and create cheese from cherished family recipes. British favorites such as cheddar were quickly produced in New England and became popular across the country. As settlers began to travel westward, their dairy animals and cheese-making skills went with them, until nearly every state had its own local cheese producers. Today, there are probably just as many cheese makers in Oregon as there are in Vermont, and California — the nation's number one dairy state — may soon overtake Wisconsin as the nation's number one cheese producer.

The arrival of the Industrial Revolution in the early 19th century changed all aspects of agriculture, including cheese making. Factories replaced farm kitchens, and giant machines replaced home cheese presses. Today, major companies make and ship millions of pounds of cheese to outlets all over the world. In 2008, Kraft Foods alone sold more than $7.5 billion worth of cheese.

The terms "big wheel" or "big cheese" originally referred to people who were wealthy enough to purchase a whole wheel of cheese.

The world's most famous cheeses

No one knows for sure how many varieties of cheese exist in the world today because many locally made cheeses are only created and consumed in their home environment. However, there are thousands of cheeses recognized worldwide, including cheeses from Africa, India, China, and Tibet. However, to most American consumers, the fine cheeses of Europe and Great Britain are the most recognizable, along with cheeses that are uniquely American in character. The world's best-known cheeses include the following:

Asiago: This Italian cow's milk cheese comes in two basic types: fresh and aged. Fresh Asiago is a firm, slightly sweet, and nutty-flavored cheese, which is usually served with bread or crackers as a snack. Aged Asiago, also called Asiago d'Allevo, is a much drier-textured cheese, usually grated, and used in recipes.

Brie: This semi-soft, round French cheese, with its edible rind, is a national favorite in France and the United States. It is often spread on crusty bread or baked in a pastry, so the center is warm and runny.

Camembert: This is another semi-soft French cheese with an edible rind. However, true Camembert is made from raw cow's milk, so it does not travel well and is not available in the United States. As is true for many European cheeses, several versions of "Camembert" are made and marketed in the United States, but true Camembert lovers recognize only the Camembert cheese made from raw milk in the French province of Normandy.

Cheddar: To many people, when you say "cheese," they think "cheddar." The first cheddars were English cheeses, but many fine types of cheddar are made in the United States today. Cheddar is made with a process called "cheddaring," where the curds are broken up and mixed with salt before the cheese is pressed and aged. Cheddar is a firm slicing cheese that can come in shades of white and yellow and, depending on how long it is aged, can be very mild or sharp. Mild cheddar has a higher moisture content and silkier texture, while aged cheddar is drier and crumbles more easily.

Colby: This cheese is uniquely American. It is similar in color and texture to cheddar, but it usually has a milder flavor and contains a bit more moisture than most cheddars. It is a favorite snacking and sandwich cheese.

Edam: This round, red-waxed ball of cheese is famous in the Netherlands, its original home. Edam is cream-colored and firm-textured with a mild, creamy flavor. It can also be found flavored with caraway seeds. Like many other European cheeses, Edam is now made in the United States as well.

Feta: Probably the best-known Greek cheese, feta is a brine-cured cheese with a semi-firm, crumbly texture. Feta was originally made with goat's and sheep's milk, but today, most commercially produced feta is made from cow's milk. Feta is often used in salads and recipes. Due to its crumbly nature, it is not a particularly good slicing cheese.

Gorgonzola: Like many cheeses, this Italian blue cheese takes its name from the region in which it was first produced. Unlike Roquefort, Gorgonzola is a cow's milk cheese. It has a very high fat content, almost 50 percent, and its veins are blue or green. The cheese itself has a creamy, almost sweet flavor, but the veins have the "bite" associated with blue cheese.

Gouda: This is another cheese from our Dutch friends. Like Edam, Gouda is a firm, waxed cheese. It slices well for sandwiches and snacks, and it also melts in the fondue pot. However, Gouda is often aged to be sharper than Edam, and some varieties of Gouda are smoked over apple wood or cherry, giving them a delicate smoky flavor.

Limburger: This washed rind cheese has long been famous for its pungent odor. It was originally made in the Limburg region of Germany. Today, Limburger is also made in one factory in Monroe, Wisconsin. Limburger's smell is due to the bacteria that inhabits its rind. As the cheese ages, the smell gets stronger, and the cheese becomes soft enough to spread instead of crumbly. People who love Limburger describe it as addictive. People who hate it say it smells like unwashed feet. Limburger is eaten as a snack cheese or in a sandwich. The classic Limburger sandwich consists of rye bread, Limburger, mustard, and sliced onions.

Monterey Jack: Like Colby, this is an American original, first produced near the town of Monterey in what is now California. Accounts vary as to the "inventor" of this cow's milk cheese, but it is probably an offshoot of a mild Spanish cheese first made by Franciscan monks who immigrated to California. Monterey Jack is used as a snack, on sandwiches, and in recipes, notably in many Tex-Mex dishes. The mild flavor of the cheese balances the hot spices of the dishes.

Mozzarella: Thanks to its popularity in Italian-American dishes such as pizza, mozzarella may be the most easily recognized cheese on this list. The original Italian mozzarella is made from water buffalo's milk, but most of the mozzarella consumed today comes from cow's milk. It can be sliced or shredded, eaten as a snack, or used in recipes. It is usually mild in flavor, but some aged and smoked mozzarellas have a sharper taste.

Mascarpone: This incredibly rich — 60 percent to 75 percent butterfat — cream cheese is most often used in dessert recipes such as tiramisu and cheesecakes, but it is also eaten fresh, either with fruit or with honey. It was originally created in Italy, but is now made in many countries, including the United States. Because it is a fresh cheese with no rennet or other additives, it must be consumed within a few days of its creation.

Paneer: Sometimes spelled "panir," this Indian cheese is a fresh curd cheese made without the addition of rennet. It is made by adding lemon juice, vinegar, or citric acid to the milk mixture. The resulting cheese is pressed until firm and eaten in salads, grilled, pan-fried, or even barbequed.

Parmesan: Like mozzarella, this Italian cheese is well-known in the United States due to its use in dishes such as pizza and pasta. The traditional Italian Parmesan is often called Parmigiano-Reggiano, named for the region where it is still produced. It is a cow's milk cheese that is usually aged until it becomes quite dry in texture, with a salty, sharp flavor. However, like many other European cheeses, American companies also produce their own versions of "Parmesan" cheese. Parmesan is a hard cheese, usually grated and used in recipes.

Provolone: This Italian cheese is one of the *pasta filata*, or spun paste, family of cheeses, produced through a kneading process that removes moisture and makes the cheese elastic in texture. It is a cow's milk cheese and can be eaten fresh or aged. The longer provolone is aged, the sharper the flavor. Provolone is usually eaten as a snack cheese, and it is also used in many Italian recipes.

Ricotta: Originally made in Italy, traditional ricotta is made from **whey**, the liquid that is pressed or squeezed from the milk mixture during the cheese-making process. Ricotta comes in soft curds, somewhat like cottage cheese in its texture. Because it is a fresh cheese with no additives, it must be made and used quickly. Most ricotta is used in recipes, especially lasagna and other pasta dishes and desserts such as cheesecake.

Romano: Like its cousin Parmesan, Romano is a hard grating cheese, usually used in Italian recipes. True Romano is made from sheep's milk, and it tends to be sharper in flavor than Parmesan. In addition to being sharp, Romano is quite salty.

Roquefort: Probably the most famous blue cheese in the world, true Roquefort can only be made in limestone caves found in one region in France. Created with sheep's milk, Roquefort gets its distinctive blue "veins" from ***Penicillium roque-forti***, a specific mold that is a distant cousin of the penicillin we use to cure illness. Roquefort is eaten mainly as a snack with bread and fruit. Genuine French Roquefort commands a premium price, $25 to $30 per pound from most cheese sellers. In the United States, it is frequently used as an ingredient in premium blue cheese salad dressings at fine restaurants. The Kraft Corporation also sells a salad dressing that they bill as "made with genuine Roquefort cheese."

Stilton: This British cheese is famous for its sharp and complex flavor. It is a blue cheese, made by introducing mold spores into the ripening cheese. It is made in only three counties in all of England and is one of only 17 British products to be granted a "protected designation of origin" status by the European Commission. Stilton is eaten as a snack cheese and is used in many recipes, including salads, omelets, and sauces.

Cheese Myth:

The moon is made from Swiss cheese.

Fact: Nearly everyone heard this story at some point in childhood. It is hard to know how the story got started, except that the moon's craters resemble the "holes" found in Swiss cheese. Many popular cartoons portray the moon as a giant round of cheese. Thanks to the moon mission in 1968, it can now be stated with certainty that it is not an edible product of dairy.

Cheese Making Today

Despite the spread of what we might call corporate cheese, artisan — or handmade cheese — is available all over the world. There are thousands of small producers, hobby farmers, and food enthusiasts who value the taste, nutrition, and quality of cheese made in small batches with few tools and fewer artificial chemicals. These fine cheeses are available through mail order and Internet sites, in gourmet and organic shops, and at farmer's markets.

Why Make Cheese?

The flavor factor

So if there are so many cheeses available, why would anyone want to make cheese at home? Perhaps the best reason is also the simplest. Homemade cheese has the best taste. While some cheeses travel well, many do not, and some of the cheeses available in your local market had to travel a long way to reach your table. If cheese is improperly aged or stored, it can lose much of its flavor. Some commercial cheeses are not aged long enough to fully develop their flavor. There is nothing more disappointing that an "aged" cheddar that tastes like a processed cheese slice.

The fresh factor

Some of the best fresh cheeses should be created and consumed within a day or two. Fresh cream, cottage, and farmer's cheeses have a delicacy of flavor that can be enjoyed most by coming directly from the kitchen to your table. As you learn to make cheese, you can also customize the flavor to suit your palate. Perhaps you want a cheese with a stronger dill flavor than the local producer provides, or maybe you crave the fire of habanero peppers in your Monterey Jack.

The quality quest

Food safety is another reason to make your own cheese. Maybe you want to use your own pesticide-free herbs in your cheese, or you have a source for milk that is higher in butterfat and lower in growth hormones and antibiotics than commercially produced milk. You may even have someone in your house that is lactose-intolerant, and you want to produce cheese he or she can actually eat. With the right recipe, this is possible.

The economic aspect

Finally, there is the economic aspect, especially if you are already raising dairy animals. While not every hobbyist cheese maker becomes a professional, most professional cheese makers started out as hobbyists. There is an ever-growing market for quality, handcrafted cheese, and you may find there is a ready market in your area for your cheesy creations. At the very least, you can have the satisfaction of knowing that if there ever is a cheese shortage, you and your family will not have to suffer.

Chapter Two

The Cheese Menu

The Categories

As mentioned in Chapter 1, there are as many types of cheese as there are cheese makers. Some types, such as cheddar, are known all over the world. Others might only be produced in a small village dairy. However, nearly all cheeses can be divided into a few basic categories, anywhere from three to 15, depending on which expert you consult. In this book, the cheeses are divided into six broad categories. The fun for a true cheese enthusiast is the variations within these categories:

1. Fresh cheeses

These cheeses are exactly what they claim to be: freshly made with very few additives. Because fresh cheeses are not aged or ripened, most have a very mild flavor and a soft, creamy texture. While some will keep for a week or so in the refrigerator, most fresh cheeses need to be created and consumed quickly. It is because of few ingredients and simple techniques that fresh cheeses are perhaps the best bet for the beginning cheese maker. Popular fresh cheeses include cream cheese, farmer's cheese, feta cheese, cottage cheese, and fromage blanc.

2. Semi-soft cheeses, with and without washed rinds

These cheeses are still soft, but they tend to be a bit firmer than their fresh cousins. Their flavors also vary more because they are treated to produce a **rind**, which is an edible coating on the outside of the cheese. The cheeses ripen as the rind does, which gives them richer, more complex flavors. The longer cheeses ripen, the deeper the flavor becomes. In addition, many rinds are washed in flavorful ingredients such as salt **brine**, cider, wine, or brandy, which add distinct flavors to the taste of the cheese. Some rinds are known as **blooming rinds** and are created when the cheese is treated with natural bacteria to help the rinds develop. Other cheeses in this category have what are called **washed rinds**. These rinds occur when the ripening cheese is repeatedly washed in a solution such as brine (salt and water), wine, beer, or cider. Washed rinds are very important to the development of flavor in these cheeses, as they provide a protective coating allowing the cheese inside to ripen without spoiling, thereby deepening the flavor of the final product. The most famous **blooming rind cheeses** include two French classics, Camembert and Brie. **Washed-rind cheeses** include Muenster, Gruyère, brick, and Limburger.

3. Semi-firm or semi-hard cheeses

This is perhaps the largest category of cheeses. These varieties are created from cut and pressed curds. They are made from all types of milk, and they feature flavors from mild to wild. Some are aged for only a few days, others for a month or longer. While making cheeses in this category takes time, they are not usually difficult to produce. Some of the best-known semi-hard cheeses are Colby, Monterey Jack, Gouda, and Edam.

4. Pasta filata (spun paste) cheeses

Some experts include these cheeses in the semi-firm category, but they have one important difference in their production: these cheeses have spun or pulled filaments that must be worked by hand in order for the finished cheese to possess its unique "springy" texture. These cheeses require careful handling so the pliant texture does not become rubbery. The most famous *pasta filata* cheeses are mozzarella and provolone.

5. Hard or aged cheeses

These cheeses are among the most time-consuming for the cheese maker because they must be aged for months in order to fully develop their distinct, robust flavor and texture. The longer these cheeses are aged, the sharper and drier they become. Like semi-firm cheeses, these recipes involve pressed and aged curds. The best-known hard cheeses include most cheddars, Swiss, Parmesan, and Romano.

6. Blue cheeses

The first blue cheese was supposedly created by accident when a French shepherd boy left his lunch bag containing a piece of fresh cheese inside a cave in the Roquefort region of France. Before he had a chance to retrieve his lunch, a pack of wolves tried to make a lunch of his sheep. He fought off the wolves and moved his flock, forgetting about his stored lunch. When he finally retrieved the sack some weeks later, mold had worked its way into the sheep's milk cheese, giving it veins of rich flavor. Thus, Roquefort was born, the cheese often referred to as, "the king of cheese and cheese of kings."

Perhaps fittingly, the "king of cheese" is the most difficult for the home cheese maker to produce. First, the fresh cheese must be cooked and placed into a mold. Then, *Pencillium roqueforti*, a special blue mold, must be introduced. The cheese must be aged in a perfect cold, damp environment for at least three months, and the developing mold must be scraped and smeared into the cheese every 20 to 30 days. Finally, the cheese is wrapped and aged in a slightly less cold refrigerator for up to six months. It is indeed a labor of love, but one that the true blue cheese aficionado may be willing to undertake. In addition to Roquefort, popular blue cheeses include Stilton and Gorgonzola.

The "other" cheeses

Some people might argue that there is yet another category of cheese. This is the type first eaten by many of us, usually in the form of a grilled cheese sandwich with a cup of tomato soup on the side. This is, of course, pasteurized processed cheese, the cheese that comes in loafs, jars, cans, and plastic-wrapped slices. It is the most recent cheese category, causing a great debate. The true gourmet chef would not consider pasteurized processed cheese a true category of cheese.

Pasteurized processed cheese is cheese — of a sort. It was first invented in Switzerland, but the U.S. patent for the process was granted to James L. Kraft in 1916. His company, Kraft Foods, went on to create the processed cheese single in 1950 — a recognizable part of the sandwich world today. Kraft Foods is still the world's largest producer of pasteurized processed cheese foods. They make everything from plastic-wrapped singles to individually packed trays of spreads and crackers, complete with a tiny plastic knife for spreading.

Pasteurized processed cheese is usually created from a mixture of other cheeses, often "scraps" of cheese that result when regular cheeses are cut into wheels or blocks for sale. These scraps are mixed with **emulsifiers**, additives that allow these scraps to bond, creating a mixture that gives the cheese its smooth, melting quality. Other additives, including salt, food coloring, and whey or other dairy by-products are added before the mixture is heated and packaged. Most processed cheeses have a flavor similar to cheddar, and the flavor can range from sharp to mild.

Processed cheese has some obvious benefits over natural cheeses. First, it melts superbly, which is not always true of other types of cheese. Second, it has a much longer shelf life than most traditional cheeses. A can of aerosol snack cheese will last almost indefinitely, and it does not need refrigeration. On the other hand, processed cheeses are usually higher in salt and preservatives than their "natural" cousins, so there is a definite trade-off between health and convenience.

If you wish to use processed cheese, it is helpful to understand the different terms surrounding this product. The Federal Food and Drug Administration created a set of specific definitions that cover processed cheese products:

- **Pasteurized processed cheese:** This product must be 100 percent cheese, with no vegetable oil or other fillers. The best-known pasteurized processed cheese is the plastic-wrapped slice, such as Kraft Singles.

- **Pasteurized processed cheese food:** It must contain at least 51 percent cheese. The snack cheese in an aerosol can is probably the most familiar form of this product.

- **Pasteurized processed cheese product:** This is basically cheese-flavored mystery product. Under the FDA rules, because it contains less than 51 percent cheese, it cannot be advertised as cheese. Many "cheese-flavored" cracker sandwiches contain this product.

- **Pasteurized processed cheese spread:** This is that yummy stuff that comes in the cans and jars. Again, it is not exactly cheese. Perhaps the best-known example of this is Velveeta, the bright yellow, loaf-shaped product often melted to make nachos or macaroni and cheese. Velveeta and other cheese spreads are highly stable; they will not spoil or go bad. At the same time, they are also high in fat and salt and lower in nutritional value than real cheese.

While we are discussing definitions, this may be a good time to talk about cheese names. In Europe, many types of cheeses — most notably Roquefort, Gorgonzola, and Pecorino Romano — are protected by trade and copyright agreements between countries. Thus, you may buy many types of blue cheese in France, but if you buy a cheese labeled "Roquefort," that cheese must come from the Roquefort region; it must be manufactured, aged, and packaged by the only companies allowed to use the Roquefort name. However, the American government never signed the agreements that protect specific cheese names; so many American cheese makers produce and sell "Roquefort" cheese that has no connection to France, knowing that the Roquefort name stands for quality blue cheese, even to people who know little about cheeses. The cheese may be just as tasty, but the true cheese purist would never call such a cheese "Roquefort."

Gas bubbles, which expand during the aging process, make the holes in Swiss cheese. The longer Swiss cheese is aged, the more large holes it will develop.

Nutritional Value of Cheese

Is cheese good for you? That probably depends on whom you ask. A cheese company's representative would naturally say, "Yes." On the other hand, your cardiologist might say, "No." However, some basic nutrition facts about cheese are not in dispute.

- Cheese is an excellent source of protein. The amount of protein people should consume varies depending on gender, age, weight, and physical condition, but a range of 40 to 70 grams is recommended for most people. A one-ounce serving of cheese provides 7 grams of an adult's recommended daily requirement of this important nutrient.

- Cheese, like all milk products, is also an outstanding source of calcium. Studies regularly claim that many children and adults in the United States are not getting their needed calcium. One tasty way to boost your calcium intake is by adding cheese to your diet. Just one ounce of almost any cheese provides up to 20 percent of the recommended daily amount of calcium, which is 1,000 milligrams for most adults, and many people eat more than one ounce.

- Cheese is low in carbohydrates. Some experts believe that diets high in protein and low in carbohydrates help burn fat.

- Many cheeses are also rich in vitamins and minerals, including Vitamin B, magnesium, and phosphorus.

So, if cheese is such a wonder food, why is it often given a bad rap? Unfortunately, there are some drawbacks to cheese that the health-conscious person must consider.

- Cheese can be high in fat. Some cheeses, such as part-skim mozzarella and string cheese, are quite low in fat, but many of the richest, most satisfying varieties, including cream cheeses, cheddar, and blue cheese, contain significant amounts of saturated fat and cholesterol.

- Cheese is salty. Again, not every cheese is high in sodium, but many are, especially cheddars and blue cheeses.

- Cheese is high in calories. While low-fat cheeses average about 70 calories per ounce, hard cheeses, including cheddar, and rich, creamy cheeses such as Brie average 110 to 130 calories per ounce. Again, most people do not eat just a once ounce serving of cheese, which is about the size of a pair of dice.

So what is a cheese lover to do? First, if you are healthy, relax. Most doctors would agree that moderate consumption of cheese can be part of a healthy diet. However, if you are overweight or have high blood pressure, high cholesterol, or any other health problem, you should talk to your doctor or a dietitian about what types of cheese will benefit your diet. With limitless possibilities for different cheese varieties, there are bound to be some types that will work for you. Also, health concerns are among the best reasons to make your own cheese because you can learn to control nutritional content of your cheese instead of relying on a giant corporation to do it for you. For example, while a few cheeses, such as Brie and the blue cheese family absolutely require the use of whole milk, many other varieties can be made with low-fat milk. In addition, the amount of salt used in the recipes in this book are up to half as much as the sodium levels found in commercial cheeses and processed cheese products. Because you are making the cheese fresh and aging it to your taste, it does not need the massive amount of salt required to make cheese shelf-stable, to travel cross-country, or be stored in warehouses for weeks at a time.

Cheese Myth:

If you want to catch a mouse, bait the trap with cheese.

Facr: Actually, cartoon rodents to the contrary, mice are not that fond of cheese. They will eat it, as they will eat many human foods, but if you really want to attract a mouse to a trap, bait it with peanut butter, chocolate, or bacon instead of Brie, Swiss, or cheddar.

A Note to the Lactose Intolerant

A significant percentage of the population is **lactose intolerant**. Lactose, also called milk sugar, is a natural ingredient found in milk and milk products. The largest concentration of lactose is found in whey. People who are lactose intolerant have difficulty digesting milk and milk products and may suffer from gas, bloating, and diarrhea. Obviously, this is a huge hurdle to overcome in order to enjoy cheese. However, the gates of Cheeseland are not necessarily closed to those with lactose intolerance. If you or someone you feed suffers from this condition, try these tips:

- **Enjoy cheeses made with goat's milk.** For most people, goat's milk produces far fewer symptoms of lactose intolerance than the same products made from cow's milk because the proteins in goat's milk are more easily broken down in the digestive system.

- **Eat hard, aged cheeses such as cheddar.** Soft cheeses, which contain more whey, have a higher concentration of lactose than hard cheeses, so they produce more symptoms.

- **Try eating yogurt-based cheeses.** There are recipes for yogurt-based cheeses included in this book. Yogurt contains bacteria, which aids in digestion and may help with the symptoms suffered by the lactose intolerant.

- **Add one of the commercial preparations designed to help lactose intolerance, such as Lactaid, before you make a batch of cheese.** Put this additive directly in the milk, and let it be absorbed at least 24 hours before making the cheese. The milk is slightly sweeter when this type of additive is used, but the quality of the final product should be comparable to untreated milk, as well as much easier for the sensitive person to digest.

- **Eat cheese with other foods, especially starches.** Breads and crackers seem to absorb much of the lactose in dairy products such as cheese, and as a result, many people who suffer from lactose intolerance find their symptoms are reduced when starches and cheese are eaten together.

Now that we have explored types of cheeses and the benefits of each, it is time to meet the main ingredient, the one element that all cheeses have in common: milk.

Chapter Three

Milk: Everything the Cheese Maker Needs to Know About the Primary Ingredient

Even schoolchildren know the primary ingredient in any cheese is milk. Mammals, of course, produce milk. In theory, milk from any animal could be used in cheese making, and in some parts of the world, milk from "exotic" creatures such as reindeer and yaks is, indeed, turned into cheese. However, most cheeses are made from cow's, goat's, or sheep's milk, or a mixture of all three.

The Dairy Cow and Cow's Milk Cheeses

Here in the United States, the cow is queen of the dairy world. There are approximately 9 million dairy cows on 60,000 farms in the United States, producing almost 21 billion gallons of milk per year. There are six types of dairy cows: Holstein-Friesian, Jersey, Guernsey, Brown Swiss, Ayrshire, and Milking Shorthorn. Holsteins are the highest-producing breed of dairy cow, but true dairy lovers claim Jersey cows give the most delicious milk. Most cheeses can be made with cow's milk. Familiar cow's milk cheeses include cheddar, Colby, mozzarella, and Monterey Jack.

The Dairy Goat and Goat's Milk Cheeses

While the United States relies on cows, the rest of world looks to goats to provide most of their dairy needs. There are valid reasons why dairy goats are preferred

instead of dairy cows. Goats are hardier than cows; they can thrive in tougher terrain and are much more disease-resistant than cows. Dairy goats also require less pasture and they can survive on much lower-quality forage. They are cheaper to buy, cheaper to own, and easier to handle because they weigh only one-tenth of the weight of the average Holstein. Goat's milk is also naturally homogenized and lower in lactose, which is good news for the lactose intolerant. Additionally, because the proteins in goat's milk are smaller than those in cow's milk, it is easier for many people to digest. Many milk aficionados find that goat's milk is much richer and creamier-tasting than cow's milk. In addition, a 4-ounce serving of goat's milk has 13 percent more calcium, 25 percent more vitamin B-6, and 47 percent more vitamin A than the same size serving of cow's milk. At one time, it was difficult to find goat's milk in the United States, but today there are many small goat farms in almost every state, and goat's milk is becoming more readily available at gourmet, health food, and organic stores, as well as farmer's markets.

The six breeds of dairy goats recognized by the American Dairy Goat Association are:

- **The Alpine:** As their name indicates, these goats originally came from the French, Swiss, and German Alps. These goats are fairly large and come in many colors. They produce more milk on average than any other breed.

- **LaMancha:** This goat was first bred in the United States. It is a cross between a short-eared Spanish goat and several breeds of Swiss goats. Its most outstanding characteristic is its tiny "elf" ears.

- **Nubian:** This goat originally came from the Far East. It does not give as much milk at the Alpine, but it is known for the high quality, high fat milk it produces.

- **Oberhasli:** Like the Nubian, this fawn-colored goat produces less milk than some other breeds, but its milk has a high fat content, which makes it ideal for many types of cheese production.

- **Saanen:** This goat is also an excellent milk producer and, as a bred, is very gentle and easy to handle. It is sometimes called "the living marshmallow" for its placid nature.

- **Toggenburg**: These brown, medium size goats are good but not outstanding milk producers. They are very sturdy and adapt well to different environments.

Famous goat's milk cheeses include feta, Halloumi, and chèvre. However, recipes for many cheeses that are normally made with cow's milk can be adapted for goat's milk. These include cream cheese, ricotta, and cheddar. Even blue cheese, Brie, and Gouda can be made from goat's milk. Goat's milk also makes delicious butter and yogurt.

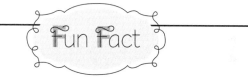

Mighty Mouse, the cartoon superhero, is vulnerable to only one substance: Limburger cheese. It acts on him the way kryptonite affects Superman.

The Dairy Ewe and Sheep's Milk Cheeses

A third form of dairy production comes from sheep's milk. Sheep are considered to be the first animals domesticated for their milk, along with their wool. Like goats, sheep require less space and less food than cows, and they can graze on a wider range of plants. Sheep's milk is also ideal for both yogurt and cheese making because it is higher in fat and milk solids than cow's milk. For this reason, it takes almost half as much sheep's milk than cow's milk to produce a pound of cheese. In addition, the flavor of sheep's milk lends itself to cheese making, and several of the world's most famous cheeses are made with sheep's milk, including Roquefort, ricotta, Pecorino Romano, and Manchego. A Spanish proverb observes, "Ewes (female sheep) for cheese, goats for milk, cows for butter."

The disadvantage to using sheep's milk is finding it. There are only a few breeds of dairy sheep commonly kept in the United States, most notably the East Friesian and the Lacaune. Dairy sheep produce less milk than both cows and goats, and few producers in the United States raise sheep for milk. In addition, sheep do not produce milk at all from October to February each year, according to the Wisconsin Sheep Dairy Cooperative, so even if you can find a sheep dairy, fresh milk is simply not available for several months at a time. Fortunately, sheep dairy producers discovered how to freeze milk for shipment to cheese makers and other producers, so frozen sheep's milk is becoming more readily available throughout the United States. At the same time, because fewer people raise sheep for milk, it is still a fairly rare commodity. Your best bet is to check local farmer's markets and organic stores to find local producers.

Deciding Which Milk to Use

While some cheeses traditionally are made with only one type of milk, almost any cheese can be made using the milk of another animal. There are slight differences in taste and texture, but the conveniences of getting the type of milk readily available in your area may be important to you. Or, the health benefits of using goat's milk when making cheese may outweigh any other considerations for your family. No matter what you value in milk, there are other considerations to be factored into your milk purchase. When it comes to cheese making, all milk is not created equal.

Commercially produced milk

The milk available in your local dairy case is not ideal for cheese making for several reasons. First, commercially sold milk is **pasteurized**. Pasteurization is a process created by French chemist Louis Pasteur in the 19th century. It involves heating milk and other food products such as beer, apple cider, and maple syrup, killing bacteria that cause the product to spoil. Some milk is even **ultra-pasteurized**, heated to much higher temperatures than those used in the standard pasteurization process. This process extends the shelf life of milk by up to three months.

Advocates of pasteurization say this process protects consumers from food poisoning. Opponents claim pasteurization kills probiotic, or good bacteria, that would protect people from these same food-borne illnesses. In addition, there is growing evidence that some of the bacteria pasteurization is designed to kill are actually heat-resistant. In response, some producers are now using cold pasteurization, involving ionized radiation, instead of heat pasteurization. The effectiveness and possible drawbacks of this type of pasteurization are still up for debate among milk experts.

Whatever the health benefits of pasteurization, there is no question that removing bacteria from milk makes it very difficult, if not impossible, to produce cheese. Cheese producers who are forced to rely on pasteurized milk must use additives such as **mesophilic starter cultures** and **calcium chloride** to replace the bacteria missing in pasteurized milk. These additives are readily available through online supply companies; however, using them can be tricky because too much or too little of any additive will change the composition of the cheese. Most artisan cheese producers try to use as few additives as possible.

Another problem with commercially produced milk is its fat content. While many consider fat a bad word, it is absolutely essential in cheese production. While there are cheeses that can be made from low-fat milk, such as farmer's cheese and part-skim mozzarella, most homemade cheeses require natural milk fat in order for curds to form and the cheese to age properly. Taste and texture can be seriously compromised if you do not use whole milk with the right percentage of milk fat.

Commercially produced milk has other drawbacks as well. There are concerns about how animals that produce commercial milk are raised. Many do not have access to pasture, and some activists claim commercial dairy cows are confined in small stalls for their entire milking lives, force-fed and force-milked until they go dry, at which time they are sent to slaughter. In addition, most commercial dairies rely on heavy doses of antibiotics and growth hormones to keep cows producing. There are concerns these substances may be passed on through the milk to the consumer.

If your only option is commercially available milk, then research different brands before you buy your milk. Read the labels and choose milk with higher fat content. Never try to make cheese, yogurt, or butter using ultra-pasteurized milk. The high heat used in the process destroys all the microbes that create cultures and chemical reactions. In addition, note whether the milk is **homogenized** or

non-homogenized. The difference is simple. Non-homogenized milk has a layer of cream rising to the top of the container. In homogenized milk, the cream is mixed throughout the milk. For higher-fat cheeses such as cream cheese, blue cheese, and some varieties of cheddar, non-homogenized milk is preferred. However, most recipes can be made with homogenized milk. The result will just be a slightly denser and less creamy cheese. Whatever milk you choose, try to get the freshest available and feel free to experiment with the different options. Just remember, different cheeses require milk with very different characteristics.

Cheese Myth:

Cheese "binds you up," causing constipation.

Fact: Mothers have been telling their children for generations that if he or she eats too much cheese, the child will not "go" for a week. In reality, cheese is no worse at causing constipation than many other foods. Constipation is caused by not enough fiber in the diet, and cheese is not a high-fiber food. If you wish to avoid constipation, be sure to eat cheese with high-fiber foods, including whole grain breads or crackers and fruit.

Raw milk

So, what is the artisan cheese maker without a herd of cows, goats, or sheep to do? There are several possibilities, depending on location and the resources available. First, consider using **raw milk** for cheese making. Raw milk is milk that has not been pasteurized. Until Pasteur came along, everyone who drank milk drank it raw. There is a grass-roots raw milk movement in the United States today driven by people who believe the dangers of raw milk — most notably the possibility of death due to bacteria — are exaggerated by commercial producers. Raw milk advocates believe for many commercial producers, pasteurization is about economics, not safety, because pasteurized and ultra-pasteurized milk can be shipped over long distances and stored on refrigerator shelves for longer periods of time. Many European cheeses, such as Roquefort, Camembert, and Parmesan are made with raw milk. Cheese gourmets believe raw milk, which has beneficial bacteria and a high fat content, gives fine cheeses their flavor and nutritional value.

Unfortunately, many states have laws against the sale of raw milk in commercial establishments; therefore, it is often impossible to buy raw milk at local markets. However, most states allow producers to sell raw milk directly to the consumer and almost every state has producers who do so. Be sure you understand the laws regarding raw milk in your state, especially if you plan to produce cheese for resale.

Organic milk

If you cannot or do not wish to obtain raw milk, organic milk may be the best option for making quality cheese. Animals that are allowed to graze freely and are not subjected to antibiotics and growth hormone injections during their lives produce organic milk. Most organic dairies are small operations, so the producers have much greater control over milk quality. You might even want to visit an organic dairy in your area and observe how the animals are treated and the milk is handled. Organic milk is widely available in grocery stores, health food and organic markets, and farmer's markets. It usually costs between $1.50 and $2.00 more per gallon than commercially produced milk, but for cheese making, the higher quality and possible health benefits are worth it.

Fun Fact

Some cheeses, especially those with yogurt as one of the main ingredients, actually help the digestive system due to the high concentration of helpful bacteria.

Raising your own milk

For serious cheese makers who have the necessary resources, it is possible to privately produce milk. For example, a small herd of dairy goats can provide enough milk for the hobby cheese maker and are fairly easy to raise and handle. There is a wealth of available information on dairy goat farming that can be found at local extension offices, the Farm Service Administration, local 4-H programs, in books, on websites, and through professional organizations. Raising dairy animals is not for everyone; however, it can be a satisfying experience for the whole family, and you will be able to control the quality of the milk used in your cheeses.

CASE STUDY: RAW MILK CHEESE FROM CRICKET CREEK FARM

Cricket Creek Farm
1255 Oblong Road
Williamstown, MA 01267
www.cricketcreekfarm.com
info@cricketcreekfarm.com
413-458-5888 (p)

Cricket Creek is trying to bring a little bit of Italy to Massachusetts. Starting in 2007, owner Judith "Jude" Sabot began making two raw milk cheeses, Maggie's Round and Tobasi, which are her own unique recipes based on the popular Italian Toma and Tallegio varieties. With the help of a small herd of Brown Swiss and Jersey dairy cows, Cricket Creek's cheese is crafted for gourmet shops and farmer's markets in the area, as well as online sales. By 2010, they hope to produce up to 20,000 pounds of their delicious cheeses. The Cricket Creek cheese maker's key to success is simple but applicable to many endeavors: "Keep good records and don't get discouraged."

Chapter Four

It's All a Matter of Chemistry

You do not need a chemistry degree to successfully make cheese. Still, just as yeast has an enormous impact on the creation of a loaf of bread, chemical reactions are vital in turning milk into cheese, and different chemicals create very different cheeses. It is important to at least understand which chemicals perform which tasks in the cheese-making process. So, it is time to examine the role chemistry plays in making delicious curds.

Rennet

The one chemical needed to create most cheeses is rennet. As we learned in Chapter 1, rennet, the substance produced in the stomach of young calves and sheep, reacts with milk and heat to begin the chemical reactions to produce cheese. Rennet causes the milk to coagulate and separate into curds, which are then washed, pressed, molded, flavored, and otherwise shaped into cheese. Rennet was originally found in the stomachs of young animals, notably lambs and calves. The fourth stomach of a calf has the highest concentration of rennet known to nature.

For thousands of years, cheese makers could only obtain rennet from young animals, so they often had to wait until spring, when young animals were plentiful, and they could kill one for its stomach lining. The lining was usually dried

and sliced into strips, which were later soaked in hot water to obtain the rennet. Today, however, while animal rennet is still available, scientists developed vegetable-based rennet as well. Both types of rennet are inexpensive and readily available through cheese-making suppliers; they come in both liquid and tablet form. For large batches of cheese, liquid rennet is more economical, but for small batches, a tablet or part of a tablet of rennet is easier to measure and work with.

Starter Cultures

In addition to rennet, most cheese recipes need some type of starter culture. These are stains of beneficial bacteria that create the reactions that turn milk into cheese. When making simple, fresh cheeses, you can "grow" the starter culture you need by simply leaving the milk out at room temperature for 24 hours. As the milk sours, the lactose changes to lactic bacteria, which react with the milk and begin to produce the separation of curds and whey that eventually becomes cheese. However, most commercially produced, homogenized milk will not produce lactic bacteria because the original lactose has been seriously impacted by the milk's processing. Therefore, you may have to add specific starter cultures to the milk in order to get the process started.

There are two main types of starter cultures: mesophilic and **thermophilic**. Mesophilic cultures work at lower temperatures, from 77 to 102 degrees Fahrenheit. There are two main strains of mesophilic cultures: *Lactococcus lactis* subspecies *lactis* and *Lactococcus lactis* subspecies *cremoris*. The first is used to make most cheeses that ripen in the 77 to 86 degree range. These cheeses include cottage cheese, cheddar, Colby, and feta, as well as many others.

The second strain of mesophilic cultures — *Lactococcus lactis* subspecies *diacetylactis* and its companion, *Lactococcus lactis* subspecies *mesenteroides cremoris* — ferment more quickly than other mesophilic strains, so they create air holes in cheeses made with these cultures. This gives the cheeses a more open, lacy texture that is not as dense as, for example, the solid texture of cheddar. This texture is necessary in blue cheeses and havarti, for example.

The second type of starter culture, thermophilic cultures, is thermo — heat — activated. These include the strains *Streptococcus thermophilus, Lactobacillus delbruekii* subspecies *bulgaricus,* and *Lactobacillus helveticus.* These cultures are either used alone or in combination with each other. You need to use these cultures when creating cheeses that require a cooking temperature from 95 to 105 degrees Fahrenheit. Thermophilic cultures can even survive in temperatures as high as 140 degrees. The heat-tolerance makes these starter cultures the ideal for use in cheeses such as Parmesan, Romano, and Gruyere.

Luckily for the average cheese maker, all of these cultures are available through cheese-making supply companies. They come in freeze-dried foil packets, similar to the yeast used by home bakers. Most of these cultures will keep up to a year after purchased if stored in a freezer. If you open and use some of the culture from its foil packet, just put the packet in a plastic freezer bag, seal it, and place it back in the freezer until it is needed again. These "direct-set" cultures, as they are called, are an easy way to add the necessary good bacteria to your cheese recipe.

One other additive often used in cheese making is calcium chloride. This additive is often included when the milk in the recipe has been pasteurized because pasteurization removes calcium from the milk. The addition of calcium chloride aids in the coagulation and formation of the curd. Calcium chloride is readily available through cheese-making supply houses.

Cheese Myth:

Cheese is an aphrodisiac.

Fact: Almost every food has been credited with spectacular bedroom-enhancing properties. However, there is little evidence to support these claims for any food, including cheese. On the other hand, a fondue for two or a picnic with Brie and a crusty loaf of French bread can be very romantic, and a romantic atmosphere can only help enhance the relationship.

Temperature and Cheese Making

Heat is also an important element in the cheese-making process. Every cheese recipe specifies a particular temperature and the milk must reach that exact temperature in order for the chemical reaction to be successful. When baking, the experienced cook can often alter the temperature by turning the oven up or down to cook faster or more slowly. He or she can cook two items that require different temperatures at the same temperature, removing one from the oven a bit earlier or later than the other. This type of thermometer creativity almost never works in cheese making. If the recipe calls for milk heated to 146 degrees Fahrenheit, 145 degrees may not do it.

Cold is also vital to cheese making. Many varieties, especially aged cheeses, need to rest in an environment with particular temperature and humidity in order to fully ripen and develop ideal flavor. Therefore, you may need a refrigerator thermostat and **hygrometer**, which enable you to set your temperature and monitor humidity. Both are available through cheese supply companies, as well as in many home supply and larger hardware stores. In many cheese-making regions, caves are still ideal repositories for varieties that require careful, cool aging. *In Chapter 5, we will discuss how to create a portable cheese cave, for readers who may not have a limestone cave available.* With a minimal investment and a bit of care, your cheeses can be as cool as needed.

pH Balance and How to Check It

Some cheeses, especially aged varieties, require that you check the **pH balance**, the level of acidity in the cheese during or after the cooking process. Recipes that require such testing will tell you what the pH range of the cheese mixture should be. However, you need specific equipment to measure these levels. Fortunately, this equipment is neither expensive nor difficult to find. The easiest pH testers are the strips we all used in high school chemistry class. They turn different colors when the pH is at different levels. These strips, which come in both paper and plastic versions, are readily available at hardware stores, hobby shops, teacher supply houses, and online from many suppliers. A packet of strips costs less than $10.

If you are making cheese for commercial sale, you may want to invest in a slightly more expensive pH testing meter. The best meters are digital ones, and they provide an instant readout, without having to compare a colored strip to a chart. Digital pH meters are available online from many laboratory supply houses. These pH meters range in price from around $30 to several hundred dollars.

The Miracle of Mold

As we learned earlier, there are several varieties of cheese that rely on mold in order to develop their distinctive color, aroma, flavor, and texture. Many cheeses have rinds, an edible coating that forms on the outside of the cheese. Cheeses with "blooming" rinds, such as Brie, grow these rinds with the application of the beneficial bacteria **Penicillium candidum**. Of course, blue cheeses would be impossible to produce without various strains of *Penicillium roqueforti, Penicillium gorgonzola*, and *Penicillium glaucum*, which must be introduced as the cheese ripens. In order to ensure these molds reach into the center of the cheeses, wheels of Roquefort and Gorgonzola must be pierced with knitting needles or other objects, creating round holes into which the spores of the *penicillim* are introduced. Without these molds, Roquefort would be just another creamy cheese. As with direct-set cultures, the molds needed to produce particular types of cheese are available in powdered or freeze-dried form through cheese-making suppliers.

Clean Cheese is Happy Cheese

All molds are not good molds. If cleanliness is next to godliness, then cheese making is a very holy activity. As a general rule, the only mold or bacteria you should add to your cheese is the specific culture or mold powder listed in the recipe. Of course, no one wants dirt in any type of food, but cheese is particularly sensitive to the wrong bacteria creeping in at the wrong moment. At best, your cheese will be ruined. At worst, you, your family, or your customers could be sickened by a bad batch of curds. In order to make sure this does not happen, the cheese maker and all the equipment must be sanitized. Following are some basic methods and tips to clean cheese-making equipment:

- Hot water sterilization. Boil all pots, knives, spoons, boards, and containers for at least 10 minutes. Allow the equipment to air dry. Do not dry anything with a cloth towel because it will just spread germs back onto the equipment.

- Bleach sanitization. One-fourth cup of household bleach in one gallon of hot water will sanitize your equipment. If you use this method, be sure to thoroughly rinse all your equipment to remove the bleach residue. There are many popular flavors of cheese and none of them are bleach-flavored. Again, allow the equipment to air dry.

- Some cheese-making suppliers also offer pre-mixed chemical sanitizers that are sprayed on equipment and left to dry. These are effective but expensive, and a bleach solution, provided that the equipment is thoroughly rinsed with fresh water, is probably just as effective and much more cost-efficient.

- Wash your hands frequently, and keep your fingernails trimmed short. Do not wear rings or other jewelry on your hands when making cheese. If you must handle the cheese while it is being made, wear disposable gloves.

There is no need to become paranoid about cleanliness. There are no known occurrences of anyone dying in the United States due to a bad batch of homemade cheese. The greater risk is that contaminated cheese will simply not turn out edible, a disappointment to anyone who spends time and care on a recipe. By taking simple precautions, you can make sure your cheese is both safe and tasty.

Chapter Five

Equipment

For the beginning cheese maker, there is no reason to rush out and buy thousands of dollars worth of exotic equipment. You may already have many of the items needed to get started, and what you do not have can be purchased in any store that carries hardware, kitchen, or craft items. As you begin to make more varieties of cheese, you can add to your equipment. There are some items that all cheese makers need. We will start with those.

For the Beginning Cheese Maker

As you begin your journey into the world of cheese making, it is not necessary to carry a great deal of baggage at first. The average cook will have many of the basic items, such as a good cooking pot, thermometer, and knives. Read the suggestions below, and start with the basic equipment and supplies. As you move from simple, fresh cheeses to more complicated recipes, you may need to add to your equipment. The following equipment will be helpful:

- **The cooking pot:** There are two important considerations when choosing a pot to cook cheese. The first is size. Many cheeses require a gallon or more of milk to cook down into cheese. If the pot is too small, it will not have room for all the necessary ingredients. An 8-quart pot is a good size. You also want a pot that is not too deep and has a fairly

broad cooking surface, so the contents heat evenly and there is room to cut the cooked product into curds. The next consideration is equally important. Cheese-making pots must be made from a non-reactive material that will not clash with the chemicals involved in cheese making. Do not use aluminum or cast iron pots with cheese recipes. You need a stainless steel or enameled pot.

- **Utensils:** At the minimum, you should have one or two quality cooking spoons and knives. A long cutting knife, approximately six to seven inches, is needed when slicing curds. Ideally, knives and spoons should also be stainless steel because it is the best non-reactive material and is easy to clean. However, if you want less expensive spoons, food-grade polycarbonate, polyester, or polyethylene will work as well; although, they may not clean up as easily as stainless.

- **Thermometer:** As mentioned earlier, many cheese recipes depend on accurate temperature readings. The only way to get those readings is with an accurate cooking thermometer. The ideal thermometer will measure from 32 degrees to 225 degrees. Old-fashioned thermometers with the numbers on the side are acceptable for use, but a digital thermometer is much more accurate and easier to read, and it only costs a few dollars more. For some recipes, an instant-read thermometer, one that can be put into the mixture and read immediately, is ideal. However, other recipes call for the milk mixture to be heated gradually, a few degrees at a time, over a period of up to one hour. For that type of cheese, you may want a thermometer that gradually tracks increasing temperatures.

- **Skimmer:** While some cheeses need to be sliced into cubes while in curd form, others need small slivers cut from the curd and layered into molds. A cheese skimmer is a long-handled utensil with a round, flat disk at the end. The disk is full of small holes that pull curds from the pan. Skimmers are available in restaurant and kitchen supply stores, and the best are made from stainless steel. A stainless steel, slotted spoon will also work for skimming curds.

- **Triers:** A trier allows the cheese maker to "try" the cheese during the aging process. This tool has a long hollow rod that can be inserted into a cheese. It also has a handle that, when turned, pulls a core sample from the cheese without disturbing the rest of the wheel or batch. As with most cheese tools, stainless steel is your best bet when buying a trier.

- **Cheesecloth and butter muslin:** Most cheeses need to be wrapped and either drained or given time to rest. Cheesecloth and butter muslin are woven cotton fabrics used to wrap cheeses during the cheese-making process. Some types are more loosely woven than others; occasionally a recipe will specify "tightly woven" or "loosely woven" cheesecloth. Some recipes require two or more layers of cheesecloth to protect the cheese. Both cheesecloth and butter muslin are inexpensive and readily available at fabric and craft shops, some hardware stores, and any company that sells cheese-making supplies. Cheesecloth can be washed in very hot water, dried, and reused, but for the price, it is possible to simply have a fresh supply for each recipe. Many cheese supply companies also offer draining bags with ties or drawstrings. They are more expensive than yards of plain cheesecloth, but are often easier for the novice cheese maker to handle.

- **Bowls and colanders:** Many cheeses need to drain through a colander at some point during the process. Again, you want to make sure the colander is not made from a reactive material, so stainless steel or food-grade plastics are the best options. Make sure the colander is large enough to hold the cheese. Depending on the recipe, the colander may have to hold up to five pounds of curds, so colanders in a variety of sizes are a good investment when planning to make many varieties of cheese. You will also need a bowl under the colander to catch the whey as it drains. A glass, glazed ceramic, or food-grade bowl is best.

- **Cheese mats:** These are open-texture, woven plastic mats often placed under cheeses during the ripening process. They come in several sizes and can be re-used as long as they are properly sanitized. They can be purchased through cheese-making suppliers.

Casanova, perhaps the most famous lover in history, definitely believed in the sex-boosting power of one particular cheese: Roquefort. He declared the noble French blue cheese was "an excellent thing to restore an old love and ripen a young one."

For the Experienced Cheese Maker

As you begin to experiment with washed-rind and aged cheeses, your need for more sophisticated and specialized equipment will grow. While you may not want to pay thousands of dollars for top-of-the-line pieces, especially if you are making cheese just for yourself, good-quality items are important to ensure that your cheese turns out the way you expect. For example, if you wish to make cheddar, do not skimp on a cheese press. The pressing process is essential, and the proper amount of pressure must be produced and maintained as the cheese curds "knit" together. The following equipment will be helpful for an experienced cheese maker:

- **Racks:** Some cheeses need to rest on racks for a few hours or even a day or more. There are many good racks available in kitchenware stores and through cheese-making suppliers. Unless you are planning to make a great deal of cheese, only one or two racks to begin. If the cheese comes into direct contact with the rack, which many recipes call for, stainless steel or coated non-reactive racks are best. Standard racks are 16x12 inches.

- **A waxing pot:** Some cheeses, such as Gouda and aged cheddars, are waxed to protect their quality. In order to wax cheeses, a pot is necessary to melt the wax. An old, two-quart saucepan is ideal for this task because it is impossible to get all the wax off a melting pot.

- **Bristle brush:** If waxing cheeses, a natural bristle brush is also needed to apply the wax. Natural bristles are ideal because they hold up to the heat in the melted wax. Never use a nylon bristle brush; it will melt and leave bristles embedded in the wax. Silicone pastry brushes are also acceptable for use. As with the wax pot, the brush will never be good for any other purpose, no matter how much it is cleaned.

- **Cheese wax:** These are special types of wax designed to protect and age cheeses. Do not use paraffin or candle wax. Food-safe wax, which is available through cheese-making suppliers, is the only wax that can be used in this process. It comes in several colors to pick from, however, some cheese, such as Edam with its red coat, are traditionally coated in a particular color of wax. Therefore, if you want your cheeses to look professional, you may want to follow tradition.

- **Molds:** Not every cheese needs to be molded. Many can simply be wrapped or placed in food-grade plastic containers. However, if you are making wheels of cheese, logs of cheese, specialty goat cheese shaped into pyramids and cones, or cheeses such as French Neufchatel, which is traditionally molded into the shape of a heart, cheese molds are necessary. Molds can be made from wood; there are patterns available in many woodworking books. However, cheese-making suppliers offer a wide selection of food-grade plastic molds in every size, shape, and price range. Perhaps the most common mold is called the **tomme mold**; this is a basic mold that produces the "wheel" shape common to many cheeses, including cheddar, Colby, Monterey Jack, and many more.

- **A cheese press:** Not all cheeses require a press; however, as you tackle more advanced recipes, a press is vital, especially for cheddars or any cheese that requires steady pressure to remove whey and press curds into shape. There are many quality presses available; start with a small one and work up as cheese-making activities increase. You can also make your own cheese press. There are several different methods; this link from Fias Dairy Farm gives you complete instructions: **http:// fiascofarm.com/dairy/cheesepress.html**. Dr. David Fankhauser, a biologist and cheese-making enthusiast, also offers plans and instructions for making a home cheese press at this site: **http://biology.clc. uc.edu/fankhauser/Cheese/Cheese_5_gallons/Cheese_press/PRESS_ SETUP_00.htm**.

- **Scale:** A good kitchen digital scale is a useful tool for weighing both ingredients and finished wheels of cheese. Most standard kitchen scales weigh items up to 11 pounds, which is enough for personal production. Scales range in price from about $25 to over $100, depending on the brand and available features. You can purchase them online from cheese-making suppliers or at kitchenware stores. With a commercial cheese operation, a hanging scale with a higher weight limit or a restaurant-grade scale is needed. These are available through restaurant supply houses.

- **Storage containers:** Most cheeses can be stored in food-grade plastic containers, which are readily available. Some cheeses, especially those with strong aromas, may need to be stored in glass or ceramic containers.

As is true of all cheese-making equipment, be sure the molds, scales, presses, and containers are thoroughly washed and properly sterilized, using either the hot water or bleach methods discussed in this book.

A note about the tomme mold

In many of the recipes, you will see the words "tomme mold" listed as part of the equipment. The tomme mold is one of the most commonly used molds in cheese making. It is a round mold that produces the familiar "wheel" of cheese. There are generally two sizes of tomme molds. The larger size, 3.5x7.5 inches, produces four to 5-pound cheeses. The smaller tomme mold, measuring 2.5x5.25 inches, creates 1- to 1 1/2-pound cheeses. Both types of tomme molds are available from cheese-making suppliers.

The clean break

Many of the recipes in this book mention the need for a "**clean break**" in the curds. This means that once the curds have cooked or ripened, you need to test them by inserting a **curd knife**. This process is similar to poking a cake with a toothpick to see if it is completely baked. If the knife comes out clean, the curds will produce a clean break when they are cut. If the curds stick or cling to the knife, then they are not yet ready to be cut. In most recipes, simply wait a few more minutes before testing the curds again. In all cases, it is important to have a clean break before cutting the curds and proceeding with the rest of the recipe.

Cheese Myth:

If cheese has mold on it, just slice the mold off and eat the rest of the cheese.

Fact: Like many myths, this one contains a grain of truth. Most hard cheeses, such as cheddar, can be trimmed of their mold and consumed. However, semi-soft cheeses, including Brie and many of the pasta filata cheeses such as mozzarella and provolone, can be ruined by the invasion of mold. If these cheeses develop mold, they need to be discarded.

For the Master Cheese Maker: The Cheese Cave

The most exquisite and acclaimed cheeses are also the most difficult to make at home. Part of the problem lies, not in the creation of these cheeses, but in their care and comfort. These cheeses, including aged cheddars, Brie, and blue cheeses require weeks, and sometimes months, of carefully monitored aging and ripening before they are truly ready to be eaten or shared. The French refer to this process as **affinage**, a controlled aging of the cheese. Commercial cheese makers solve this problem with cheese caves, whether natural or artificial, which provide the ideal mixture of temperature, humidity, and light for these cheeses as they mature. However, unless you are lucky enough live next door to an abandoned limestone mine, there is probably nowhere in your home where cheeses can age. Even the basements of most modern homes are too warm and too dry to coddle these cheeses. A cheese cave is the only option. Fortunately, it is not difficult to make one. Here are some methods to create a cheese cave:

- The serious cheese maker can build a cheese cave in the basement by adding a heavily insulated extra room and setting up racks, shelves, humidifiers, thermometers, fans, and gauges of every kind. There are several very detailed online blogs from people who set up such caves, complete with materials lists, photos, and tips for maintaining temperature. However, this is only recommended for someone who plans to make and sell cheese on a fairly large scale. Otherwise, it simply is not cost-effective.

- To make a simpler cheese cave, use a refrigerator. Any size will do, but obviously, the more cheese being made, the more space needed to ripen and age it properly. This cannot be the same refrigerator where things like cola, lettuce, and lunchmeat are stored. The average kitchen refrigerator is not cool or damp enough for most delicate cheeses. If it is possible to find an old refrigerator, one without the ice dispensed in the door and energy-saving programmable thermostat, this is a better base for a cheese cave. Old refrigerators do not have the forced air and heat exchanges that the modern models have. A classic Frigidaire from the 1960s is ideal, but other models can be adapted, as long as the proper equipment to control both temperature and humidity, including a separate thermostat and a hygrometer, are available.

- Equip the refrigerator with a separate refrigerator thermostat. These are readily accessible and allow users to override a refrigerator's built-in thermostat. This is a must because the thermostats built into modern refrigerators cannot be set to 60 degrees Fahrenheit. With a separate thermostat, they can be.

- A chest-style freezer will also work, provided the standard thermostat is replaced with a warm temperature thermostat, thus ensuring the freezer's temperature can be set above freezing.

- If possible, set up your cheese cave refrigerator or freezer in the basement where the temperature is naturally cooler than the rest of the house.

- Purchase a digital combination thermometer and hygrometer, which will measure both temperature and humidity.

- Find out what temperature and humidity a particular cheese needs in order to properly affinage. During this process, most cheeses need to be maintained at 50 to 55 degrees Fahrenheit and 80 to 90 percent humidity.

- Keep the humidity high by placing pans of water in the "cave" with cheeses. Check both temperature and humidity each day and adjust as needed.

- As cheeses continue to mature, rinds may become discolored. In most cases, the cheeses can be washed and oiled once aged, thus creating a better presentation.

Affinage is a trial and error experience at best, even for the most skilled cheese makers. However, it is the only way to produce the truly great aged and blue cheeses.

CASE STUDY: THE HOME OF AMERICAN "FRENCH" CHEESE

Marin French Cheese Company
Maxx Sherman, Sales and Marketing
Manager
7500 Red Hill Road
Petaluma, CA 94952
(800)-292-6001 ext. 15 (p)
(707) 762-0430 (f)
www.marinfrenchcheese.com

Hand-crafted quality is not necessarily limited to small cheese makers. For 145 years, the Marin French Cheese Company has been making and selling a wide range of excellent cheeses, from their original soft breakfast cheese (made when Abe Lincoln was still President) to Rouge et Noir triple crème Brie and Yellow Buck Camembert. Carefully selected milk from local dairies is delivered to their 700-acre facility near Petaluma, California, where master cheese makers constantly create award-winning cheeses. For Marin French, this location is ideal because "in Petaluma, our cows, land, and climate is similar to that of France. We produce European-style cheese." Sales and marketing Manager Maxx Sherman said, "We create the recipe, and we have many employees that work in our production facility (kitchen) to recreate the same product every day of production. Our cheeses are handmade, and consistency is our number one challenge. Our cheeses taste a little bit different every day due to the stages of affinage (aging and ripening of the cheese). We taste most of our cheeses every week at a production meeting. I eat our cheese seven days a week." In order to achieve that consistency, Mr. Sherman urges cheese makers to "write down everything you do during the making of the cheese every day, and taste every batch of cheese during the entire life of the cheese."

The Cheese Maker's Best Friend: The Cheese Journal

While carefully following recipes will avoid most problems, cheese making is still an art, not an exact science. Many factors, from the amount of rennet in the mixture to the amount of humidity in the air, can affect the final product. Therefore, the new cheese maker should start a cheese journal and use it to record the process. If something does go wrong with a batch of cheese, notes from a journal can help pinpoint and correct the problem. Better yet, if a finished cheese is extraordinary, you will know exactly how to reproduce it in the next batch. In addition, if cheese is being marketed, it is especially important to be able to ensure quality control, and the information kept in a cheese journal will be invaluable.

What does a cheese journal look like? Ideally, it is portable and easy to use even while making the cheese. For that reason, keeping notes on a computer is probably not the best method.

The simplest cheese journal is a spiral or loose-leaf notebook. The spiral version is perhaps more portable, but the information in a loose-leaf binder can be added to and reorganized as notes grow. A loose-leaf binder will also open flat on any surface. This makes it easier to consult and to add notes as cheese is created.

If you wish, a simple information sheet can be designed. Copy or print it off as many times as necessary and store it in the notebook when it is completed. Here is a sample sheet, with the information that should be tracked while following recipes.

Date started: _____

Name of recipe: _____

Amount of milk used: _____

Type of milk used (cow's, goat's, or sheep's): _____

Quality of milk (organic, pasteurized, whole, reduced-fat, etc.): _____
_____

Rennet added (yes or no): _____

If yes, amount of rennet used: _____

Milk temperature when rennet was added: _____

Other additives and amounts used (mesophilic starter, bacteria, etc): _____
_____

Milk temperature when additives were introduced: _____

Cooking time: _____

Hottest cooking temperature: _____

Draining time: _____

Resting time: _____

Curds cut? If so, how large: _____

Salt added? Quantity: _____

Herbs added? Type and quantity: _____

Pressed (yes or no): _____

If pressed, length of time in press: _____

Weight used in press: _____

Air dried? If so, length of time dried: _____

Waxed (yes or no): _____

Date waxed: _____

Aged (yes or no): _____

Temperature for aging: _____

Humidity for aging: _____

Date sampled: _____

Comments: _____

This seems like a great deal of information, and it is not necessary to make all these notes each time a simple batch of cream cheese is made. However, if attempting one of the master cheeses in this book, a complex cheese such as Brie, or a cheese like cheddar whose taste is dependent on proper aging, better results in future batches will occur if all of the information is saved from the first batch. If problems do happen, it will be much easier to pinpoint and fix the issue quickly with the right information. Alternately, if cheese turns out exactly the way it should, it will be nice to know that the ingredients, measurements, and other factors have been recorded.

Despite the fact that blue cheeses are created using mold spores, other types of mold on these cheeses ruin their flavor. If blue cheese has a gray or pinkish mold on the surface of the cheese, it is no longer good to eat.

Shelf life of cheese

Every cheese has a life of its own, a span of time when it is at its best. However, that varies widely from one cheese to another. For example, ricotta cheese is only edible for a few days after it is made. At the other end of the timeline, many cheddars and hard cheese such as Parmesan and Romano only get better with age. Indeed, many cheeses must be aged for a period of days, weeks, or even months before they are ready to eat. The recipes in this book include suggested shelf life and aging times for each type of cheese.

Chapter Six

Getting Started: Confidence-Building Recipes

Now that you know more than you ever dreamed about the world of cheese, it is time to start making your own versions of this wonderful food. However, before you begin, there are a few tips that are helpful for any recipe, no matter how easy or complex. Using the checklist below will help save time and frustration and increase the chances of success with cheese making. This should be a fun process, not a milk-fueled headache. Before starting your recipe:

- Make sure you have all the ingredients necessary. This may sound obvious, but there is nothing worse than being in the middle of a recipe and realizing you do not have enough rennet or are a quart short on milk.

- Remember to make sure that whatever milk being used is not ultra-pasteurized. No matter what the recipe, ultra-pasteurized milk will not produce cheese.

- Gather all equipment before getting started. When you are boiling three gallons of milk, you do not want to be rummaging in the drawer for a thermometer.

- Make sure you have a large enough workspace. Space is needed on the stove for pots, space on the counter for colanders and draining bowls, and possibly space for racks or shelves to allow cheese to rest. It is also a

good idea to have the sink clear in case rinsing or draining is necessary during the process.

- Bring milk to room temperature before beginning your recipe. Since almost all cheese recipes require heated milk, it will save time if the milk is already at 65 to 70 degrees Fahrenheit, rather than 40 degrees Fahrenheit.

- Read through new recipes before beginning. Most cheeses require very specific cooking and draining times. You do not want to start what you think is a 15-minute recipe, only to discover that it takes two hours.

- Follow the recipe precisely, at least at first. Most cooks love to experiment, and as you learn more about how the various cheeses behave, you can begin to add your own touches. For now, however, trust the time-tested recipes in this book.

Simple Dairy Recipes

The same ingredients and techniques that give us cheese also produce other wonderful dairy products. Because most of these products are fresh, they do not require rennet or long periods of aging and need fewer molds and other specialized equipment. These are excellent ways for the beginning cheese maker to get familiar with the dairy cooking processes. Best of all, they are delicious.

Crème fraîche

Prep time: 5 minutes
Cooking time: 10-15 minutes
Resting time: 12 hours

Like Julie Andrews teaches the children in *The Sound of Music*, "Let's start at the very beginning. A very good place to start." Crème fraîche is not cheese; it is a dairy product similar to sour cream. It is an excellent project for the beginning cheese maker because the recipe incorporates many elements of cheese making: fresh milk, an acid to create a chemical reaction, and heat and time to finish the process. Crème fraîche is also a simple recipe with wonderful results, so it will build your confidence and get you ready to tackle more complicated cheese creations. Crème fraîche can be used in the place of sour cream in many recipes. In fact, because it has a higher temperature tolerance than sour cream, it works even better in sauces because it will not separate during the cooking process. The resulting crème fraîche will be thick and tangy with a richer texture than sour cream. It is wonderful over fresh fruit, especially berries, and it can be stored in the refrigerator for up to a week.

Ingredients/Equipment:

17 ½ oz cream

1 oz buttermilk or plain yogurt

A 1-qt saucepan, preferably with a non-stick interior

A bowl

A spoon

A linen or "flour sack" cotton towel. Use a smooth-finish towel, not velour or one with terry loops

Kitchen thermometer

Directions:

1. Over medium heat, pour the cream into the saucepan. Heat it over low heat to between 98°-100° Fahrenheit.

2. Remove the pan from the heat. Pour the cream into a bowl. Add the buttermilk or yogurt and stir thoroughly.

3. Cover the bowl with the towel and leave it overnight (a minimum of 12 hours) in a warm place in order for the fermentation to take place. You can leave the bowl on the back of the stove or on the kitchen counter, provided there is not a cold air register nearby.

Clotted cream

Prep time: 5 minutes

Resting time 12-24 hours

Cooking time: 1 hour, 30 minutes

The British earned our gratitude with many great cultural contributions — Shakespeare, James Bond, Monty Python — but perhaps our greatest gratitude should be reserved for this simple invention: clotted cream. Smoother than whipped cream, thicker than crème fraîche, and with a faint buttery savor, clotted cream is simply delicious over any kind of fruit, or as a topping for scones, pound cake, or waffles. Use the freshest, non-homogenized milk you can find, preferably organic.

Ingredients/Equipment:

4 qts of fresh non-homogenized milk

Heavy large saucepan, preferably enameled (to prevent scorching)

Directions:

1. Pour milk into a large stainless steel or enameled pot and cover with a clean cloth. Let stand for 12 hours if the room is quite warm (over 77° Fahrenheit) or up to 24 hours in a cooler environment.

2. Place the pot over low heat and slowly warm milk until very hot but not boiling. It is vital that you not boil the milk, which is why slow heat is essential. You will see the surface of the milk barely quivering. Control the heat so it continues to quiver but not boil. Hold the cream as close to this steady temperature for one hour, by adjusting or briefly turning off the heat as necessary.

3. Turn off heat and let milk cool.

4. When cool, move pot very carefully into the refrigerator. Do not jostle it any more than necessary. When completely chilled, skim off the thick cream and store it in jars in the refrigerator. Use the skimmed milk remaining for cooking or making cheese that requires skim milk.

Homemade buttermilk

Prep time: 10 minutes

Resting/ripening time: 24 hours

Traditional buttermilk is the liquid left after churning butter. It is somewhat sour and tangy, with a slightly thickened texture. Some people enjoy drinking buttermilk, but more people use it in recipes, especially sauces and baked goods. It has a fairly long shelf life due to the presence of lactic bacteria, which keeps other types of harmful bacteria from growing. Here is a simple recipe to make your own buttermilk.

Ingredients/Equipment:

2 qts whole or 2% milk (whole milk will produce a thicker finished product)

¼ tsp aroma mesophilic culture

2-qt glass jar with tight-fitting lid

Directions:

1. In a double-boiler, heat milk to 185° Fahrenheit and keep it at that temperature for at least 30 minutes.

2. Let the milk cool to about 78° Fahrenheit. You can do this quickly by putting the pot of milk into a sink full of cool water.

3. Sterilize the glass jar and lid by rinsing with boiling water. Drain well. Fill with milk.

4. Sprinkle the culture over the surface of the milk. Let stand for several minutes to allow culture to rehydrate. Put the lid on the jar and shake well until blended.

5. Let ripen at room temperature for 24 hours.

6. Store in the refrigerator for up to three weeks.

Simple homemade yogurt

Prep time: 2 minutes

Resting time: 12 hours

Yogurt is a traditional dairy product that is believed to have originated in Eastern Europe. It is rich in active cultures that aid in digestion. There is also evidence that the probiotics in yogurt may help strengthen the immune system. Yogurt is an excellent choice for the lactose intolerant, as the cultures help break down the milk proteins more easily. Of course, there are many brands of commercial yogurt available, but they are often loaded with sugar. By making it homemade, cooks can control the sugar content and add any fruit, herbs, or other flavors. Yogurt starter culture is available through cheese supply companies, or you can simply use a carton of plain commercial yogurt. Just make sure the label says, "with active cultures." Once you make your first batch of yogurt, it is OK to save the starter for the next batch.

Ingredients/Equipment:

4 cups nonfat milk

1 ½ tbsps plain yogurt with active cultures or commercial yogurt starter culture, available through cheese-making suppliers

Lidded 1-qt container

Whisk

Gas or electric oven or heating pad

Directions:

1. Pour milk — either goat's or cow's — into container.

2. Add yogurt with live cultures or starter culture. Whisk together thoroughly.

3. Place sealed container in warm spot for 12 hours. If you have a gas oven with a pilot light, you can place the container at the back of the stove over the pilot light, or set the oven on warm until the "ready" light goes off, then turn off the oven, turn on the light inside the oven, and place the container in the oven overnight. You can also place a heating pad on the kitchen counter, turn it on "low," and place the container on the pad.

4. Refrigerate the finished yogurt before serving. You can mix in fruit, honey, or jam to make a sweet yogurt.

Bulgarian-style yogurt

Prep time: 20 minutes
Cooking time: 45-50 minutes

Resting time: 4-6 hours

Draining time: 1-2 hours if desired

This yogurt requires a specific type of culture called Bulgarian yogurt culture. Like the other cultures and mold powders required for these recipes, it is available through cheese-making suppliers. This yogurt needs to be cooked to a very high heat, so a good thermometer is essential. Bulgarian-style yogurt has a thicker, more custard-like consistency than other yogurts. Like all yogurts, it can be sweetened with honey or mixed with fruit or jam.

Ingredients/Equipment:

1 qt whole cow's milk

1 tsp Bulgarian yogurt culture powder

Non-reactive cooking pot

Larger pot for cold water bath

Whisk

Thermometer

Cheesecloth

Colander

Ceramic or glass bowl

Directions:

1. In a large, heavy-bottomed, non-reactive pot, warm milk over medium heat to 176° Fahrenheit, stirring gently to prevent milk from scorching. Turn off heat. Cover pot and hold for five minutes.

2. Remove pot from heat and place in a cold water bath, (a larger pot filled with cold tap water and ice cubes) to cool milk as quickly as possible to 115° Fahrenheit. Stir or whisk the milk mixture to speed up the cooling process.

3. Remove ½ cup of warm milk from the pot. Dissolve the dry yogurt culture in the warm milk and stir back into the larger pot. Cover pot and let it sit four to six hours or until firm.

4. Refrigerate pot overnight.

5. If a thicker yogurt is desired, strain through a cloth-lined colander for one to two hours.

6. Place finished yogurt in a covered container and refrigerate for up to two weeks while eating.

Quick cooked yogurt

Cooking time: 15-20 minutes
Resting time: 4-5 hours

If it is necessary for the yogurt to be finished quicker, use this cooked recipe. This version uses the commercial starter culture, but like the previous recipe, it creates homemade yogurt with no extra sugar. You may sweeten it with honey or mix it with fruit. You can certainly add granulated white sugar, but it will give the yogurt an odd, gritty feel in the mouth, so honey is a better alternative.

Ingredients/Equipment:

1 qt whole or low-fat milk, either cow's or goat's
1 packet of yogurt starter culture
Stainless steel or enameled cooking pot
Larger pot for water bath
Whisk
Storage container
Kitchen thermometer

Directions:

1. Heat milk to 180° Fahrenheit.

2. Remove milk from heat and cool to 110° Fahrenheit.

3. Dissolve packet of starter culture in two tablespoons of milk. Add to heated milk mixture.

4. Cover pan of milk. Place pan of milk in larger pan that is half-filled with water. Heat until the milk is 114° Fahrenheit and keep at that

temperature approximately four hours or until yogurt has cooked to the desired consistency. Spoon into lidded container and place in refrigerator.

The world's easiest butter

Prep time: 10-15 minutes

Making butter was a popular project for Girl Scouts and kids in programs such as 4-H. However, the process took forever — this is a much easier recipe, and the freshness and quality of the finished product is superb. Be sure to use heavy cream that has not been ultra-pasteurized.

Ingredients/Equipment:

2 cups heavy cream
¼ tsp salt, or to taste
Food processor, blender, or electric hand mixer
Glass or ceramic mixing bowl
Wooden or food-grade plastic spoon

Directions:

1. Pour cream into food processor, blender, or bowl.

2. Process, blend, or whip for approximately ten minutes. Watch carefully and stop when the butter begins to appear.

3. Lumps of butter will separate from the buttermilk. The buttermilk can be reserved for cooking and baking, especially pancakes and muffins.

4. Drain the butter from the buttermilk and add salt.

5. Place butter into a bowl and press with the back of a cooking spoon to further drain the liquid.

6. Pack the salted butter into a container with a lid and store in the refrigerator.

Jalapeño butter

Prep time: 10 minutes
Resting time: 15 minutes

Once you master making your own butter, the possibilities are almost endless. This recipe, using fresh chopped jalapeños and parsley, is a wonderful addition to the dinner table. Imagine a dab of this butter melting in a mound of mashed potatoes. Picture it slathered over corn on the cob or spread across a hot corn muffin. Ole!

Ingredients/Equipment:

½ cup fresh butter, softened
1 tsp finely chopped fresh parsley
1 tsp finely chopped fresh jalapeño peppers
Small bowl
Fork

Directions:

1. Place butter in a small bowl. Beat lightly with a fork until creamy. Add parsley and jalapeño and mix well. Let stand for 15 minutes at room temperature to allow flavors to blend.

2. Store tightly covered in refrigerator for up to one week.

Morel mushroom butter

Prep time: 1 hour, 15 minutes
Resting time: 15 minutes

The morel is a very popular wild mushroom found in many parts of the United States and southern Canada. This recipe is a great way to combine fresh morels and homemade butter. The resulting spread is especially good on top of grilled meats or on an omelet. Just be sure you get your mushrooms from a reliable source. While poisonings are rare, they can happen. Never eat any mushroom unless you are sure it is a safe variety.

Ingredients/Equipment:

½ cup diced fresh or dried morel mushrooms
1 cup salted butter, softened
1 tbsp finely ground shallots
¼ tsp black pepper
Small bowl
Fork

Directions:

1. If using dried morels, rise and soak in lukewarm water for one hour or until softened. Drain and pat dry with a paper towel.

2. Slice morels into small pieces; set aside.

3. Place butter in a bowl. Beat with a fork until creamy. Add morels, shallots, and pepper and mix well to blend evenly. Let stand for 15 minutes at room temperature to develop the flavors.

4. Serve immediately or store tightly covered in the refrigerator for up to five days.

Simple, Fresh Cheeses

The recipes in the next section are all for fresh cheeses, using various types of milk. A few use rennet or other cultures, but most rely simply on milk, heat, and time to create the finished product. The recipes make fairly small batches, so they are good recipes to try first. Also, most can be flavored with fruit, herbs, and other add-ins to produce different creations. All of these cheeses have a fairly short shelf life and will keep up to about a week in the refrigerator.

Yogurt cheese

Prep time: 5 minutes
Resting time: 12-48 hours

As mentioned earlier, some people have difficulty digesting milk products such as cheese. For these lactose intolerant individuals, yogurt cheese may be the answer. Because it contains active bacteria cultures, it is easier for many people to digest. This simple recipe can be used as a spread, in cooking, or as a substitute for sour cream. Be sure to use plain yogurt with active cultures. The longer you let the yogurt rest, the thicker the finished product will be.

Ingredients/Equipment:

12 oz plain yogurt with active cultures or 12 oz homemade yogurt
Cheesecloth
Colander or strainer
Bowl

Directions:

1. Line the strainer or colander with two layers of cheesecloth.

2. Put the colander or strainer into a larger bowl for draining.

3. Pour the yogurt through the cheesecloth layers.

4. Cover with plastic wrap and place in the refrigerator.

5. After 12 hours, the yogurt will have the consistency of sour cream and can be used in dips or sauces.

6. After 36-48 hours, the yogurt will firm up to the consistency of cream cheese.

7. Remove the yogurt cheese from the cheesecloth. Add salt, herbs, or other flavorings if you wish. A teaspoon of sea salt, a teaspoon of minced garlic, and a teaspoon of dill results in a spread delicious on crackers or bagels.

Lactic cheese

Prep time: 20 minutes

Cooking time: 30 minutes

Resting time 12 hours

Draining time: 6-12 hours

This is a simple, fresh cheese that can be "dressed up" with a combination of herbs and other flavorings. It can be made with pasteurized milk, and you may use either cow's or goat's milk. Goat's milk will give the cheese a slightly stronger, tangier flavor. Because rennet is added to the mixture, lactic cheese can be stored longer than many other fresh cheeses, up to two weeks in the refrigerator. This is a delicious snack cheese.

Ingredients/Equipment:

1 gal pasteurized milk, either cow's or goat's milk

½ tsp mesophilic starter

3 drops liquid rennet

Kosher or pickling salt to taste

Ground black pepper to taste

Sweet paprika to taste

2 tsps fresh chopped chives

1 clove chopped fresh garlic

Non-reactive cooking pot

Thermometer

Cheesecloth or butter muslin

Colander

Glass or ceramic mixing bowl

Distilled water

Directions:

1. Using sterilized equipment, pour milk into cooking pot. Warm over medium heat to 86° Fahrenheit. Remove from heat. Add starter culture and mix thoroughly.

2. Dilute rennet in ⅓ cup of cool distilled water. Add to milk mixture, stirring gently with an up-and-down motion. Cover and let sit at room temperature (at least 72° Fahrenheit) for 12 hours or until mixture firms up. It should look something like yogurt at this point.

3. Pour the curd through a cheesecloth-lined colander. Tie the corners of the cloth to make a bag and hang the curd over the sink to drain for 6-12 hours, or until mixture achieves the thickness you wish. A room temperature of at least 72° Fahrenheit will encourage draining.

4. Place the curds into a bowl and mix in salt, pepper, and other seasonings.

5. Store in a covered bowl in the refrigerator for up to two weeks.

Gervais

Prep time: 25 minutes
Cooking time: 35 minutes
Resting time: 24 hours
Draining time 4-6 hours
Pressing time: 6-8 hours

Gervais is a delicious soft cheese made from a mixture of milk and cream. The cream gives this cheese a silkier texture and a richer taste. Gervais is an unusual fresh cheese because it is pressed, not simply drained. Like many fresh cheeses, gervais lends itself to the addition of herbs and spices. Try chopped dill or thyme, or mix in *Herbes de Provence*, a Mediterranean blend of herbs that includes bay leaf, thyme, orange peel, and rosemary. *Herbes de Provence* is available at gourmet and specialty stores.

Ingredients/Equipment:

2 ⅔ cups pasteurized whole milk
1 ⅓ cups pasteurized heavy cream
½ tsp mesophilic starter
1 drop liquid rennet
Salt (optional)

Herbs (optional)

Non-reactive cooking pot

Thermometer

Cheesecloth

Colander

1 small tomme mold

4 small (2 ¼ inch x 1 ¾ inch) round molds

Glass or ceramic mixing bowl

Distilled water

Directions:

1. Using sterilized equipment, pour milk and cream into cooking pot. Warm over medium heat to 80° Fahrenheit. Remove from heat. Add starter culture and mix thoroughly.

2. Dilute rennet in two tablespoons of cool distilled water. Add to milk mixture, stirring gently with an up-and-down motion. Cover and let sit at room temperature for 24 hours.

3. Pour the curd through a cheesecloth or muslin-lined colander. Tie the corners of the cloth to make a bag and hang the curd over the sink to drain for four to six hours, or until the mixture stops dripping. You may need to open the bag and scrape down the sides of the cloth once or twice to encourage draining.

4. Place the curds in a fresh piece of cloth and place in a tomme mold. Put the mold in a cheese press. Press at 15 pounds of pressure for six to eight hours.

5. Remove cheese from press and un-mold into a bowl. Mix in salt to taste. Cheese should be creamy and smooth. If it is lumpy, force it through a strainer. Add herbs if desired to taste.

6. Place cheese into four small molds lined with wax paper.

7. Store in the refrigerator for one to two weeks.

Buttermilk cheese

Prep time: 15 minutes

Cooking time 45-55 minutes

Resting/Ripening time: 24 hours

Draining time: 6-7 hours

Buttermilk makes a very tangy fresh cheese that has the consistency of fine cottage cheese or ricotta. Buttermilk cheese is delicious eaten with a spoon as a side dish, or it can be used in any recipe that calls for ricotta. It gives a sharper flavor to pasta dishes, and it balances the sweetness of other ingredients in homemade cheesecake. Because the curds of buttermilk cheese are very fine, use a clean linen towel to strain the curds from the milk during the cheese-making process.

Ingredients/Equipment:

4 qts freshly made buttermilk

Salt to taste

Non-reactive cooking pot

Thermometer

Colander

Linen towel

Glass or ceramic mixing bowl

Wooden spoon

Directions:

1. Pour the buttermilk into a bowl and cover with a clean cloth. Let ripen at room temperature for 24 hours to further develop the milk's **acidity**.

2. In a large non-reactive cooking pot, warm the ripened buttermilk over medium heat to 162° Fahrenheit, stirring gently to prevent scorching. The solids will separate from the whey. Remove from heat and let stand for six to seven minutes.

3. Pour contents of pot through a cloth-lined colander. Tie the four corners of the cloth together to form a bag. Insert a wooden spoon through

the knot and hang the bag over the cooking pot. Drain for six to seven hours or until desired texture is reached. Remember that cheese will firm up slightly once it is refrigerated. Remove curds from cloth and add salt to taste. Store in a covered container in the refrigerator for up to two weeks.

Fromage frais

Prep time: 10 minutes
Cook time: 15-20 minutes
Rest time: 4-8 hours

This is a classic French cheese used in recipes or eaten with bread or fruit. It has a very creamy consistency and a mild, milky flavor. Unlike many of the fresh cheeses, it uses liquid rennet instead of the tablet form. It also keeps a bit longer than some other fresh cheeses. You can store it for up to two weeks in the refrigerator.

Ingredients/Equipment:

4 qts whole cow's milk
¼ tsp mesophilic culture
2 drops liquid rennet
Kosher or sea salt to taste
Stainless steel cooking pot
Spatula
Kitchen thermometer
Cheesecloth
Colander
Smooth-finish towel
Bowl
Storage container

Directions:

1. In stainless steel pan, heat milk to 77° Fahrenheit, stirring gently to prevent scorching.

2. Remove milk from heat. Let stand five minutes.

3. Sprinkle half a teaspoon of mesophilic culture on the surface of the milk. Using the spatula and an up-and-down motion, gently work culture into milk. Do not stir or whip milk.

4. Dilute rennet in a tablespoon of cool water. Add to milk mixture in the same manner as the culture.

5. Cover and sit in a draft-free spot for 12 hours.

6. Ladle curd into cheesecloth-lined colander and let drain for up to eight hours. The longer it drains, the firmer the final product. Feel free to open the bundle and check the consistency or remove a spoonful of cheese and then return it to the bag without affecting the process. The cheese is fully drained when the bundle is damp but not dripping.

7. Place finished cheese in container and salt if desired. Store in refrigerator.

Fromage blanc

Prep time: 10 minutes
Cooking time: 10 minutes
Resting time: 45 minutes

Fromage blanc, or "white cheese" in French, is one of the easiest fresh cheeses to make. It has a wonderful, creamy texture, and it is very versatile. Drizzled with honey or preserves, it works beautifully with fresh fruit. You can also add chopped fresh herbs such as chives, dills, or rosemary, and serve fromage blanc with breads or crackers as an appetizer.

Ingredients/Equipment:

2 qts whole milk
1 cup heavy cream
2 cups fresh buttermilk
2 tbsps fresh lemon juice, with no pulp or seeds
½ tsp salt
Non-reactive saucepan

Mixing bowl

Thermometer

Colander

Cheesecloth

Ladle

Directions:

1. In a large, heavy saucepan, combine the milk and cream.

2. In a separate bowl, thoroughly mix the buttermilk and lemon juice. Add this mixture to the milk and cream, and heat on low until the mixture reaches 175° Fahrenheit, using a kitchen thermometer to frequently check the temperature.

3. While the mixture is cooking, stir only twice, using a wide, heatproof spatula. This mixture needs only a few slow, gentle strokes when you stir it each time.

4. As soon as the thermometer reads 175° Fahrenheit, remove the pan from the stove and let the mixture sit for ten minutes.

5. Line a big colander or mesh drainer with cheesecloth or butter muslin. Use two layers and position the colander over a large bowl. Using a ladle or large cooking spoon, transfer the cooked mixture into the cheesecloth.

6. Let the mixture drain until most of the whey has drained, about two to three minutes.

7. Take the ends of the cheesecloth and tie them together, forming a bag or pouch. Hang this over the bowl and let the mixture continue to drain and firm, about 40 minutes.

8. Serve at once with honey, preserves, or fruit, or refrigerate up to a week. If you want a savory flavor, mix in three tablespoons of finely chopped fresh herbs and then let the finished product refrigerate overnight so that the cheese absorbs the flavors of the herbs.

Lemon cheese

Prep time: 5 minutes
Cooking time: 20 minutes
Resting time 60-90 minutes

This is a simple, creamy cheese with a tangy lemon flavor. It goes especially well in sauces for seafood. It can also be dressed up with the addition of fresh herbs such as dill, basil, or chives, or add finely minced capers. Drizzled with honey, it becomes a lovely dessert cheese.

Ingredients/Equipment:

½ gal whole milk
¼ cup freshly squeezed lemon juice, with pulp and seeds removed
Stainless steel or other non-reactive cooking pot
Thermometer
Cheesecloth
Large colander

Directions:

1. Pour the milk into a stainless steel pot and heat to 165° Fahrenheit, stirring frequently to prevent milk from scorching. Check temperature with a kitchen thermometer.

2. As soon as the milk reaches the desired temperature, remove from heat and stir in the lemon juice. Let the milk rest for 15 minutes. You will begin to see curds forming.

3. Transfer the mass to a cheesecloth-lined colander with a deep bowl underneath. Tie the cheesecloth ends into a bundle and suspend the mass above the colander, using a wooden spoon passed through the knot and resting on the edges of the colander. Let the cheese drain one hour or until the whey stops dripping.

4. Unwrap the cheese and transfer it to a bowl. Add salt and herbs if desired.

5. Store in an airtight container in the refrigerator for up to one week.

Chèvre

Prep time: 20 minutes

Cooking time: 25 minutes

Resting time: 24 hours

Draining time: 6-7 hours

Chèvre is the French word for goat. Thus, chèvre cheese is made from goat's milk. There are many types of chèvre cheese available, from soft and spreadable to crumbly or sliceable. Traditional soft chèvre cheese is often molded into cylinders, cones, or small pyramids. Obviously, this does not affect the flavor, but it makes for an appealing presentation. Molds specifically designed for soft chèvre cheese are available from cheese-making suppliers. Soft chèvre has a thick and creamy consistency that is very similar to cream cheese, but it does have a slightly sharper, tangier flavor from its goat's milk base. Soft chèvre is often flavored with herbs or peppercorns for variety. This recipe uses dill, but thyme, rosemary, or mint would work as well, or you can roll the finished cheese in whole green peppercorns or red pepper flakes.

Ingredients/Equipment:

4 qts whole goat's milk

¼ tsp mesophilic culture

1 drop liquid rennet

Pickling (canning) or kosher salt to taste

2 tbsps dried dill weed, rosemary, or thyme (optional)

Whole green peppercorns or crushed red pepper flakes (optional)

Non-reactive cooking pot

Larger pot for hot water bath

Thermometer

Draining bag

Bowl

Skimmer

Directions:

1. Using sterilized equipment, pour milk into a cooking pot and place pot in larger **hot water bath** — a larger pot of water that will act as a double boiler, allowing you to heat the milk but protect it from scorching. Over medium heat, warm milk to 77º Fahrenheit, stirring gently to prevent scorching. Remove milk from heat.

2. Sprinkle culture over surface of milk. Let stand for five minutes. Using skimmer and an up-and-down motion, gently work the culture into the milk while disturbing the surface of the milk as little as possible.

3. Dilute rennet in one tablespoon of cool distilled water. Using skimmer and the same gentle motion, work rennet into milk mixture. Cover and allow mixture to rest for 24 hours at room temperature.

4. Tip pot slightly to drain off collected whey. Using skimmer, ladle curd into a draining bag or cloth-lined colander. Let drain for six to seven hours or until desired thickness is reached. Be aware that cheese will thicken further once it is refrigerated.

5. Remove cheese from bag and place in a bowl. Add salt. Mix in herbs if desired or gently shape cheese into a log and roll in peppercorns. Store chesse in a covered container in the refrigerator for up to two weeks.

Brousse

Prep time: 20 to 30 minutes
Cooking time: 15 minutes
Draining time: 6 hours

Brousse was originally made in the village of Rove, near the city of Marseille in the South of France. For this reason, it is often called Brousse du Rove. Local farmers made this cheese from the milk of a particular breed of goat. The cheese was packed into small cone-shaped molds and sold at the local markets to be taken home and eaten fresh. Brousse is very soft, almost runny, and it has a slightly acidic flavor. It has a fairly high fat content, almost 45 percent. Brousse is usually eaten as a dessert cheese, either drizzled with honey or simply sprinkled with sugar.

Ingredients/Equipment:

1 qt goat's milk
¼ cup white vinegar
Cheesecloth
Colander
Non-reactive cooking pot
Thermometer
4 Brousse molds or other small cone-shaped cheese molds
Skimmer
Distilled water

Directions:

1. Using sterilized equipment, pour milk into a cooking pot. Over medium heat, warm milk just to the boiling point, stirring gently to prevent scorching. Remove from heat.

2. Dilute vinegar in ¾ cup of cool distilled water and add to milk, stirring quickly with skimmer. Continue stirring vigorously until milk curdles and small flakes of cheese rise to the top of the pot.

3. Using skimmer, ladle curds into a cloth-lined colander. Let drain over a bowl for two to three minutes. Using your hands or a spoon, fill the molds, packing curd down. Tap molds slightly to ensure they are completely filled at the bottom.

4. Place molds in a basket or bowl so they stand upright. Let them drain for about six hours. Place molds in the refrigerator and unmold cheeses as you use them. Brousse should be eaten fresh, no more than 24 hours after it is made.

Sheep's milk Brousse

Prep time: 20 minutes
Cooking time: 20 minutes
Rest Time: 12 hours

This is a fresh sheep's milk cheese that is made in a mold. It has a delicate texture and sweet flavor. Because it is not made with bacteria or preserved with salt, this cheese must be kept cold and eaten within a few days of its creation. It is mostly eaten as a dessert cheese. Pair it with preserves, honey, or a sweet dessert liqueur for a sophisticated treat.

Ingredients/Equipment:

2 qts sheep's milk (thawed frozen sheep's milk will work)
1/8 tsp liquid rennet
8 St. Marcellin molds (small plastic molds that are shaped like large thimbles and available from cheese supply houses)
Stainless steel cooking pot
Skimmer (a tool that skims slivers of curd from the surface of a mixture)
Spatula
Kitchen thermometer
Sink full of ice cubes and cold water
Cheese mats
Plastic draining container

Directions:

1. Pour milk into cooking pot. Heat over medium heat until temperature reaches 175° Fahrenheit, stirring gently to prevent milk from scorching.

2. Remove from heat and place pot into sink full of ice water. Let mixture cool to 100° Fahrenheit, stirring constantly.

3. Dilute rennet in two tablespoons of cool distilled water. Add to mixture and use spatula to gently work rennet into mixture using up-and-down motion. Do not stir, beat, or whisk.

4. Cover and let sit for 15 minutes.

5. Using a skimmer, gently skim slivers of curd from the mixture and put them into the molds, giving each layer time to settle before adding more slivers of curd. Mound the curd above the top of the mold. As it settles, it will flatten.

6. Place molds on cheese mats in a draining container. Cover container and put into the refrigerator to drain. Let drain for 12 hours.

7. Un-mold the cheeses just before eating. Consume this cheese within two days of production.

Mizithra

Prep time: 20 minutes
Cooking time: 25 minutes
Draining time: 17 hours

Mizithra is a traditional fresh cheese made in country kitchens throughout Greece. It is mild and creamy, with a rich and gentle flavor. Unlike its cousin feta, mizithra is not brined, so it has less of a salty flavor. Mizithra is traditionally made from goat's milk, but whole cow's milk will also work. Just be sure to use whole milk or the finished cheese will not have the pleasing creamy texture you seek.

Ingredients/Equipment:

3 qts whole milk
1 tbsp pickling or kosher salt
½ tsp liquid rennet
Cloth-lined colander
Non-reactive cooking pot
Thermometer
Whisk
Cheesecloth
Distilled water

Directions:

1. Using sterile equipment, pour milk into a non-reactive pot. Over medium heat, warm milk to 90° Fahrenheit, stirring gently to prevent scorching. Remove from heat and stir in salt.

2. Dilute rennet in ¼ cup cool distilled water. Add to milk and, using a gentle up-and-down motion, draw rennet into the milk until well

blended. Cover and set aside at room temperature for 30-60 minutes or until a firm curd forms.

3. Using a whisk, gently break up curd, stirring until curd pieces are approximately ½ inch in size. Let stand for two to three minutes. Using skimmer, stir gently for five minutes.

4. Gently pour curd into a cloth-lined colander and let drain for one hour. Scrape cheese into the center of the cloth. Gather the four corners of the cloth together and tie to create a bag. Hang the bag and let it drain over the sink for five hours at room temperature.

5. Place colander in a bowl and place the bag in the colander. Allow to drain for 12 hours in the refrigerator.

6. Remove the cheese from the cloth and place in a container. Store in the refrigerator for up to two weeks.

Fresh cottage cheese

Prep time: 15 minutes
Cook time: 1 hours, 15 minutes
Resting time: 20 hours

There seems to be no middle ground with cottage cheese. People either love it or loathe it. Of course, homemade cottage cheese has a flavor that cannot be matched by the kind in the plastic carton. This is a fairly simple recipe, but timing is crucial. In order for the curds to turn out well, they *must* have their full resting time.

Ingredients/Equipment:

1 gal fresh cow's milk
4 oz mesophilic starter culture
¼ tablet rennet
Glass or ceramic bowl
Distilled water
Linen towel

Stainless steel whisk
Non-reactive cooking pot
Thermometer
Cheesecloth
Colander
Ice water

Directions:

1. Mix the milk with the mesophilic starter.

2. Add the rennet to two tablespoons of cool distilled water. Combine thoroughly, then add the mixture to the milk and starter, whisking for at least five minutes.

3. Cover with a smooth linen or cotton towel and let the mixture ripen at room temperature, around 70° Fahrenheit, for a full 20 hours, both to allow the curd to form and to give the flavor time to develop.

4. Using a sharp, steel knife cut the whole curd into 1/2-inch cubes.

5. Let these curds firm up for 15 minutes.

6. Place the curds into a large, heavy saucepan and heat very slowly for about 30 minutes until the curds reach 110° Fahrenheit. Use a kitchen thermometer to check the temperature.

7. Cook for an additional 45 minutes at 110° Fahrenheit. Stir the curds frequently to keep them breaking apart. As you cook, the curds will shrink and begin to sink to the bottom of the pot.

8. Line a colander with cheesecloth and pour out the cooked curds. Let the result drain for five minutes.

9. Keeping the curds in the cloth, lift them from the colander and dunk them repeatedly into a bowl of ice water for three to four minutes. This will give the curds their firm, almost "squeaky" texture in the mouth.

10. Remove the curds from the cheesecloth and place them into a bowl or lidded container.

11. Add two tablespoons of fresh cream for a richer texture. Season with salt, pepper, or herbs such as chives and dill.

Goat's milk cottage cheese

Prep time: 45 minutes
Cooking time: 1 hour, 30 minutes
Resting time: 18 hours, 20 minutes
Draining time: 5-10 minutes

Goat's milk tends to add a tangier, deeper flavor to any cheese recipe. As previously discussed, it is also easier for many people to digest. This cottage cheese recipe requires careful cooking. If you want a milder flavor, dip the bag of curds into a bowl of ice water several times and allow the curds to drain for five minutes between each dunking. This cottage cheese is particularly good when mixed with fruit, such as pineapple chunks or mandarin oranges slices.

Ingredients/Equipment:

2 gals pasteurized whole goat's milk
¾ tsp mesophilic starter
4 drops liquid rennet
2 tbsps heavy cream (optional)
Pineapple chunks or mandarin orange segments, drained (optional)
Glass or ceramic bowl
Distilled water
Linen towel
Stainless steel whisk
Non-reactive cooking pot
Thermometer
Cheesecloth
Colander
Ice water in a bowl

Directions:

1. Start with sterilized equipment. Heat the milk to 72° Fahrenheit. Stir in starter culture.

2. Dilute rennet in ¼ cup cool distilled water. Add to milk mixture, stirring gently for one minute.

3. Cover and let milk sit for 12-18 hours at warm room temperature (72° Fahrenheit) to coagulate. The curd will be quite soft.

4. Cut the curd into ½-inch cubes. Rest for 15 minutes.

5. Place pot back on heat. Gradually heat to 90° Fahrenheit, increasing temperature no more than three degrees every five minutes. This step should take approximately 30 minutes.

6. Continue to increase temperature until it reaches 102° Fahrenheit. Once this temperature is reached, cook mixture at 102° Fahrenheit for 30 minutes or until curds are firm.

7. Let curds sit five minutes.

8. Pour off the whey. Pour the curds into a cloth-lined colander. Allow them to drain for five to seven minutes. If desired, dip bundle in ice water and let curds drain. Repeat this step three or four times if desired. The more the curds are rinsed, the milder the final taste will be. However, be sure to rinse curds in ice water at least once.

9. Place the curds in a bowl and break up any matted pieces. Add cream if desired. Salt to taste. Add fruit if desired before serving.

10. Store in a covered container in the refrigerator for up to two weeks.

Simply delicious cream cheese

Prep time: 25 minutes
Cook Time: 15 minutes
Resting time: 3-4 days

This is another simple recipe that requires only a few ingredients and a great deal of patience to allow the cheese to reach its fullest flavor potential. A bagel's best friend, this cheese is also a great ingredient in cheesecake, pound cake, or any recipe that calls for the richness of real cream cheese.

Ingredients/Equipment:

4 cups non-ultra pasteurized half and half

1 cup non-ultra pasteurized whipping cream

2 tbsps buttermilk

1 tsp salt

Heavy saucepan

Thermometer

Glass or glazed ceramic mixing bowl

Colander

Cheesecloth

Directions:

1. Pour both creams into a heavy saucepan. Mix them together, and then heat them slowly until they reach 90° Fahrenheit, using a kitchen thermometer.

2. Take the pan off the heat and add the buttermilk.

3. Pour the mixture into a sanitized mixing bowl, ideally one that is glass or glazed ceramic. Cover the bowl with plastic wrap and surround the bowl with several thicknesses of kitchen towels, which will hold in the heat and help "cook" the cheese.

4. Place the bowl in a warm area and leave it for 24 hours.

5. Check on the mixture. It should be fairly firm, like yogurt, and it should not lean up the side of the bowl, if the bowl is tilted. If it is not yet firm, cover again and let it sit for 6-12 hours.

6. When the mixture is firm, pour it into a cheesecloth-lined colander with a drip bowl under it. Let it drain for 15 minutes, then cover the new cheese with the cheesecloth, place the colander in a bowl that is deep enough to hold it, and cover everything with plastic. Place the bowl and colander in the refrigerator for 12 hours.

7. Remove the curd from the cheesecloth. Discard the whey, or save it for cooking.

8. Lightly salt the curds, and add herbs if desired.

9. Shape the curds into balls, rewrap them in a fresh piece of cheesecloth, and put them back into the colander. Cover the colander with more plastic wrap, and put everything back into the refrigerator for up to 48 hours. The longer the cheese drains in the refrigerator, the firmer the texture.

10. Remove the finished product and pack it into a plastic storage container. It will keep in the refrigerator for up to two weeks.

Goat's milk cream cheese

Prep time: 20 minutes
Cook Time: 15 minutes
Resting time: 24 hours

The richness of goat's milk gives this cream cheese a different flavor than the ones you might be used to. It lends itself especially well to strongly flavored herbs such as chives and rosemary. It also works wonderfully with thinly sliced smoked salmon and chopped onions on bagels or pumpernickel bread. Because it is made with goat's milk, it is also easy to digest.

Ingredients/Equipment:

1 gal fresh goat's milk
½ tsp direct-set **mesophilic-m** culture
¼ tab rennet, diluted in 5 tbsps cool water
Non-reactive cooking pot
Thermometer
Colander
Large bowl for draining
Cheesecloth

Directions:

1. Pour the milk into a 5- or 6-quart heavy pot. Heat the milk to 80° Fahrenheit, using a kitchen thermometer to check the temperature.

2. Remove the pot from the heat. Add the culture and stir well. Then add the rennet and stir again.

3. Cover the pot and let it sit for 12-18 hours.

4. Check the mixture. As with other cream cheese recipes, it should have the thickness of yogurt.

5. Place a colander in a large bowl, and line the colander with cheesecloth. Pour the mixture into the colander and let it drain until most of the whey seems to have drained through the cloth.

6. Tie the corners of the cheesecloth and hang the bundle. You can hang this from the handles of your kitchen cupboards or from your kitchen faucet if it is the right shape. You can also run the handle of a wooden spoon through the loop and balance the bundle on the rim of a bowl. No matter how you hang it, make sure that you keep a bowl under the cheesecloth bundle, to collect the extra whey that drains.

7. Let the cheese drain for three to four hours. Open the bundle and stir the cheese with a sanitized spoon or spatula, then close it and let it drain for three to four more hours.

8. Unwrap and store the finished cheese in a plastic container in the refrigerator. Like most cream cheeses, it will last up to two weeks.

Neufchatel French cream cheese

Prep time: 10 minutes
Resting time: 36 hours

Unlike most American cream cheese, Neufchatel is made with whole milk instead of cream. In France, it is usually packed into a heart-shaped mold. Many recipes add finely pureed strawberries, which give the cheese a wonderful rose color and a delicate sweetness. This is usually eaten as a dessert cheese, but it is also delicious on waffles or bagels for breakfast.

Ingredients/Equipment:

½ gal fresh whole milk

2 oz mesophilic starter culture

¼ tab rennet

½ cup pureed strawberries, raspberries, or blueberries (optional)

2 glass or ceramic mixing bowls

Linen towel

Measuring spoons

Colander

Cheesecloth

Directions:

1. Mix the milk with the mesophilic starter in a sanitized mixing bowl, preferably glass or glazed ceramic.

2. Add one-fourth tab of rennet to two tablespoons of cool water. Whisk this into the milk mixture for at least five minutes.

3. Cover with a clean, smooth-surfaced towel and set aside to ripen. Leave out at room temperature, around 70° Fahrenheit, for 15-20 hours.

4. Ladle the curds into a colander lined with fine cheesecloth. Let this drain for 30 minutes.

5. Tie the bundle, hang, and let drain for an additional eight to 12 hours.

6. Place the curds in a clean bowl and cream together gently until mixed.

7. Puree fresh or thawed frozen berries in a food processor. Drain once through a colander to remove some of the liquid. Then add to the cheese mixture.

8. Place in a sealed container in the refrigerator. The cheese will firm slightly once refrigerated. It keeps up to two weeks.

Mascarpone

Prep Time: 5 minutes

Cook Time: 15 minutes

Rest time: 12 hours

Just as Neufchatel is France's answer to cream cheese, mascarpone is Italy's entry into the cream cheese category. It is a rich and sweet cheese, perfect for desserts. Some people like to pit large green grapes and stuff them with mascarpone or fill fresh apricot halves with this cheese. It is also easy to make and keeps well in the refrigerator.

Ingredients/Equipment:

1 qt light cream

¼ tsp tartaric acid*

This ingredient is used in wine making, so many stores that carry wine making supplies, including some large liquor stores, will have tartaric acid. It can also be ordered from many cheese-making suppliers.

Heavy saucepan

Thermometer

Large spoon

Colander

Cheesecloth or clean linen towel

Directions:

1. Pour the cream into a heavy saucepan. Heat the cream to 180° Fahrenheit, using a kitchen thermometer.

2. Add the tartaric acid. Remove from heat.

3. Stir for 10-15 minutes. The mixture will thicken, and fine bits of curd will be visible.

4. Pour the mixture into a colander lined with a double layer of fine cheesecloth or a linen towel. Let it drain for an hour into a bowl beneath the colander.

5. Put the colander and bowl into the refrigerator and let the cheese continue to drain for 12 hours.

6. Scoop out the cheese and place into an airtight container. Store in the refrigerator. It will keep up to three weeks.

Simple ricotta

Prep time: 20 minutes

Cook time: 15 minutes

Rest time: 2-3 hours

The word ricotta means "recooked" in Italian. Traditional ricotta cheese is made from whey gathered from other cheeses, which is then is recooked to become this new cheese. However, not everyone has the eight quarts of whey needed to make a batch of traditional ricotta. This recipe uses fresh milk instead and yields a tasty product.

Ingredients/Equipment:

1 gal whole milk, either cow's or sheep's

¼ cup lemon juice

2 tsps kosher or sea salt

Stainless steel pot

Cheesecloth

Colander

Thermometer

Large spoon

Directions:

1. Heat the milk and lemon juice in a stainless steel pot until the mixture reaches 90° Fahrenheit. The curds should begin to separate from the whey. If they do not, let the mixture warm to 100° Fahrenheit, but do not let the milk scorch.

2. Line a colander with three layers of cheesecloth. Pour the mixture through and let it drain into a bowl below the colander. Bring the end of the cheesecloth up and tie them together.

3. Hang the cheesecloth bag above the colander and bowl. You can often slip a large wooden spoon through the knot and suspend the bag by placing the spoon across the lip of the colander.

4. Put the bundle in the refrigerator and allow it to drain for two to three hours.

5. Unwrap and remove the cheese, place in an airtight container. Add salt. You may also add minced garlic, cracked black pepper, and olive oil.

6. Use within three days.

Sweet dessert ricotta

Prep time: 10 minutes
Cooking time: 20 minutes
Resting time: 1 hour

Like the previous recipe, this ricotta is made from fresh milk instead of whey. However, this sweet version contains no salt, which means it will go bad in only two to three days. This is one treat you need to make and eat at once. It is a great cheese to serve at the end of a dinner party, along with fresh fruit, preserves, or a sweet dessert wine.

Ingredients/Equipment:

4 qts whole cow's milk
1 tsp citric acid powder
Distilled water
Non-reactive cooking pot
Thermometer
Colander
Cheesecloth
Large bowl

Directions:

1. Add the citric acid powder to 1/4 cup of cool distilled water. Make certain the powder dissolves completely.

2. In a sterilized stainless steel pan, combine the milk and the citric acid solution. Heat the milk to 190° Fahrenheit, stirring gently but constantly to make certain the milk does not scorch. Use a kitchen thermometer to monitor the temperature.

3. As soon as the mixture begins to curdle, remove it from the heat. Let the mixture stand for about ten minutes. At this point, curds will begin to rise to the top of the pot. Gently ladle the curds into a cheesecloth-lined colander over a large bowl. Allow the cheese to drain for about one hour, until the result is a soft and creamy mixture. Eat this cheese at once. It is good with fruit or drizzled with honey and spread on thin slices of pound cake or short cake.

Easy goat's milk ricotta

Prep Time: 10 minutes
Cook time: 20-30 minutes
Resting time: 2 minutes

While most ricotta cheese is made from sheep's milk, there is no reason to leave our friend the goat out of the fun. Like previous recipes, this is a whole-milk cheese that does not require whey from another batch of cheese for production. It has a slightly tangier flavor than regular ricotta.

Ingredients/Equipment:

1 gal whole goat's milk
¼ cup vinegar, either apple cider or white wine vinegar
3 tbsps melted butter, *not* margarine
½ tsp baking soda
Non-reactive cooking pot
Thermometer
Colander

Cheesecloth
Large bowl

Directions:

1. In a sanitized stainless steel pan, heat the milk to 195° Fahrenheit. Do not let the milk come to a boil.

2. Gradually stir in the vinegar. Watch the mixture for the moment when the curds begin to separate from the whey.

3. Use a slotted spoon to remove the curds from the mixture. Ladle them into a colander lined with fine cheesecloth or butter muslin.

4. Drain for two minutes, and then transfer the curds to a mixing bowl. Add the melted butter and baking soda. Mix well and pack the resulting mixture into a storage container. This cheese will keep in the refrigerator for up to one week.

Classic ricotta

Prep Time: 10 minutes
Cook time: 20 minutes
Rest time: 3-5 hours

This is a traditional ricotta made with whey. It is an easy recipe; the trick is having whey left over from another cheese-making project, such as a batch of cheddar, Monterey Jack, or Gouda. You must use fresh whey. Like all ricottas, this is a cheese that only keeps for a week or so in the refrigerator. It is best made and eaten quickly. It is also a low-yield cheese, making only enough for one or two uses.

Ingredients/Equipment:

2 gals of fresh whey from cow's milk or sheep's milk
1 qt whole milk
¼ cup cider vinegar
¼ tsp cheese salt
Herbs to taste (optional)
Stainless steel cooking pot

Kitchen thermometer
Colander
Butter muslin
Draining bowl
Storage container

Directions:

1. Place fresh whey in pot. Add whole milk. Heat to 200° Fahrenheit.

2. Turn off heat and add vinegar. Stir until you see tiny white particles of protein forming in the whey.

3. Ladle the curds into the muslin-lined colander. Drain.

4. Once mixture is cool, tie the muslin into a bundle and drain over a sink or colander.

5. Remove drained cheese from bundle and place in bowl. Add salt and herbs if desired.

Quark

Prep Time: 10
Cook time: 15 minutes
Rest time: 28 hours

No, this is not a *Star Trek* character. In German, quark means "curds." Quark is a fresh, soft cheese very popular in German cooking. It is often eaten with boiled new potatoes, as the creaminess of the quark sets off the fresh appeal of the tender young potatoes. It is also used in noodle dishes, soufflés, crepes and other desserts, and sauces.

Ingredients/Equipment:

4 qts 1 or 2% milk
4 quarts whole milk
¼ tsp mesophilic culture
¼ tablet rennet

1 tbsp kosher or sea salt, or to taste

Stainless steel cooking pot

Kitchen thermometer

Cheesecloth

Colander

Curd knife

Spatula

Clean, smooth-surface towel

Container

Directions:

1. Heat milk in cooking pot to 77° Fahrenheit, stirring gently. Remove from heat. Let stand five minutes.

2. Sprinkle mesophilic culture over surface of the milk. Using the spatula, gently work the culture into the milk in an up-and-down motion, disturbing the milk as little as possible. Do not stir, whisk, beat, or whip.

3. Dilute rennet in ¼ cup cool water and work into milk mixture the same way.

4. Cover pot of milk and let sit in a draft-free spot for 24 hours.

5. Remove towel. Tip pot gently to drain whey from surface of cheese. Using a long-bladed knife cut the curd into vertical strips about two inches wide. Let the cheese rest for five minutes and gently drain whey again.

6. Gently lift curds into cheesecloth-lined colander and let drain for four hours.

7. Remove cheese from cheesecloth and place in container. Mix in salt to taste. Cover and store in the refrigerator for up to two weeks.

Feta

Prep time: 40-50 minutes

Cook time: 15 minutes

Rest time: 8 and ½ hours

Feta is the famous salty goat's milk cheese of Greece. Here in America, it is often eaten in salads, but it works in many recipes and with bread as a snack. You can make this recipe with cow's milk, but it will not have the recognizable feta flavor. Try to get goat's milk if at all possible. If you must use cow's milk, add lipase powder to strengthen the flavor of the finished product.

Ingredients/Equipment:

1 gal pasteurized whole goat's milk or cow's milk

1/4 tsp lipase powder diluted in ¼ cup water and allowed to rest for 20 minutes (optional, use if cow's milk is used)

1 packet direct-set mesophilic starter culture

½ tablet rennet

2-4 tsps cheese salt

Stainless steel cooking pot

Kitchen thermometer

Colander

Cheesecloth

Spatula

Curd knife

Bowl

Container

Brine solution (Optional)

Directions:

1. Pour the goat's milk into the cooking pot. If using cow's milk, add the lipase first and then pour into cooking pot.

2. Heat the milk to 86° Fahrenheit. Remove from heat.

3. Add mesophilic starter culture. Cover the milk and let it sit in a warm location for one hour.

4. Dilute the rennet in 1/4 cup of water and let sit for 20 minutes. Add rennet mixture to milk mixture, working it into the milk with a gentle up-and-down motion.

5. Cover again and let sit at 86° Fahrenheit for another hour.

6. Cut the curd into ½-inch cubes. Let rest for ten minutes.

7. Gently stir curd mixture for 20 minutes.

8. Pour the curds into the cheesecloth-lined colander. Drain over a bowl or the kitchen sink for six hours.

9. Unwrap cheese and cut into 1-inch cubes. Sprinkle with salt to taste.

10. Place in covered container, put in refrigerator for four to five days to age.

11. If desired, make a brine solution for the feta, combining one-third cup salt, one teaspoon calcium chloride, and a half gallon of distilled water. Pour over finished cheese. *Note: If the milk you use comes from a commercial source, the cheese will probably disintegrate in the brine. Use the brine only if you have a farm source for your milk.*

Queso blanco

Prep time: 20 minutes
Cooking time: 50 minutes
Draining time: 6 to 7 hours

Queso blanco, or "white cheese" in Spanish, is a creamy, fresh cheese that is designed to be made and eaten quickly. Because it contains no rennet or other starter cultures, it has a very mild, milky flavor and a creamy texture. It does not "hold" well; you need to eat it no more than a week after it is made. Queso blanco is often stir-fried with vegetables or used in salads. It is popular in many areas of Latin America.

Ingredients/Equipment:

4 qts whole cow's milk
¼ cup white vinegar
Non-reactive cooking pot
Cheesecloth
Colander

Thermometer

Stainless steel cooking spoon or whisk

Directions:

1. Start with sterilized equipment. Pour milk into cooking pot over medium heat. Warm milk to 180° Fahrenheit, stirring gently to prevent scorching. Reduce heat to low and hold at this temperature for five to six minutes. The temperature may go a bit higher, but make sure it does not go above 185° Fahrenheit. Remove from heat.

2. Add vinegar. Stir milk continuously for ten minutes or until milk curdles and solids rise to the top. If milk does not curdle, add another tablespoon of vinegar and continue stirring.

3. Pour contents of pot into a cloth-lined colander. Let curds drain for 15-30 minutes. Gather the corners of the cloth together and tie to form a bag. Hang the bag over the sink and let drain for six to seven hours.

4. Unwrap cheese and place in small bowl. Cover and store in refrigerator for up to one week.

Panir (or paneer)

Prep time: 20 minutes

Cook time: 20-25 minutes

Resting time: 3 hours

Panir, also spelled "paneer," is a mild and creamy cheese from India. Like most fresh cheeses, it takes on the flavors of herbs and spices very well. Try mixing in curry powder, dry mustard, and turmeric. You could also add sesame seeds or coriander. This is a "rinsed" cheese, one that is rinsed under running water to remove the coagulating agent.

Ingredients/Equipment:

1 gal whole cow's milk

8 tbsps lemon juice

Stainless steel cooking pot
Colander
Cheesecloth
Spoon

Directions:

1. Add milk to pot under medium heat. Bring to a rolling boil, stirring frequently.

2. Reduce heat and add lemon juice. Cook for another 10-15 seconds.

3. Remove from heat and stir gently until large curds appear. If the whey is milky instead of clear, return to heat for another minute or so.

4. Once curds appear and whey is clear, remove from heat and let rest for ten minutes.

5. Remove the curds from the whey and place in cheesecloth-lined colander. Tie the cheesecloth into a knot and lift the bag out over the sink. Run a gentle stream of lukewarm water over the contents of the bag for 15-30 seconds. Gently twist the top of the cloth bundle to squeeze out more whey and water.

6. Hang and drain the bundle over the sink or place it back in the colander and place a brick or filled bowl of water on the bundle. Press for two hours.

7. Unwrap cheese and add herbs or seasonings as desired. This cheese keeps in the refrigerator for up to two weeks, if stored in a covered container.

Chenna

Prep time: 45 minutes
Cooking time: 20-25 minutes
Resting time: 10 minutes
Pressing time: 45 minutes

Chenna is similar to paneer. However, it is whipped while still warm to give it a velvety, whipped cream consistency. Unflavored chenna is used in recipes for many

Indian sweets. It can also be flavored with herbs and spices. Try curry powder, cumin, or coriander. Chenna is also shaped into a patty and lightly fried for a snack, as in this recipe.

Ingredients/Equipment:

1 gal whole cow's milk

8 tbsps lemon juice

Minced green chilies (optional)

Herbs and spices (see suggestions above)

Olive oil for or clarified butter for frying

Stainless steel cooking pot

Colander

Cheesecloth

Spoon

Directions:

1. Add milk to pot under medium heat. Bring to a rolling boil, stirring frequently.

2. Reduce heat and add lemon juice. Cook for another 10-15 seconds.

3. Remove from heat and stir gently until large curds appear. If the whey is milky instead of clear, return to heat for another minute or so.

4. Once curds appear and whey is clear, remove from heat and let rest for ten minutes.

5. Remove the curds from the whey and place in cheesecloth-lined colander. Tie the cheesecloth into a knot and lift the bag out over the sink. Run a gentle stream of lukewarm water over the contents of the bag for 15-30 seconds. Gently twist the top of the cloth bundle to squeeze out more whey and water.

6. Return the wrapped cheese to the colander. Place a 5-pound weight on top of the wrapped cheese and press for 45 minutes.

7. Unwrap the still-warm cheese and place it on a smooth, clean surface. Break it apart and press with a clean cloth to remove any remaining whey.

8. Knead the cheese by **pressing** it with your palm and the heel of your hand. Gather up the cheese with a spatula and continue to knead it for up to ten minutes or until the cheese is light and velvety without any grainy texture.

9. Add minced chilies, salt, herbs, or other seasonings to taste.

10. Shape cheese into flat patties and fry lightly if desired or store worked cheese in a covered container in refrigerator for one to two weeks.

English farmer's cheese

Prep time: 45 minutes
Cook time: 20 minutes
Resting time: 30 hours

This mild white cheese is made in molds. Use either 8-inch Brie molds or 4-inch Camembert molds. Either way, look for a classic round, flat cheese mold for this particular recipe. This is not a difficult cheese to make, but because it is molded and drained onto cheese mats, it involves a few more steps and is a good cheese to try before moving on to more complicated recipes. This cheese can also be made with low-fat milk, so it is a good choice for people concerned about high-fat cheeses. The finished cheese is a bit firmer than some white cheeses; it slices well and can be eaten on muffins or drizzled with olive oil and herbs.

Ingredients/Equipment:

10 qts whole or low-fat cow's milk
¼ tsp mesophilic starter culture
¼ tsp calcium chloride
¼ tsp liquid rennet
4 tsps pickling, kosher, or sea salt
2 8-inch Brie molds or 4 4-inch Camembert molds
Stainless steel cooking pot

Larger pot for hot water bath

Kitchen thermometer

Colander

Cheesecloth

Spoon

Curd knife

Spatula

Cheese mats

Rack

Cheese board

Large plastic container, big enough to hold the rack

Directions:

1. Pour milk into cooking pot. Place pot in larger pot half-filled with water for hot water bath. Warm milk to 90° Fahrenheit, stirring gently.

2. Sprinkle mesophilic culture over the surface of the milk and let stand for five minutes. Using spatula and an up-and-down motion, work starter into milk. Do not stir, beat, whisk, or whip.

3. Dilute calcium chloride in ¼ cup of cool distilled water. Work into milk mixture as you did with starter culture.

4. Dilute rennet in ¼ cup of cool distilled water. Work into milk mixture as you did with starter culture.

5. Cover milk mixture and let rest for one hour, maintaining temperature at 90° Fahrenheit. You may have to put the milk back into a warm bath, or let the milk rest on a heating pad. Either way, you must monitor the temperature carefully.

6. Test the curds with your knife. You should get what is called a "clean break" — your knife should cut cleanly into the curds without dragging. If this does not happen, let mixture rest another 15 minutes before cutting.

7. Place a rack inside a large, square plastic container. On the rack, place a cutting board, and then cover the board with cheese mats. On the mats, place the two 8-inch or four 4-inch molds.

8. Cut across the cheese mixture, creating thick slices of curd. Layer these slices into the molds. If the whey is still draining as you cut deeper into the curd, wait before making more slices. Continue until all the curd is layered into the molds.

9. Cover the draining container with the molds inside and let everything rest for 12 hours at room temperature.

10. Flip the cheeses over in their molds and let them drain for another 12 hours. If the cheeses stick, use a knife to gently loosen them from the mats before turning.

11. Sprinkle cheeses with salt and place them on clean mats in a clean container.

12. Refrigerate for six to eight hours until firm. Remove from the molds.

13. Wrap each cheese in waxed paper or parchment paper and store in the refrigerator for up to ten days.

Chapter Seven

Expanding Your Horizons: Semi-Firm, Ripened, and Brine-Washed Cheeses

At this point, you have experienced the satisfaction of making your own cheese. You have discovered the mystery is not such a mystery after all. You have enjoyed cream cheese, cottage cheese, and various fresh cheeses that can be eaten right away or used in recipes. Now, however, it is time to move on to the broader world of cheese making. In this section, you will learn how to make some of the most popular cheeses in America, everything from Monterey Jack for your sandwich to mozzarella for your pizza. These cheeses are particularly satisfying because they can be made and stored for future use or given to friends without the worry of whether they will be eaten right away.

A Note on Brine and Washed-Rind Cheeses

As we learned in Chapter 2, cheeses with rinds come in two types. There are blooming rind cheeses, which are treated with specific molds to produce the rind's edible natural coating on the outside of the cheese. Many other cheeses are washed in either salt brine, a mixture of salt and water, or liquids such as beer or wine to produce a rind. Recipes usually tell you whether you need a brine. All rinds can be eaten. If you do not brine the cheese, the cheese may not come out the way the recipe intends. Because the brine is salty, it gives a salty taste to the cheese. Each

Photographs courtesy of ChiotsRun.com

washed-rind cheese recipe included in this book has its own instructions for the washing solution, but here is a simple salt brine solution that can be used with many cheeses. This brine can also be used on meats such as pork and turkey.

Basic salt brine

Ingredients/Equipment:

1 gal distilled water
1 ½ cups kosher or pickling salt
Cooking pot

Directions:

Many salt-brined cheeses require brine that is 18 to 22 percent salt. In order to create brine, heat the water and add the salt, stirring until dissolved. Unless the recipe specifies hot brine, let the brine cool before using.

CASE STUDY: "HAPPY COWS" PRODUCING RAW MILK CHEESE

Three Sisters Farmstead Cheese Company
24163 Road 188
Lindsay, CA 93247
(559) 562-2132 (p)
(559) 562-0911 (f)
www.threesisterscheese.com

The Three Sisters Farmstead Cheese Company produced its first wheel of cheese in 1999. Owner Marisa Simoes raises her own herd of Jersey cows to provide the freshest ingredients for her award-winning and completely original raw-milk cheeses, Serena and Serenita. She feels that the best part of cheese making is "receiving public praise for an outstanding product that you worked so hard to produce." She also recognizes the "challenge of keeping a steady inventory of a cheese aged a year or more when your sales are not consistent."

The company produces approximately 25,000 pounds of cheese per year or 500 pounds each week. Serena is ripened for 12 to 18 months, giving it "an intense, nutty flavor," while Serenita is aged for two to five months, which produces a cheese that is "sweet and savory, with subtle herbal flavors and a buttery texture." Both cheeses are sold through wholesale distributors to fine restaurants and gourmet shops. Simoes also offers a gift box of Serena and Serenita through **http://threesister-scheese.foodzie.com**.

Semi-Firm Cheeses

The semi-firm cheeses are perhaps the most versatile of all the cheeses. Like soft cheeses, they melt well and can be used in many recipes. Like the hard cheeses, they can be aged or smoked to vary flavor. They last longer than many fresh cheeses, but like fresh cheeses, they make terrific snacks, and many semi-firm cheeses go well with fruit. Semi-firm cheeses feature some of the most familiar and beloved varieties, including Monterey Jack, Swiss, Gouda, and many more.

Monterey Jack

Prep time: 25 minutes
Cooking time: 45 minutes
Resting time: 3 days
Aging time: 30-90 days

Monterey Jack is a true American cheese, created in Monterey County, California in the 19th century. Often called Jack cheese, it is a snacking and sandwich cheese, but is also used in many Tex-Mex recipes. It can be mild or sharp, depending on how long it is aged. It is usually cream colored. Commercial cheese makers often combine pieces of Monterey Jack with pieces of Colby to create an orange-and-white cheese called Colby Jack or Cojack.

Ingredients/Equipment:

2 gals whole cow's milk

Note: *For a grated Monterey Jack, use skim milk instead of whole milk, the finished product will have a texture similar to Parmesan.*

1 packet direct-set mesophilic starter culture or 4 oz prepared starter culture

½ tablet rennet

1 tbsp cheese salt

Cheese wax

Stainless steel cooking pot

Wax melting pot

Kitchen thermometer

Plastic mold for hard cheese, 7 ¾x8 in

Curd knife

Colander

Cheesecloth

Directions:

1. Heat the milk to 90° Fahrenheit. Add the mesophilic starter and stir thoroughly.

2. Cover and let rest at 90° Fahrenheit for 30 minutes.

3. Stir rennet into 1/4 cup of cool distilled water. Add to milk mixture, stirring gently for one minute.

4. Cover again and let rest for 30-45 minutes at 90° Fahrenheit, until the curds give a clean break (slice cleanly) when tested.

5. Cut curd into ¼-inch cubes and let rest for 40 minutes.

6. Heat curds to 100° Fahrenheit, increasing temperature gradually, about 5° for every five minutes. Stir frequently to keep curds from **matting**.

7. Maintain curds at 100° Fahrenheit for 30 minutes, stirring occasionally.

8. Let rest for five minutes. Pour off whey to the level of the curds.

9. Let curds rest another 30 minutes, stirring occasionally to prevent curds from matting together. Keep the temperature at 100° Fahrenheit.

10. Line a colander with cheesecloth and remove the curds from the whey, ladling them into the colander. Sprinkle with salt and mix. Let drain.

11. Line a mold with cheesecloth and transfer the curds. Press with a brick or other 3-pound weight for 15 minutes.

12. Remove the cheese and peel away the cheesecloth. Turn the cheese over and rewrap it in the cheesecloth. Press for 12 hours.

13. Remove the cheese from the mold. Unwrap it and place it on a clean surface or a cheese rack to air dry. Turn the cheese twice a day until the surface of the cheese is dry to the touch. This will take two to three days, depending on humidity.

14. Coat the cheese with wax.

15. Age the cheese at 55° Fahrenheit for 30-90 days, turning it over at least once a week. The longer you age it, the sharper it will be.

American-style cheese

Prep time: 20 minutes
Cooking time: 2 hours, 20 minutes
Resting time: 2 hours
Pressing time: 6 hours

Even though we might not admit it, most of us love the smooth consistency and slightly tangy but never overwhelming flavor of American cheese slices. Indeed, for many children, "American" cheese is the only cheese there is. This recipe will produce a cheese with that comforting flavor and texture, but without all the salt and preservatives that often go along with the wrapped slice. Be sure to monitor the heat carefully during the cooking process; this cheese needs fairly high heat to come together.

Ingredients/Equipment:

1 gal whole milk
½ cup powdered milk
1 cup cultured buttermilk
½ tsp liquid rennet
¼ tsp annatto coloring (optional)

Non-reactive cooking pot
Thermometer
Colander
Cheesecloth
Cheese knife
Cheese press
1 tsp cheese salt or kosher salt
Tome mold
Distilled water

Directions:

1. Combine the whole milk and powdered milk. In a non-reactive pot, warm the buttermilk to 86° Fahrenheit. Add the rest of the milk mixture. Let sit at room temperature for 90 minutes.

2. Mix rennet into ¼ cup of cool distilled water. Add to milk mixture. Add **annatto** coloring if you wish cheese to be yellow. Let rest for 30 minutes, keeping the mixture warm but not cooking it. Wrap the pot in a towel or put pot in a sink full of warm water.

3. Check for a clean break. If clean break is not present, let mixture rest for another 10 to 15 minutes.

4. When clean break is present, use cheese knife to cut curds into ½-inch cubes.

5. Return pot to heat and warm to 86° Fahrenheit. Hold at this temperature for 30 minutes.

6. Slowly warm temperature to 104° Fahrenheit, stirring frequently. Hold for 60 minutes at 104° Fahrenheit.

7. Remove pot from heat and pour into cloth-lined colander, draining off any whey. Cut curds again. While still warm, work salt into cheese curds. Pack curds while still warm into cloth-lined mold.

8. Place mold in cheese press and press for four hours at 15 pounds of pressure. Remove cheese from press, unwrap, turn, and rewrap. Return

cheese to mold and place mold back in press. Press for eight hours at 15 pounds of pressure.

9. Once pressed, cheese is ready to eat. Wrap and store in the refrigerator.

Mysost

Prep time: 10 minutes
Cooking time: 6-10 hours
Resting time: 12 hours

Mysost is a Scandinavian cheese, most often served for breakfast. It is made from whey that is cooked down for many hours, until the resulting cheese has a lovely caramelized color and flavor. Mysost is a great cheese to use whey from for another cow's milk cheese. It is time-consuming, but the resulting cheese is unique and well worth the effort. The finished cheese can be frozen for up to four months.

Ingredients/Equipment:

Fresh whey from 2 gals of cow's milk
1 cup heavy cream
Cooking pot
Slotted spoon
Electric blender
Rectangular cheese molds or food grade plastic containers
Kitchen sink filled with ice water

Directions:

1. Pour the fresh whey (no more than three hours old) into the pot and bring to a boil. Watch carefully. Foam will appear on the surface once the whey is boiling.

2. Skim off foam with a slotted spoon and reserve foam in a covered container at room temperature for later.

3. Allow the whey to boil slowly over low heat in an uncovered pot. It will need to boil at least six hours, perhaps as long as ten hours.

4. Once the whey boils down to 75 percent of its original volume, start stirring frequently to prevent the mixture from sticking. Add the reserved foam.

5. As the whey thickens, add the cream.

6. Remove the mixture from the heat and pour carefully into a blender.

7. Hold down the top of the blender with a potholder or oven mitt. The whey will be very hot, and if the lid on the blender is not held down, it may pop off.

8. Blend at medium speed for one minute until smooth and creamy.

9. Pour the mixture back into the pot and continue to cook over low heat, stirring constantly.

10. Once the mixture cooks to the consistency of fudge, remove from heat and plunge pot into kitchen sink filled with ice cubes and cold water.

11. Continue stirring the mixture until it is cool enough to pour into molds.

12. Let molded cheese cool overnight.

13. Remove from molds, wrap, and refrigerate or freeze.

14. Slice mysost and serve it with toast for breakfast.

Mozzarella

Prep time: 20 minutes
Cook time: 3-4 hours
Rest time: 2-3 hours

Mozzarella is one of America's favorite Italian cheeses. The average American eats over 13 pounds of mozzarella cheese each year, mostly in shredded form on pizzas. Of course, much of that is commercially processed and prepackaged, but artisan mozzarella is becoming more and more popular. Fresh mozzarella is delicious in salads. It is also good sliced with fresh tomatoes, drizzled with olive oil and sprinkled with herbs, and it is a mainstay of many Italian dishes. Classic mozzarella was made with buffalo's milk, but cow's milk will work fine. Whole milk gives the best flavor.

Ingredients/Equipment:

1 gal whole cow's milk

1/8 tsp direct-set thermophilic culture

¼ tablet of rennet

Stainless steel cooking pot

Larger pot for double boiler

Brine pot

Kitchen thermometer

Curd knife

Colander

Cheesecloth

Draining bowl

Wooden spoons

New latex gloves

pH testing strips

Directions:

1. Pour milk into cooking pot and heat to 90° Fahrenheit. Add starter culture.

2. Let mixture rest for 45 minutes.

3. Add rennet to mixture and stir for five minutes. Let the mixture rest at 90° Fahrenheit for one hour.

4. Insert a curd knife and check to see if there is a clean break. If so, remove from heat and cut mixture into ½ inch cubes.

5. Reheat the mixture to 90° Fahrenheit for 30 minutes.

6. Slowly raise temperature to 105° Fahrenheit; this should take approximately 30 minutes.

7. Cook at 105° Fahrenheit for five to ten minutes.

8. Pour mixture into cheesecloth-lined colander and drain whey.

9. Return mixture to cook pot and place cook pot inside larger pot that is half-full of water at 105° Fahrenheit. The water in the larger pot must stay at 105° Fahrenheit.

10. Continue to cook mixture at 105° Fahrenheit for two to three hours, periodically draining off extra whey and stirring the curds so they heat evenly. As the whey continues to be drained, the curds will form a paste at the bottom of the cook pot.

11. Test the pH of the curds; this should be between 5 and 5.3. If it is not in this range, continue cooking and check the pH again until it hits the 5 to 5.3 goal.

12. Cut the cooked curds into half-inch cubes again and place them in four cups of water that is heated to 170° Fahrenheit.

13. Using two wooden spoons, press the curds together into a ball.

14. Once the curds form into a ball, remove them from the hot water and work them with your hands, making sure your hands are protected from the heat by latex or other heat-resistant gloves.

15. Stretch and knead the ball until you are satisfied with the texture. It should be springy but not rubbery.

16. Plunge the ball of cheese into a cold (55° Fahrenheit) 18 percent brine solution. Let the cheese soak in the solution for one hour.

17. Remove the cheese from the brine, wrap in waxed paper or parchment paper, and place in the refrigerator. It is ready to eat.

Smoked mozzarella

Prep time: 1 hour, 10 minutes
Cook time 4-15 hours

For a real treat, try smoked mozzarella. Smoking adds a delicate flavor and aroma to mozzarella cheese, and a home smoker will work well for this recipe. Smoked mozzarella is an incredible appetizer, and it works well with mushrooms, marinated peppers, and other ingredients in an antipasto platter. Smoked mozzarella also adds an extra level of taste to pasta dishes, and it works very well with chicken on a pizza. Be sure to use apple or cherry wood chips rather than hickory or mesquite chips, since the stronger-smelling chips will create smoke that can overwhelm the flavor of the cheese.

Ingredients/Equipment:

1 batch of mozzarella cheese (*see previous recipe*)
Home smoker
Cherry or apple wood chips

Directions:

1. Soak the wood chips in water for one hour.

2. Sit a rack inside your home smoker, or wrap the mozzarella in cheesecloth and hang it from the top of the smoker.

3. Smoke on low heat (65-85° Fahrenheit). This prevents butterfat from being drawn from the cheese.

4. Smoke for 4-15 hours.

Asadero

Prep time: 60 minutes
Cooking time: 2 hours, 10 minutes
Resting time: 1 hours, 30 minutes
Chilling time: 15 minutes
Brining time: 30 minutes

Asadero is a Mexican "spun paste" cheese. It is similar in texture and flavor to freshly made mozzarella. Asadero means "roastable," and this cheese is famed for its melting qualities; it will melt smoothly without getting oily. Asadero is the cheese of choice for genuine Mexican quesadillas. Be sure to wear heat-resistant, new rubber gloves when handling the curds for this cheese.

Ingredients/Equipment:

8 qts whole cow's milk

¼ tsp thermophilic culture

¼ tsp liquid rennet

¼ tsp calcium chloride

Bowl of ice water

Stainless steel cooking pot

Brine pot

Thermometer

Curd knife

Colander

Cheesecloth

Cutting board

Wooden spoons

New rubber gloves

Measuring cup

Directions:

1. Start with sterilized equipment. Pour milk into a cooking pot that is placed into a hot water bath. Over medium heat, warm milk to 99° Fahrenheit, stirring gently as the milk warms. Remove from heat.

2. Sprinkle the culture over the surface of the milk and let stand for five minutes. Using skimmer, gently draw the culture down into the milk with an up-and-down motion, doing your best not to break the surface of the milk. Return pot to hot water bath. Cover and let ripen for 45 minutes.

3. Dilute calcium chloride in ¼ cup of cool distilled water and add to milk, using the same up-and-down motion.

4. Dilute rennet in ¼ cup of cool distilled water and add to the mixture, again using an up-and-down motion to disturb the surface as little as possible. Cover pot again and let it sit for 45 minutes.

5. Check mixture for a clean break. If curds do not break clean, let them sit for another ten minutes. Once a clean break is achieved, use the skimmer and curd knife to cut curd into ¾-inch cubes. Let curds settle to the bottom of the pot and rest for five minutes. Then stir for 30 minutes.

6. Using a measuring cup, remove approximately ⅓ of the whey from the pot. To do so, dip out whey until you can see the surface of the curds. Make sure you measure the whey you removed.

7. Replace the volumes of removed whey with hot water to bring the temperature to 108° Fahrenheit, adjusting with more hot or cool water as needed but not exceeding the amount of whey removed. Stir the mixture continuously for 30 minutes. Let curds settle and hold, maintaining temperature for one hour.

8. In a separate pan, heat five quarts of water to 185° Fahrenheit.

9. Pour curds into cloth-lined colander and let drain until they are matted together. Place mass on a cutting board and cut into 2-inch cubes. Place cubes in a large bowl and pour water heated to 185° Fahrenheit over them to soften. Wearing heat-resistant gloves, knead and pull cheese underwater until it melts together into one mass.

10. Return cheese to board and knead mass until shiny and smooth. Shape into a smooth ball. Plunge ball of cheese into a bowl of ice water for 15 minutes to chill and firm.

11. Immerse chilled cheese in brine solution for 30 minutes. Remove from brine, pat dry.

12. Use cheese immediately or wrap tightly and store in refrigerator for up to two weeks.

Provolone

Prep Time: 30 minutes

Cook time: 50 minutes

Rest time: 36-48 hours

Brining time: 12 hours

Ripening time 2 to 12 months

Provolone, like mozzarella, is a *pasta filata* cheese that must be worked by hand in order to obtain the right texture. It has a slightly creamier texture and flavor than mozzarella, and it can also be smoked. Like mozzarella, it is eaten fresh or used in various Italian recipes. The major difference between the two cheeses is that provolone develops a rind and mozzarella does not.

Ingredients/Equipment:

1 gal non-homogenized whole cow's milk

¼ tsp direct-set thermophilic culture

¼ tsp mesophilic culture

¾ tsp liquid rennet

¾ tsp calcium chloride

Cool brine solution

Stainless steel cooking pot

Larger pot for hot water bath

Brine pot

Skimmer

Kitchen thermometer

Curd knife

Colander

Cheesecloth

Draining bowl

Cheese rack

Cheese mats

Wooden spoon

New latex gloves

Olive oil

Directions:

1. Pour milk into cooking pot. Place pot in hot water bath under low heat, heating milk to 96° Fahrenheit. Turn off heat.

2. Sprinkle both thermophilic and mesophilic cultures over the milk's surface. Let rest for five minutes. Using skimmer or a spatula and an up-and-down motion, gently introduce both cultures into the milk. Do not stir, beat, or whisk. Cover and rest for 45 minutes.

3. Dilute calcium chloride in ¼ cup of cool distilled water. Add to milk mixture using the same up-and-down motion.

4. Dilute rennet in ¼ cup of cool distilled water. Add to milk mixture using the same up-and-down motion.

5. Cover mixture and let rest for approximately one hour.

6. Uncover and test with curd knife for a clean break. If curd is still fragile, cover and let rest for another 15 minutes.

7. Using a curd knife and a skimmer, break mixture into 1/2-inch cubes. Let stand five minutes to firm up curds.

8. Return curd mixture to low heat in hot water bath and gradually warm curds to 115 ° Fahrenheit. Stir gently and continually through this process. Make sure it takes 30 minutes for the curds' temperature to reach 115° Fahrenheit. Adjust temperature as needed to ensure that the full 30 minutes are used.

9. Place curds in cheesecloth-lined colander and drain whey. The curds should form a solid mass.

10. Place the mass of curds on a cutting board and slice into 1-inch cubes. Place these cubes in the cooking pot and cover with water heated to 145° Fahrenheit. Let this mixture stand until the water temperature drops to 130° Fahrenheit. This will take one to two hours.

11. Wearing gloves for protection from the heat, pick up the cubes and work them into a large ball, kneading and shaping the mass under the water. Once you have a large ball, pull it out of the water and stretch it

into a rope shape. Loop it back on itself and stretch it again until it is a shiny and smooth mass. Do not let the cheese get too cool or it will become brittle. If it begins to cool, place it back in the water and warm it again before stretching it more.

12. Once the cheese is smooth and shiny, shape it into a ball or pear shape and place it in a bowl of ice water to firm up for about 20 to 30 minutes.

13. Place the cooled cheese in the pot of brine solution. Let it rest for 12 hours at room temperature, turning it once after six hours.

14. Remove cheese from brine. Place on a rack and let it air dry for one to two days, turning it periodically.

15. Place the cheese on a cheese mat in a ripening container and put into a controlled cooling environment. Cure at 62°-65° Fahrenheit and 80 to 85 percent humidity. Turn cheese daily for the first two weeks, then once a week after that.

16. If spots of mold appear, wipe cheese with a solution of a teaspoon of salt dissolved in one-fourth cup vinegar.

17. After the cheese has cured for one month, wipe the rind with olive oil. Repeat monthly as the cheese cures.

18. Cure cheese for two to four months to serve as a slicing cheese or 6-12 months if a hard grating cheese is desired

Pepper Jack cheese

Prep Time: 45 minutes
Cook Time: 1 hour, 30 minutes
Resting Time: 72 hours
Aging Time: 1-4 months

The only way to make Monterey Jack better is to add hot peppers to the mix. The advantage to this recipe over the store-bought version is that you can control the peppers and the heat. Use chopped jalapeños, crushed red pepper, or even habeneros. This cheese is wonderful with bread or crackers, and it is also delicious in any number of Tex-Mex recipes. Try it shredded on a bowl of chili or use it to top tacos.

Ingredients/Equipment:

2 gals whole cow's milk
1 package direct-set mesophilic starter
½ tsp liquid rennet
1 tbsp pickling or kosher salt
¼ cup finely diced jalapeno peppers
¼ cup finely diced habanero peppers (optional; substitute another ¼ cup of jalapeno peppers or ¼ cup of crushed red pepper flakes if preferred)
Non-reactive cooking pot
Larger pot for hot water bath
Colander
Cheesecloth
Skimmer
Large (3.5x7.5 in) tome mold
Curd knife
Cheese press
Cheese mat
Thermometer
Ripening container
Cheese wax
Natural bristle brush

Directions:

1. Using sterilized equipment, pour the milk into the cooking pot and place the pot in a hot water bath on the stove. Heat the milk to 88° Fahrenheit. Add the mesophilic starter and stir thoroughly. Cover pot and increase heat to allow mixture to ripen for 30 minutes at 90° Fahrenheit. Monitor the temperature throughout this process.

2. Add the finely chopped peppers. Stir until the peppers are well blended throughout the mixture.

3. Dilute rennet in 1/2 cup of cool distilled water. Using skimmer and an up-and-down motion, mix rennet into milk, disturbing the surface of the milk as little as possible. Cover and let sit for 30 minutes, maintaining the temperature at 90° Fahrenheit.

4. Check for a clean break. If curds do not break clean, cover again and let sit for ten minutes. If clean break is achieved, use skimmer and curd knife to cut curds into 1/4- inch cubes. Cover again and let sit for about 40 minutes at room temperature.

5. Heat the curds slowly to 100° Fahrenheit, increasing the temperature by two degrees approximately every five minutes. Depending on the temperature of the mixture when you begin, this may take up to 35 minutes. Gently stir the mixture throughout this process to keep the curds from matting.

6. Once the mixture reaches 100° Fahrenheit, maintain that temperature for 30 minutes, again stirring occasionally to keep the curds from matting. Remove the pot from the heat and let curds sit for five minutes.

7. Gently pour off the whey to the level of the curds.

8. Return the pot to the heat and warm mixture to 200° Fahrenheit. Maintain the curds at this temperature for 30 minutes, stirring frequently to prevent the curds from matting.

9. Ladle the curds into a cheesecloth-lined colander placed in the sink or over a larger bowl. Sprinkle mixture with salt. Let drain for ten minutes.

10. Pack the curds into a cheesecloth-lined tomme mold. Pull the cloth up around the mixture and wrap and smooth the cloth over the top. Put lid on mold.

11. Place in cheese press or put a 3 pound weight on top of the mold and press for 15 minutes.

12. Remove cheese from the weight, peel away cheesecloth, and turn cheese over. Rewrap cheese and place it back in the press or under a 10-pound weight. Press at ten pounds of pressure for 12 hours.

13. Remove the cheese from the press, unwrap and place it on a clean surface to dry at room temperature. Turn the cheese twice a day until it is dry to the touch. Drying may take up to three days.

14. Place the cheese in the refrigerator for five to six hours, then remove and wax it with two coats of cheese wax, letting it dry between coats.

15. Age the waxed cheese at 55° Fahrenheit for one to four months, depending on how sharp you wish the finished cheese to be. Turn the cheese over at least once a week as it ages.

Edam

Prep time: 60 minutes
Cook time: 2 hours
Rest time: 10 minutes
Pressing time: 14 hours
Brining time: 12 hours
Drying time: 2-3 days
Ripening time: 1-2 months

Along with Gouda, Edam is one of the best-known and loved cheese exports from the Netherlands, the region known as Holland. Edam is instantly recognizable by its ball shape. It is a mild and creamy cheese, good for snacks, sandwiches, recipes, and fondues. Edam is made with cow's milk; you can use either whole or 2-percent milk, but whole milk will produce a creamier cheese with a softer texture.

Ingredients/Equipment:

16 qts whole or 2% cow's milk
½ tsp mesophilic culture
¾ tsp calcium chloride
¾ tsp liquid rennet

18% brine solution
Non-reactive cooking pot
Second non-reactive pot for warm whey
Large pot for hot water bath
Distilled water
Colander
Cheesecloth
Skimmer
Curd knife
Bowl for drained whey
Cheese press
Cheese mat
Thermometer
Ripening container
Cheese wax
Natural bristle brush

Directions:

1. Start with sterilized equipment. Pour milk into a cooking pot that is placed into a hot water bath. Over medium heat, warm milk to 88° Fahrenheit, stirring gently as the milk warms. Once milk reaches 88° Fahrenheit, remove from heat.

2. Sprinkle the culture over the surface of the milk and let stand for five minutes. Using skimmer, gently draw the culture down into the milk with an up-and-down motion, doing your best not to break the surface of the milk. Return pot to hot water bath. Cover and let ripen for 30 minutes; maintain temperature at 88° Fahrenheit.

3. Dilute calcium chloride in ¼ cup of cool distilled water and add to milk, using the same up-and-down motion.

4. Dilute rennet in ¼ cup of cool distilled water and add to the mixture, again using an up-and-down motion to disturb the surface as little as possible. Cover pot again and let it sit for 30 minutes; maintain the 88° temperature.

5. Check mixture for a clean break. If curds do not break clean, let them sit for another ten minutes. Once a clean break is achieved, use the skimmer and curd knife to cut curd into 1/2-inch cubes. Let curds settle to the bottom of the pot and rest for five minutes.

6. Return pot to heat and begin to slowly warm curds to 92º Fahrenheit, stirring slowly and adjusting heat to make sure it takes 15-20 minutes for curds to come to 92º Fahrenheit. Do not heat too quickly. Once 92º Fahrenheit is achieved, let curds settle to the bottom of the pot.

7. Drain off enough whey to expose the surface of the curds. Reserve drained whey in a large clean pot.

8. Replace the drained whey with an equivalent amount of warm distilled water to bring the curds to 99º Fahrenheit. Stir continuously for 30 minutes, maintaining the temperature at 92º Fahrenheit.

9. Let curds settle and begin to mat together. Drain off whey, adding half to the reserved whey in the second pot and draining the other half through the prepared mold to warm it. Fill the warmed mold with curds. Pull up cheesecloth around the curd bundle and fold cloth neatly over the top of the bundle. Put on the mold lid.

10. Place mold in cheese press. Press at 12 pounds of pressure for 30 minutes.

11. Warm the pot of reserved whey to 122º Fahrenheit. Remove the cheese from the press and unwrap it. Place cheese in whey for 20 minutes, turning it three times to make sure all surfaces of the cheese are exposed to the whey.

12. Remove cheese from whey solution, rewrap and place in the mold again. Place mold in the cheese press and press at 16 pounds of pressure for seven hours. Remove cheese from press, unwrap, turn, and rewrap. Place the cheese back in the press and press at 16 pounds of pressure for another seven hours.

13. Remove cheese from press and unwrap it. Place cheese in brine solution for 12 hours, turning once during this process.

14. Remove cheese from brine and let it dry on a cheese mat placed on a rack at room temperature for two to three days, turning the cheese once daily. You may wax the cheese at this stage or ripen it un-waxed.

15. If ripening without wax, place the cheese on a clean cheese mat in a ripening container. Ripen at 50-54º Fahrenheit and 85 percent humidity. Every second day, wipe cheese with a brine-soaked cloth.

16. If waxed cheese is desired, coat cheese with two coats of wax, using a natural bristle brush and letting each coat of wax dry. Then ripen cheese at 50-54º Fahrenheit and 85 percent humidity. Turn cheese once a week to ensure even ripening.

17. With either waxed or un-waxed cheese, let cheese ripen for a minimum of two months. You may continue to ripen cheese for a third month if a stronger flavor is desired.

Havarti

Prep time: 60 minutes
Cook time: 70 minutes
Rest time: 10 hours
Ripening time: 4 weeks

A classic Danish cheese, havarti is semi-firm and has a somewhat open, lacy-looking texture throughout. It is often served as a snack or in sandwiches, but it also works well in fondues and recipes. Most havarti is fairly mild-tasting, but if it is ripened past the initial four weeks, it becomes deeper and richer in flavor. In addition, some havarti has dill or other herbs added for more flavor, and there is also a smoked version of this versatile cheese.

Ingredients/Equipment:

16 qts whole cow's milk
½ tsp mesophilic culture
¾ tsp calcium chloride
¾ tsp liquid rennet

⅓ cup pickling or kosher salt

Non-reactive cooking pot

Large pot for hot water bath

Colander

Cheesecloth

Large round mold

Skimmer

Curd knife

Measuring cup

Cheese press

Cheese mat

Thermometer

Ripening container

Cheese wax

Measuring cup

Brush

Directions:

1. Start with sterilized equipment. Pour milk into a cooking pot that is placed into a hot water bath. Over medium heat, warm milk to 90° Fahrenheit, stirring gently as the milk warms. Once milk reaches 90° Fahrenheit, remove from heat.

2. Sprinkle the culture over the surface of the milk and let stand for five minutes. Using skimmer, gently draw the culture down into the milk with an up-and-down motion, doing your best not to break the surface of the milk. Return pot to hot water bath. Cover and let ripen for 30 minutes, maintain temperature at 90° Fahrenheit.

3. Dilute calcium chloride in ¼ cup of cool distilled water and add to milk, using the same up-and-down motion.

4. Dilute rennet in ¼ cup of cool distilled water and add to the mixture, again using an up-and-down motion to disturb the surface as little as possible. Cover pot again and let it sit for 45 minutes, maintaining the temperature at 90° Fahrenheit.

5. Check mixture for a clean break. If curds do not break clean, let sit for another ten minutes. Once a clean break is achieved, use the skimmer and curd knife to cut curd into half-inch cubes. Stir gently for ten minutes; curds will shrink slightly during this process. Let curds settle to the bottom of the pot.

6. Using a measuring cup, remove five quarts or about ⅓ of the whey from the pot until you can just see the surface of the curds. Replace the whey with an equal amount of distilled water, which is already heated to 170° Fahrenheit. This should make the mixture 100° Fahrenheit. If necessary, raise the temperature by adding more hot water, or lower it by adding cool water.

7. Add the salt to the pot, stirring constantly. Hold the mixture for 30 minutes at 100° Fahrenheit, stirring every five minutes or so to keep the curds from sticking together or matting. After 30 minutes, let curds settle and mat at the bottom of the pot.

8. Pour curds into cloth-lined colander. Using skimmer, break up curds slightly to release extra whey. Fill a prepared, cheesecloth-lined mold with curds, packing the mixture tightly to ensure that there are no air pockets between the curds. Pull up cloth round the curds, wrapping and smoothing it across the top of the bundle. Put on the mold lid.

9. Place mold in cheese press or place a 5-pound weight on top. Press lightly for 20 minutes.

10. Remove cheese from the press and redress by unwrapping the cheese, turning it over in the mold, rewrapping it, and pressing again. Continue to press the cheese for six to eight hours.

11. Remove the cheese from the press. Unwrap it and place it on a cheese mat in a ripening container. Cover and ripen at 54° Fahrenheit and 90 percent humidity for four weeks. Turn cheese once a day during the first week, draining any additional whey from the bottom of the container. After the first week, turn cheese once every two days.

12. After four weeks of ripening, remove cheese from container. Using cheese wax and a natural bristle brush, coat cheese with two or three

layers of wax, allowing each coat to dry before applying the next coat. Store in the refrigerator and serve or continue to ripen to taste. Cheese will become sharper and slightly drier as it ripens further.

Gouda

Prep time: 60 minutes

Cook time: 90 minutes

Rest time: 25 minutes

Pressing time: 8-12 hours

Brining time: 12 hours

Drying time: 2-3 days

Ripening time: 6 weeks-3 months

Gouda was originally a farmhouse cheese from Holland, but it is now made in several countries, including the United States. It has a firm and silky texture and a flavor that can vary from mild and almost sweet to sharp. Smoked Gouda is also popular, as is Gouda with herbs or chilies added. Like Edam, Gouda is usually coated with red wax as a preservative. The Dutch invented this method of waxing cheese when it was discovered that waxed cheeses could be easily stacked and transported by ship without spoiling. Gouda is an excellent snacking cheese and also works well in many recipes.

Ingredients/Equipment:

16 qts whole cow's milk

½ tsp mesophilic culture

¾ tsp calcium chloride

¾ tsp liquid rennet

18% brine solution

Non-reactive cooking pot

Large pot for hot water bath

Distilled water

Colander

Cheesecloth

Skimmer
Curd knife
Large round mold
Cheese press
Cheese mat
Thermometer
Ripening container
Cheese wax
Natural bristle brush

Directions:

1. Start with sterilized equipment. Pour milk into a cooking pot that is placed into a hot water bath. Over medium heat, warm milk to 85° Fahrenheit, stirring gently as the milk warms. Once milk reaches 85° Fahrenheit, remove from heat.

2. Sprinkle the culture over the surface of the milk and let stand for five minutes. Using skimmer, gently draw the culture down into the milk with an up-and-down motion, doing your best not to break the surface of the milk.

3. Dilute calcium chloride in ¼ cup of cool distilled water and add to milk, using the same up-and-down motion.

4. Dilute rennet in ¼ cup of cool distilled water and add to the mixture, again using an up-and-down motion to disturb the surface as little as possible. Cover pot again and let it sit for 30 minutes, maintaining the 85° Fahrenheit temperature.

5. Check mixture for a clean break. If curds do not break clean, let them sit for another ten minutes. Once a clean break is achieved, use the skimmer and curd knife to cut curd into ½-inch cubes. Let curds settle to the bottom of the pot and rest for five minutes. Gently stir curds for five minutes, and then let them settle for five minutes again.

6. Using a measuring cup, remove six cups of whey from the pot, taking care not to disturb the curds at the bottom of the pot.

7. Replace the drained whey with an equivalent amount of distilled water heated to 140° Fahrenheit to bring the curds to 92° Fahrenheit. Stir curds gently for ten minutes, maintaining the temperature at 92° Fahrenheit.

8. Let curds settle and begin to mat together. Drain off whey until curds are just exposed and replace with an equal amount of distilled water heated to 110° Fahrenheit, which will bring the temperature of the pot to about 98° Fahrenheit. Stir continuously for 20 minutes. The curds will shrink to the size of navy beans. Once they shrink, let them stand for ten minutes.

9. Drain whey, pouring it through the prepared mold to warm it. The curds will be knit together at this point. Using your washed hands, break off chunks of curd and place them in the prepared mold, mounding them up in a cone shape. Curds will continue to drain and will lose volume. Pull up cheesecloth around the curd bundle and fold cloth neatly over the top of the bundle. Put on the mold lid.

10. Place mold in cheese press or put a 5-pound weight on the mold. Press at five pounds of pressure for 30 minutes.

11. Remove cheese from press and unwrap it. Turn cheese over, rewrap it, and return it to the press or place a ten to 12-pound weight on it. Press at 10-12 pounds of pressure for 12 hours.

12. Remove cheese from press. Unwrap it and place it in a brine solution for 12 hours, turning it once during this process.

13. Remove cheese from brine and let dry on a cheese mat placed on a rack at room temperature for two to three days, until cheese is dry to the touch. Turn cheese daily during this process.

14. Place cheese on a clean mat in a ripening container and ripen at 50° Fahrenheit and 85 percent humidity for one week.

15. Coat cheese with two or three coats of wax, using a natural bristle brush and letting each coat of wax dry. Then ripen cheese at 50° Fahrenheit

and 85 percent humidity for five weeks to three months. Turn cheese once a week to ensure even ripening.

Hot chili Gouda

Prep time: 60 minutes

Cook time: 90 minutes

Rest time: 25 minutes

Pressing time: 8-12 hours

Brining time: 12 hours

Drying time: 2-3 days

Ripening time: 6 weeks-3 months

This is a spicy variation on the classic Gouda. Gouda purists might argue against the addition of hot peppers, but their bite contrasts wonderfully with Gouda's creamy texture and mild, milky flavor. It is wonderful as a snacking cheese. It also makes an unexpected addition to Tex-Mex dishes. The recipe is similar to Gouda, with one extra step in the middle of the process.

Ingredients/Equipment:

16 qts whole cow's milk

½ tsp mesophilic culture

¾ tsp calcium chloride

¾ tsp liquid rennet

18% brine solution

1 medium fresh jalapeno pepper or 4 tbsp hot pepper flakes

Non-reactive cooking pot

Large pot for hot water bath

Distilled water

Colander

Cheesecloth

Skimmer

Curd knife

Cheese press

Cheese mat
Thermometer
Ripening container
Cheese wax
Natural bristle brush

Directions:

1. Start with sterilized equipment. Pour milk into a cooking pot that is placed into a hot water bath. Over medium heat, warm milk to 85° Fahrenheit, stirring gently as the milk warms. Once milk reaches 85° Fahrenheit, remove from heat.

2. Sprinkle the culture over the surface of the milk and let stand for five minutes. Using skimmer, gently draw the culture down into the milk with an up-and-down motion, doing your best not to break the surface of the milk.

3. Dilute calcium chloride in ¼ cup of cool distilled water and add to milk, using the same up-and-down motion.

4. Dilute rennet in ¼ cup of cool distilled water and add to the mixture, again using an up-and-down motion to disturb the surface as little as possible. Cover pot again and let it sit for 30 minutes, maintain the 85° Fahrenheit temperature.

5. Check mixture for a clean break. If curds do not break clean, let them sit for another ten minutes. Once a clean break is achieved, use the skimmer and curd knife to cut curd into 1/2-inch cubes. Let curds settle to the bottom of the pot and rest for five minutes. Gently stir curds for five minutes and then let them settle for five minutes again.

6. Using a measuring cup, remove six cups of whey from the pot, taking care not to disturb the curds at the bottom of the pot.

7. Replace the drained whey with an equivalent amount of distilled water heated to 140° Fahrenheit to bring the curds to 92° Fahrenheit. Stir curds gently for ten minutes, maintaining the temperature at 92° Fahrenheit.

8. Boil the hot pepper flakes or the finely chopped fresh jalapeno in four cups of water for ten minutes. Let cool.

9. Let curds settle and begin to mat together. Drain off whey until curds are just exposed and replace with an equal amount of distilled water heated to 110º Fahrenheit, which will bring the temperature of the pot to about 98º Fahrenheit. Stir continuously for 20 minutes. The curds will shrink to the size of navy beans. Once they shrink, let them stand for ten minutes.

10. Drain whey, pouring it through the prepared mold to warm it. The curds will be knit together at this point. Add the boiled peppers and water. Using hands protected with gloves, mix the peppers into the curd. Break off chunks of curd and place them in the prepared mold, mounding them up in a cone shape. Curds will continue to drain and will lose volume. Pull up cheesecloth around the curd bundle and fold cloth neatly over the top of the bundle. Put on the mold lid.

11. Place mold in cheese press or put a 5-pound weight on the mold. Press at five pounds of pressure for 30 minutes.

12. Remove cheese from press and unwrap it. Turn cheese over, rewrap it, and return it to the press or place a ten to 12-pound weight on it. Press at 10-12 pounds of pressure for 12 hours.

13. Remove cheese from press. Unwrap it and place it in a brine solution for 12 hours, turning it once during this process.

14. Remove cheese from brine and let dry on a cheese mat placed on a rack at room temperature for two to three days, until cheese is dry to the touch. Turn cheese daily during this process.

15. Place cheese on a clean mat in a ripening container and ripen at 50º Fahrenheit and 85 percent humidity for one week.

16. Coat cheese with two or three coats of wax, using a natural bristle brush and letting each coat of wax dry. Then ripen cheese at 50º Fahrenheit and 85 percent humidity for five weeks to three months. Turn cheese once a week to ensure even ripening.

Liptauer

Prep time: 30 minutes

Cooking time: 1 hour, 30 minutes

Resting time: 15 minutes

Draining time: 36-40 hours

Ripening time: 17 days

Liptauer is a Hungarian cheese. After it is made, it is often turned into a cheese spread with the addition of paprika, mustard, caraway seeds, onion, and butter. The recipe for this spread is listed in the following recipe. However, Liptauer can be eaten "as is," and when served in its natural state, it is a mild and unassertive cheese with a faintly salty taste. Liptauer is always made from sheep's milk.

Ingredients/Equipment:

8 qts sheep's milk

¼ tsp mesophilic culture

¼ tsp liquid rennet

2 tbsps pickling (canning) or kosher salt

Stainless steel cooking pot

Colander

Thermometer

Brick mold

Cheesecloth

Skimmer

Cheese knife

Cheese matting

Ripening container

Measuring cup

Distilled water

Directions:

1. As always, begin with sterilized equipment. Pour milk into non-reactive cooking pot. Warm milk over low heat to 80° Fahrenheit, stirring gently. Turn off heat.

2. Sprinkle culture over the surface of the milk and let stand for five minutes. Using the skimmer and a gentle up-and-down motion, work the culture into the milk as gently as possible.

3. Dilute rennet in ¼ cup of cool distilled water and work into milk mixture in the same manner. Cover pot and return to heat. Let sit for one hour, maintaining temperature at 80° Fahrenheit throughout this time.

4. Check for a clean break. If clean break is not present, wait an additional five to ten minutes. Once clean break is present, use a long-bladed knife and skimmer to cut curd into 1-inch cubes. Let stand for ten minutes to firm up curds.

5. Using a measuring cup, carefully dip off any whey that has collected on the surface of the curds. Using skimmer, gently ladle curds into a cloth-lined colander. Let drain for one hour, gently moving the curd once or twice with the skimmer to help drain. Gather the four corners of the cloth together and tie to form a bag. Hang and let drain for 12-18 hours or until it no longer drips.

6. Remove curd from bag. Using your hands, press curd into prepared brick mold, filling it completely. Place on a rack in a draining container and let drain at room temperature for 24 hours, turning the cheese once in the mold during this time.

7. Remove cheese from mold. Place on a clean mat in a ripening container. Ripen at 54° Fahrenheit and 85 percent humidity for ten days, turning daily.

8. After ten days, remove the cheese from container and trim off all the rind. Cut cheese into ½-inch cubes. Place cubes in bowl and toss with salt until well blended. Pack cheese down well. Cover bowl and ripen 54° Fahrenheit six to seven days.

9. When ripened, the cheese should have a soft, buttery texture. Using a food mill or blender, grind the cheese into a smooth paste. Place in a bowl, cover, and store in the refrigerator up to two weeks. Use cheese on its own or in the traditional Liptauer spread, described below.

Traditional Liptauer spread

Ingredients/Equipment:

8 oz Liptauer cheese

4 oz butter, softened

1 tsp paprika

½ tsp prepared mustard (any kind will do, but coarse-ground adds more flavor and texture)

½ tsp caraway seeds

1 small onion, grated

½ tsp anchovy paste (optional)

Bowl

Fork

Directions:

1. In a bowl, using a fork or small whisk, blend together butter and cheese until smooth.

2. Add paprika, mustard, caraway seeds, onion, and anchovy paste if desired. Blend together until color is a uniform light red. Pack into a small bowl or jar and store covered in the refrigerator for up to two weeks. Serve with crusty bread, radishes, rye crackers, or celery sticks. This spread also goes well with beer.

Bel Paese

Prep time: 50 minutes

Cook time: 90 minutes

Rest time: 7 hours

Brining time: 6 hours

Ripening time: 3-6 weeks

The name of this Italian cheese means "beautiful country." A man named Egidio Galbani originally developed Bel Paese in Italy around 1906. It is a semi-soft, sweet, fast-ripening cheese. It is made in the United States as well as Italy. It is usually served as a snack or as part of an antipasto platter.

Ingredients/Equipment:

8 qts whole cow's milk

¼ tsp thermophilic culture

½ tsp calcium chloride

½ tsp liquid rennet

18% brine solution

Non-reactive cooking pot

Large pot for hot water bath

Distilled water

Colander

Skimmer

Stainless steel curd knife

Cheese press

Large (3.5x7.5 in) tomme mold

Cheese mat

Drying rack

Thermometer

Draining container

Ripening container

Cutting board

Directions:

1. Prepare draining container by setting a rack inside. Cover the rack with a cutting board, followed by a cheese mat, then a tomme mold.

2. Start with sterilized equipment. Pour milk into a cooking pot that is placed into a hot water bath. Over medium heat, warm milk to 108° Fahrenheit, stirring gently to avoid scorching. Once milk reaches 108° Fahrenheit, remove from heat.

3. Sprinkle the culture over the surface of the milk and let stand for five minutes. Using skimmer, gently draw the culture down into the milk with an up-and-down motion, doing your best not to break the surface of the milk.

4. Dilute calcium chloride in ¼ cup of cool distilled water and add to milk, using the same up-and-down motion.

5. Dilute rennet in ¼ cup of cool distilled water and add to the mixture, again using an up-and-down motion to disturb the surface as little as possible. Cover pot again and let it sit for 30 minutes, maintaining the 108° Fahrenheit temperature.

6. Check mixture for a clean break. If curds do not break clean, let them sit for another ten minutes. Once a clean break is achieved, use the skimmer and curd knife to cut curd into ⅜-inch cubes. Let curds settle to the bottom of the pot and rest for five minutes.

7. Using skimmer and maintaining temperature at 108° Fahrenheit, stir curds for 20 to 30 minutes or until shrunken and beginning to mat together. Let settle for five minutes.

8. Drain the whey from the pot until the surface of the curds is visible.

9. Gently ladle curds into prepared mold. Place lid on mold. Place mold in draining container and put lid on container to keep curds warm. Let curds drain for six to seven hours, turning mold once each hour. The cheese should be firm enough to handle but still soft.

   *Important: unlike most other molded cheeses, this one does not get wrapped in cheesecloth.

10. Remove cheese from mold and place in 18 percent brine solution for six hours, turning once during this time.

11. Remove cheese from brine and pat dry with a clean, lint-free towel. Place cheese on a clean cheese mat in a ripening container and ripen at 40-42° Fahrenheit and 80-90 percent humidity. Turn cheese every other day and drain any extra whey from the bottom of the container. Wipe

cheese with a dry paper towel each time you turn it. After about ten days, the cheese will begin to form a moist coating.

12. Wash cheese twice a week with a cloth dipped in a brine solution. After three weeks, remove cheese from ripening container. Clean cheese by wiping it again with the brine-soaked cloth and drying it completely with a paper towel. Wrap in foil and store in refrigerator for up to three weeks.

13. If you wish a sharper cheese, apply two coats of wax to cheese and place waxed cheese back in ripening container. Continue to ripen at 40-42° Fahrenheit and 80-90 percent humidity for a total of up to six weeks.

CASE STUDY: NOT "SHY" WHEN IT COMES TO MAKING CHEESE

Shy Brothers Farm LLC
P.O. Box 422
Westport, MA 02791
(508) 333-2926 (p)
(508) 636-8827 (f)
www.shybrothersfarm.com

Started in 2006, Shy Brothers Farms is a relative newcomer to the world of artisan cheese. Milking more than 120 Holstein and Ayrshire cows, Shy Brothers produces semi-soft, bloomy-rind cheeses for "great chefs, gourmet shops, and farmer's markets," as well as online to customers throughout the U.S. Partner Barbara Hanley notes that making cheese for sale can be a challenge: "There's a difference between home kitchen cheese and artisanal cheese…A home recipe is fun, but it may not translate to larger batches." Like most cheese makers, she admits that, "the most enjoyable aspect of cheese making is tasting!" Her greatest challenge has been "learning how the seasonal changes in milk affect the process." Shy Brothers also employs a unique quality control step. "Besides the scientific-based standards, the essential question is: Would I serve this at a dinner party?"

Hanley advises the beginning cheese maker: "When a good cheese maker tells you that he or she threw out a lot of cheese for months when they were learning, don't think, 'Oh, not me, I will never have to do that!'" Shy Brothers obviously learned from all those batches of cheese, having won both regional and national awards for their products.

Washed Rind and Ripened Rind Cheeses

Many cheeses have rinds, an edible coating that forms on the cheese during the ripening process. Some rinds are produced by bathing the cheese in salt brine, wine, brandy, or cider during the ripening process. Other rinds form due to specific bacteria that are rubbed into the cheese as it ripens. In order for the rind to form properly, the cheese must be cared for tenderly. Cheeses need to be turned, wiped, or washed at specific intervals as specified in the recipes and need full ripening time in order to develop their distinctive flavors.

Brie

Prep time: 1 hour, 10 minutes

Cooking time: 2 hours

Resting time: 10 minutes

Draining time: 24 hours

Ripening time: 5-6 weeks

The cheese throne has many pretenders. Cheddar, Stilton, Roquefort, and Parmesan have all laid claim to the title "king of cheeses." However, in 1815, a group of European ambassadors — men who knew something about gourmet food — formally proclaimed French Brie *roi des fromages* (the king of cheeses). Brie is a soft, creamy cheese with an edible rind created by a particular mold. Like many cheeses, Brie becomes stronger as it ages. Some people prefer to eat Brie when it is "young," after only three to four weeks of ripening. Others prefer their Brie *fort*, or strong, ripened up to six weeks. A whole round of Brie is sometimes baked with slivered almonds on top and served warm. It is wonderful with crusty French bread of course, and it also goes well with many types of fruit.

Ingredients/Equipment:

8 qts whole cow's milk

¼ tsp mesophilic culture

⅛ tsp *Penicillium candidum* mold powder

½ tsp calcium chloride

½ tsp liquid rennet

Stainless steel cooking pot

Larger pot for hot water bath

Pickling or kosher salt

Cheesecloth

Two 8-inch half-Brie molds

Cheese mats

Ripening container

Thermometer

Curd knife

Skimmer

Measuring cup

Cheese ripening paper

Directions:

1. Begin by sterilizing all equipment. Prepare a draining container by placing a rack inside. Place a cutting board on top of the rack. Cover the rack with matting. Place molds on top of all.

2. Pour milk into non-reactive cooking pot and place in larger pot partially filled with water. Warm milk over medium heat to 88° Fahrenheit, stirring gently. Turn off heat.

3. Sprinkle culture and mold powder over the surface of the milk and let stand for five minutes. Using the skimmer and a gentle up-and-down motion, work the culture and mold powder into the milk as gently as possible.

4. Dilute calcium chloride in ¼ cup of cool distilled water and work into milk mixture in the same manner.

5. Dilute rennet in ¼ cup of cool distilled water and work into milk mixture in the same manner. Cover pot and return to heat. Let sit for 1 ½ hours, maintaining temperature at 88° Fahrenheit throughout this time.

6. Check for a clean break. If clean break is not present, wait an additional five to ten minutes. Once clean break is present, use a long-bladed knife and skimmer to cut curd into 1-inch cubes. Let stand for five minutes to firm up curds.

7. Using a skimmer, stir curd very gently, lifting from the bottom all around the perimeter of the pot for five to ten minutes, or until pieces of curd start to shrink slightly and edges become rounded. Let curds settle.

8. Using a measuring cup, drain off whey until you can see the surface of the curds.

9. Using a skimmer, carefully ladle curds into prepared molds. Ladle a spoonful of curds into one mold, then the other, and repeat. It will take time for the curds to drain down, but the curds will eventually fit into the two molds. Do not be tempted to add a third mold. Let curds drain for two hours. Carefully lift cheese and mold together and flip over. Repeat in two hours, then repeat again in another two hours. Cover the container and let cheese drain overnight.

10. Flip cheeses in the morning and let them drain for another two hours. By this time, the cheeses will have been draining for approximately 24 hours. Remove cheeses from molds and prepare a mat in a ripening container.

11. Sprinkle the top of each cheese with one teaspoon of salt. Turn salted side of cheese down on the mat in a clean container and salt the other side of the cheeses. Cover with lid.

12. Let cheese ripen at 50° 55° Fahrenheit and 90 percent humidity. Flip cheeses daily and remove any drained whey. Wipe container with clean paper towel. Keep covered and make sure the cheese does not become dry.

13. After about one week, a fine fuzzy white mold will begin to grow on the cheeses. Continue to turn daily. Once cheeses are fully covered in white fuzzy mold, wrap them in cheese-ripening paper and return to container. (Cheese-ripening paper is a special white paper coated with paraffin on one side. It is available from cheese-making supply houses.)

14. After another week, the cheeses will begin to soften. They are ready to eat at four to five weeks, or continue to ripening for a total of six weeks. Once cheese has ripened, keep it wrapped and stored in the refrigerator. Brie will continue to ripen in storage, but more slowly due to the colder temperature.

Camembert

Prep time: 1 hour, 10 minutes
Cooking time: 2 hours
Resting time: 10 minutes
Draining time: 24 hours
Ripening time: 4 weeks

Camembert is another famous soft French cheese with an edible mold rind. It was originally made in the Normandy region of northern France, and it is still very popular there today. Some people confuse Brie and Camembert, and the two cheeses do have a similar pedigree. However, Camembert, which is made in a smaller mold, ripens more quickly than Brie and is not quite as strong in flavor. However, like Brie, Camembert becomes stronger if it is aged longer. Eat it young to fully enjoy the mild creaminess.

Ingredients/Equipment:

8 qts whole cow's milk
¼ tsp mesophilic culture
⅛ tsp *Penicillium candidum* mold powder
½ tsp calcium chloride
½ tsp liquid rennet
Stainless steel cooking pot

Larger pot for hot water bath

Pickling or kosher salt

Cheesecloth

4 4-inch Camembert molds

Cheese mats

Ripening container

Thermometer

Curd knife

Skimmer

Measuring cup

Cheese ripening paper

Directions:

1. Begin by sterilizing all equipment. Prepare a draining container by placing a rack inside. Place a cutting board on top of the rack. Cover the rack with matting. Place molds on top of all.

2. Pour milk into non-reactive cooking pot and place in larger pot partially filled with water. Warm milk over medium heat to 88° Fahrenheit, stirring gently. Turn off heat.

3. Sprinkle culture and mold powder over the surface of the milk and let stand for five minutes. Using the skimmer and a gentle up-and-down motion, work the culture and mold powder into the milk as gently as possible.

4. Dilute calcium chloride in ¼ cup of cool distilled water and work into milk mixture in the same manner.

5. Dilute rennet in ¼ cup of cool distilled water and work into milk mixture in the same manner. Cover pot and return to heat. Let sit for 1 ½ hours, maintaining temperature at 88° Fahrenheit throughout this time.

6. Check for a clean break. If clean break is not present, wait an additional five to ten minutes. Once clean break is present, use a long-bladed knife and skimmer to cut curd into 1-inch cubes. Let stand for five minutes to firm up curds.

7. Using a skimmer, stir curd very gently, lifting from the bottom all around the perimeter of the pot for five to ten minutes, or until pieces of curd start to shrink slightly and edges become rounded. Let curds settle.

8. Using a measuring cup, drain off whey until you can see the surface of the curds.

9. Using a skimmer, carefully ladle curds into prepared molds. Ladle a spoonful of curds into each mold in turn, and repeat. It will take time for the curds to drain down, but the curds will eventually fit into the four molds. Do not be tempted to add a fifth mold. Let curds drain for two hours. Carefully lift cheese and mold together and flip over. Repeat in two hours, then repeat again in another two hours. Cover the container and let cheese drain overnight.

10. Flip cheeses in the morning and let them drain for another two hours. By this time, cheeses will have been draining for approximately 24 hours. Remove cheeses from molds and prepare a mat in a ripening container.

11. Sprinkle the top of each cheese with one teaspoon of salt. Turn salted side of cheese down on the mat in a clean container and salt the other side of the cheeses. Cover with lid.

12. Let cheese ripen at 50°-55° Fahrenheit and 90 percent humidity. Flip cheeses daily and remove any drained whey. Wipe container with clean paper towel. Keep covered and make sure the cheese does not become dry.

13. After about one week, a fine fuzzy white mold will begin to grow on the cheeses. Continue to turn daily. Once cheeses are fully covered in white fuzzy mold, wrap them in cheese-ripening paper and return to container. (Cheese-ripening paper is a special white paper coated with paraffin on one side. It is available from cheese-making supply houses.)

14. After another week, the cheeses will begin to soften. They are ready to eat at three to four weeks. Once cheese is ripened, keep it wrapped and stored in the refrigerator. Camembert will continue to ripen in storage, but more slowly due to the colder temperature.

Coulommiers

Prep time: 1 hour, 10 minutes

Cooking time: 1 hour, 30 minutes

Resting time: 10-20 minutes

Draining time: 18-20 hours

Ripening time: 3-4 weeks

This French cheese is similar in character to Brie and Camembert, but because it ripens for a shorter time, it does not have as strong a flavor. Its flavor is often described as buttery or faintly nutty. Coulommiers is also a bit firmer in texture; it does not have the "runny" quality often associated with Brie. Like other mold-ripened cheeses, the rind is edible, but much of the cheese's sharpness is in the rind, so if you prefer a milder flavor, just discard the rind.

Ingredients/Equipment:

10 qts whole milk

¼ tsp mesophilic culture

⅛ tsp *Penicillium candidum* mold powder

¼ tsp calcium chloride

¼ tsp liquid rennet

4 tsps pickling or kosher salt

Stainless steel cooking pot

Larger pot for hot water bath

Cheesecloth

2 8-inch half-Brie molds

Cheese mats

Cheese rack

Ripening container

Thermometer

Curd knife

Skimmer

Measuring cup

Cheese ripening paper

Directions:

1. Begin by sterilizing all equipment. Prepare a draining container by placing a rack inside. Place a cutting board on top of the rack. Cover the rack with matting. Place molds on top of all.

2. Pour milk into non-reactive cooking pot and place in larger pot partially filled with water. Heat the milk over medium heat to 90° Fahrenheit, stirring gently. Turn off heat.

3. Sprinkle culture and mold powder over the surface of the milk and let stand for five minutes. Using the skimmer and a gentle up-and-down motion, work the culture and mold powder into the milk as gently as possible.

4. Dilute calcium chloride in ¼ cup of cool distilled water and work into milk mixture in the same manner.

5. Dilute rennet in ¼ cup of cool distilled water and work into milk mixture in the same manner. Cover pot and return to heat. Let sit for 1 ¼ hours, maintaining temperature at 90° Fahrenheit throughout this time.

6. Check for a clean break. If clean break is not present, wait an additional 15 minutes. Once clean break is present, use a long-bladed knife and skimmer to cut the curd into 1-inch cubes. Let stand for five minutes to firm up curds.

7. Using a skimmer, carefully ladle curds into prepared molds. Ladle a spoonful of curds into one mold, then the other, and repeat. It will take time for the curds to drain down, but the curds will eventually fit into the two molds. Do not be tempted to add a third mold. Let curds drain for four to five hours.

8. Carefully lift cheeses in their molds and flip over. Let drain for another 12 hours or overnight. Flip cheeses again and let them drain for another three hours.

9. Remove cheeses from molds and prepare a mat in a ripening container.

10. Sprinkle the top of each cheese with one teaspoon of salt. Turn salted side of cheese down on the mat in a clean container and salt the other side of the cheeses. Cover with lid.

11. Let cheese ripen at 50°-55° and 90 percent humidity. Flip cheeses daily and remove any drained whey. Wipe container with clean paper towel. Keep covered and make sure the cheeses do not become dry.

12. After 10-12 days, a fine fuzzy white mold will begin to grow on the cheeses. Continue to turn daily. Once cheeses are fully covered in white fuzzy mold, wrap them in cheese-ripening paper and return to container. Cheese-ripening paper is a special white paper coated with paraffin on one side. It is available from cheese-making supply houses.

13. After another two weeks, the cheeses will be soft and creamy around the edges but still firm in the center with a somewhat chalky texture. They can be eaten three to four weeks after you begin to ripen them. Store ripened cheeses in the refrigerator for up to ten weeks.

Crottin

Prep time: 30 minutes
Cooking time: 25 minutes
Resting time: 20-24 hours
Draining time: 24 hours
Ripening time: 2-4 weeks

Crottin (pronounced "crow-tan") is a French goat's milk cheese with a mold-ripened rind. Due to the addition of a particular culture, *Flora Danica*, finished rounds of Crottin have a faintly fruity aroma and taste, especially when young. As this cheese ripens further, it takes on an earthy, almost gamey tang. *Flora Danica* culture is available through cheese and wine making suppliers.

Ingredients/Equipment:

1 gal whole goat's milk
⅛ tsp *Flora Danica* culture
⅛ tsp *Penicillium candidum* mold powder

Pinch of *Geotrichium candidum* mold powder

2 drops liquid rennet

⅛ tsp calcium chloride

4 Crottin molds (round molds, 2 ½x4 ¾ in)

Stainless steel cooking pot

Larger pot for hot water bath

Cheesecloth

2 8-inch half-Brie molds

Cheese mats

Cheese rack

Ripening container

Thermometer

Curd knife

Skimmer

Directions:

1. Begin by sterilizing all equipment. Prepare a draining container by placing a rack inside. Place a cutting board on top of the rack. Cover the rack with matting. Place molds on top of all.

2. Pour milk into non-reactive cooking pot. Heat the milk over low heat to 72° Fahrenheit, stirring gently. Turn off heat.

3. Sprinkle *Flora Danica* culture over the surface of the milk and let stand for five minutes. Using the skimmer and a gentle up-and-down motion, work the culture and mold powder into the milk as gently as possible.

4. Dilute calcium chloride in ¼ cup of cool distilled water and work into milk mixture in the same manner.

5. Add both mold powders, using the same gentle motion.

6. Dilute rennet in ¼ cup of cool distilled water and work into milk mixture in the same manner. Cover pot and let sit for 18-24 hours, keeping temperature as close to 72° Fahrenheit as possible. You do not need to cook the milk mixture during this time, but it does need to rest in a warm, draft-free spot.

7.   Check for a clean break. If clean break is not present, wait an additional 15 minutes. Once clean break is present, use a long-bladed knife and skimmer to cut the curd into 1-inch cubes. Let stand for five minutes to firm up curds.

8.   Using a skimmer, carefully ladle curds into prepared molds. Ladle a spoonful of curds into one mold after another, and repeat. It will take time for the curds to drain down, but the curds will eventually fit into the four molds. Do not be tempted to add a fifth mold. Let curds drain for 24 hours or until they pull away from the sides of the molds.

9.   Prepare a clean ripening container with a clean mat inside. Place molds into ripening container. Ripen at 58° Fahrenheit and 85 percent humidity for two weeks. Turn the cheeses every other day during this period, removing collected whey from the container with a clean paper towel.

10. After two weeks, the cheeses should develop a blooming white rind. You may eat the cheeses at this point, or continue to ripen for up to four weeks.

Chaource

Prep time: 30 minutes
Cooking time: 12 hours, 25 minutes
Resting time: 5 minutes
Draining time: 36-48 hours
Ripening time: 1 week

Chaource is yet another French cheese with a ripened rind. It was first made in the 14th century in the small town of Chaource in the Champagne region of France. It is similar in appearance to Brie, but it ripens much more quickly, and it has a slightly earthy aroma and flavor, almost like mushrooms or truffles. Not surprisingly, it goes well with the wine of the region, the famous sparkling champagne. It does require long and careful cooking, so plan on having someone else to help you watch the cooking pot.

Ingredients/Equipment:

8 qts whole milk

¼ tsp aroma mesophilic culture

Pinch of *Penicillium candidum* mold powder

Pinch of *Geotrichum candidum* 15 mold powder

¼ tsp calcium chloride

2 drops liquid rennet

4 tsps pickling or kosher salt

Stainless steel cooking pot

Cheesecloth

Eight Crottin molds (small round molds, 2 ½" across by 4 ¾' high)

Cheese mats

Cheese rack

Ripening container

Thermometer

Curd knife

Skimmer

Measuring cup

Directions:

1. Begin by sterilizing all equipment. Prepare a draining container by plac-ing a rack inside. Place a cutting board on top of the rack. Cover the rack with matting. Place molds on top of all.

2. Pour milk into non-reactive cooking pot. Over low heat, warm milk to 77° Fahrenheit, stirring gently. Turn off heat.

3. Sprinkle culture and both mold powders over the surface of the milk and let stand for five minutes. Using the skimmer and a gentle up-and-down motion, work the culture and mold powder into the milk as gen-tly as possible.

4. Dilute rennet in one tablespoon of cool distilled water and work into milk mixture in the same manner. Cover pot and return to heat. Let sit

for 12 hours, maintaining temperature at 77° Fahrenheit throughout this time.

5. Remove any whey that has collected on the surface of the curd, without disturbing the curd. Using a skimmer, carefully fill the prepared molds to the top, and then continue to top off until all the curd is used. It will take time for the curd to drain down, but all the curd will fit into the four molds. Do not add more molds.

6. Place molds in prepared draining container. Cover and let drain overnight at room temperature.

7. Carefully lift cheeses in their molds and flip over. Collect any drained whey from the container. If cheeses are too delicate to flip, wait for six hours before trying again. Whether or not cheeses are successfully flipped, continue to drain cheeses for another day or until no more whey is draining.

8. Remove cheeses from molds and prepare a mat in a ripening container.

9. Place cheeses on mat. Sprinkle the top of each cheese with ¼ teaspoon of salt. Turn salted side of cheese down on the mat in a clean container and salt the other side of the cheeses. Cover with lid.

10. Let cheese ripen at 50°-55° Fahrenheit and 95 percent humidity. Flip cheeses daily and remove any drained whey. Wipe container with clean paper towel. Keep covered and make sure the cheeses do not become dry.

11. After one week, a fine fuzzy white mold will begin to grow on the cheeses. Continue to turn daily. Once cheeses are fully covered in white fuzzy mold, remove them from box and wrap in foil or plastic wrap, storing cheeses in refrigerator. Cheeses are now ready to eat.

Taleggio

Prep time: 1 hour, 30 minutes
Cooking time: 1 hour, 20 minutes
Resting time: 35 minutes

Draining time: 12 hours
Brining time: 8 hours
Drying time: 2 days
Ripening time: 4-5 weeks

Taleggio is a semi-soft cheese from northern Italy. It has a washed rind that develops during the ripening process. Taleggio melts easily, making it a great choice for hot sandwiches, fondues, and casseroles. Like many washed rind cheeses, this recipe calls for a particular ripening bacteria, in this case *Brevibacterium linens*, available through cheese-making suppliers. The traditional Taleggio is made in a square mold, but a standard tome mold will work as well. This cheese does not need to be aged, just ripened.

Ingredients/Equipment:

2 gal whole milk, either cow's milk or goat's milk
¼ tsp mesophilic culture
Pinch of *Brevibacterium linens* culture
½ tsp calcium chloride
½ tsp liquid rennet
Stainless steel cooking pot
Larger pot for hot water bath
18% cool brine solution
Draining pot
Colander
Cheesecloth
2 7 ½x6 in. molds, or one tomme mold
Cheese mats
Ripening container
Thermometer
Curd knife
Skimmer
Measuring cup
Stainless steel racks
Distilled water

Directions:

1. Using sterile equipment, pour milk into cooking pot and place into larger pot partially filled with water. Under medium heat, slowly warm the milk to 90° Fahrenheit, stirring gently. Turn off heat.

2. Sprinkle culture and *Brevibacterium linens* bacteria over the milk and let it stand for five minutes. Using a skimmer, work the additives into the milk with a gentle up-and-down motion, disturbing the surface of the milk as little as possible. Cover and let ripen for one hour, keeping the temperature at 90° Fahrenheit.

3. Dilute the calcium chloride in ¼ cup of cool distilled water. Add to milk mixture, again using gentle up-and-down motion.

4. Dilute the rennet in ¼ cup of cool distilled water and add to mixture in the same manner as previous additions. Cover pot and let it sit for 20-30 minutes. There is no need to keep the temperature constant.

5. Check for a clean break. If clean break is not present, wait another five to ten minutes. If there is a clean break, use curd knife and skimmer to cut curd into ¾-inch cubes. Let stand for five minutes. Stir gently for 30 minutes. Every ten minutes, stop and remove two cups of whey, pouring whey into a separate pot.

6. After 30 minutes, let curds settle. Pour the contents of the pot into a cloth-lined colander. Fill the square molds or the tome mold with the soft curds. Let them drain for 12 hours, turning the cheese over in the molds every two hours.

7. Remove the cheese from the molds or mold and place in an 18 percent brine solution for eight hours, turning the cheese over once during this process.

8. Remove cheese from brine and place on a rack. Allow the cheese to dry at room temperature for two days, turning once during this time.

9. Place cheese on a cheese mat in a ripening container. Ripen at 50° Fahrenheit and 90 percent humidity for four to five weeks. Wash the cheese

twice a week with a clean cloth dipped in a brine solution. When ripe, the cheese will feel softer and will bulge slightly around the middle.

10. Wrap the finished cheese in foil or parchment paper and store in the refrigerator for up to four weeks while eating.

Munster

Prep time: 50 minutes

Cooking time: 30 minutes

Resting time: 1 hour, 35 minutes

Draining time: 30 minutes

Pressing time: 24 hours

Ripening time: 5 days-3 months

Munster is a type of washed-rind cheese, usually made from cow's milk, although goat's milk can also be used. There is some debate as to which country first produced Munster; France, Denmark, and Germany all claim Munster as their cheese. It was probably first produced by monks; the word "Munster" is believed to be a variation of the Latin word for monastery. Today, Munster is produced both in Europe and the United States. The U.S. version of this cheese is usually the mildest; although, German Munster has a stronger odor, the cheese's flavor is usually fairly mild, while French Munster is politely described as "assertive" in both aroma and flavor. Like most washed-rind cheeses, Munster grows stronger as it ages. If you want a mild and creamy taste, eat it while it is "young."

Ingredients/Equipment:

1 gal whole milk (you can use cow's milk or goat's milk for this recipe)

½ tablet vegetable rennet dissolved in 1/4 cup of cool un-chlorinated water (Remember, if you are using powdered or rennet tablets, to allow 20 to 30 minutes for the rennet to fully dissolve.)

Salt (to taste)

Stainless steel cooking pot

Thermometer

Colander

Cheesecloth

Ladle

1-pound mold

Directions

1. Pour the milk into a stainless steel bowl or pot.

2. Place the bowl of milk into a hot water bath to bring the temperature of the milk to 85° Fahrenheit. Alternatively, you can heat the milk in a double boiler.

3. Remove the pot of milk from the heat and allow it to sit for five minutes.

4. Add the diluted rennet mixture and stir gently.

5. Cover mixture and allow it to sit undisturbed for an hour.

6. At this point, the curds will be a thick yogurt-like consistency.

7. Cut the curds into 1-inch cubes.

8. You can add a little salt at this point by sprinkling one to two teaspoons over the curds.

9. Allow the curds to rest undisturbed for 15 minutes.

10. Return the pot of curds to the warm water in a double boiler and very gently turn the curds. Your goal here is to gently bring the curds from the bottom of the pot to the top. Again, the emphasis is on "gentle." If you stir the curds too vigorously, it will have a negative effect on the consistency of your cheese. The gentle turning of the curds helps heat them evenly and it helps distribute the added salt.

11. Allow the curds to rest undisturbed for 15 minutes.

12. Line a colander with a large doubled piece of cheesecloth. Make sure the cloth is large enough that you will be able to bring the corners together in a bag for the cheese to drain. Place the colander over a pot to catch the whey.

13. Use a ladle to transfer the curds to the cheesecloth-lined colander.

14. Allow the curds to drain for 30 minutes.

15. Line a cheese mold with cheesecloth. Ideally, you will want to use a 1-pound mold (a mold large enough to accommodate one pound of cheese).

16. You will be pressing this cheese with 40 pounds of weight so use a mold from a cheese press, one that is made of sturdy food-grade plastic or stainless steel.

17. Place the cheese mold in a pan to catch the draining whey.

18. When the curd reaches room temperature, transfer the curds from the colander into the cheese mold. You should pack the curds rather tightly into the mold.

19. Fold the cheesecloth over the top to the cheese curd.

20. Place a follower (the lid or other piece that goes between the top of the cheese and the press) on top of the wrapped curd and press the curd with 40 pounds of pressure for 12 hours.

21. Remove the cheese from the mold and unwrap it.

22. Turn the cheese over and rewrap it.

23. Place the rewrapped cheese back into the mold and press with 40 pounds for 12 hours.

24. Lightly rub the exterior of the cheese with salt.

25. Place the cheese on a cheese mat and place a saucer on top of the cheese to prevent the top of the cheese from becoming too dry.

26. Flip the cheese once a day for five to six days, lightly salting the exterior of the cheese each tip you flip it.

27. The cheese will develop a soft rind after a couple of days.

28. The cheese is ready after it has developed the rind, but ideally, you should let it ripen for the full five to six days. The longer you allow your cheese to sit, the more intense the flavor will be. If you desire truly strong Muenster, you can let your cheese develop for as long as three

months, flipping and wiping it with a cloth dipped in brine solution each time. Muenster cheese may be frozen for up to three months. Once you slice into your Muenster cheese, you should use it within a week's time.

Esrom

Prep time: 60 minutes
Cooking time: 2 hours
Resting time: 40 minutes
Pressing time: 12 hours
Brining time: 12 hours
Drying time: 24 hours
Ripening time: 6 weeks

Esrom was originally made by monks at the Esrum Abbey in Denmark. In 1559, the Reformation forced the closure of this abbey, and the recipe for Esrom cheese was lost. In 1951, the Danish Cheese Institute announced that they recreated this recipe, and Esrom has been sold commercially ever since. While some cheese experts doubt that the actual recipe has been faithfully recreated, it is likely that this cheese is very similar to the one originally created by the monks. Esrom is an open-textured cheese like havarti, with tiny holes throughout the paste of the cheese. It develops a reddish-orange rind during the ripening process. While Esrom has a strong smell, mostly from the rind, the cheese itself is actually rather soft and buttery in flavor. It melts well and is often used in casseroles for this reason.

Ingredients/Equipment:

2 gals whole milk
½ tsp mesophilic culture
⅛ tsp *Brevibacterium linens* culture
¾ tsp calcium chloride
¾ tsp liquid rennet
Stainless steel cooking pot
Larger pot for hot water bath

18% cool brine solution

Colander

Cheesecloth

One large tomme mold

Cheese mats

Cheese press

Ripening container

Thermometer

Curd knife

Skimmer

Measuring cup

Distilled water

Directions:

1. Using sterile equipment, pour milk into cooking pot and place into larger pot partially filled with water. Under medium heat, slowly warm the milk to 90° Fahrenheit, stirring gently. Turn off heat.

2. Sprinkle culture and *Brevibacterium linens* bacteria over the milk and let it stand for five minutes. Using skimmer, work the additives into the milk with a gentle up-and-down motion, disturbing the surface of the milk as little as possible. Cover and let ripen for 30 minutes, keeping the pot covered and wrapped in a towel to retain warmth.

3. Dilute the calcium chloride in ¼ cup of cool distilled water. Add to milk mixture, again using gentle up-and-down motion.

4. Dilute the rennet in ¼ cup of cool distilled water and add to mixture in the same manner as previous additions. Return to heat. Cover pot and let it sit for 40-45 minutes at 90° Fahrenheit.

5. Check for a clean break. If clean break is not present, wait another five to ten minutes. If there is a clean break, use curd knife and skimmer to cut curd into ¾-inch cubes. Let stand for five minutes. Stir gently for five minutes. Let curds settle.

6. Using a measuring cup, remove ⅓ the whey from the top of the curd. Replace with an equal amount of distilled water heated to 90° Fahrenheit. Return heat to low and slowly warm the mixture to 95° Fahrenheit, stirring continuously. Adjust the heat as needed to make sure it takes 20 minutes for this step to occur. Do not heat mixture too quickly.

7. Turn off heat and continue to stir for another 15 minutes. Let curds settle.

8. Pour the contents of the pot into a cloth-lined colander. Fill the tomme mold with the soft curds. Pull cloth up around curd bundle and smooth it over the top. Put on lid.

9. Place mold in cheese press. Press at medium pressure (12-15 pounds) for six hours.

10. Remove cheese from press, unwrap, and redress. Replace cheese in mold and put mold back in press. Press again at medium pressure for six hours.

11. Remove the cheese from mold and place in an 18 percent brine solution for 12 hours, turning the cheese over once during this process.

12. Remove cheese from brine and place on a rack. Allow the cheese to dry at room temperature 24 hours, turning once during this time.

13. Place cheese on a cheese mat in a ripening container. Ripen at 60° Fahrenheit and 90 percent humidity for six weeks. Turn cheese daily for the first week.

14. After first week, wash cheese every second day with a cloth dipped in a brine solution, turning the cheese each time. The cheese will begin to develop a reddish-orange rind, and the cheese should feel semi-soft when pressed in the middle with a finger.

15. After six weeks, the cheese is ready to eat. Wrap the finished cheese in foil or parchment paper and store in the refrigerator for up to four weeks.

Tilsit

Prep time: 45 minutes

Cooking time: 2 hours

Resting time: 40 minutes

Draining time: 8-12 hours

Brining time: 12 hours

Drying time: 24 hours

Ripening time: 2-6 months

Tilsit was first made in Prussia (now part of Germany) by Dutch immigrants in the 19th century. Today it is made in Switzerland and is a very popular cheese there. It is semi-firm and fairly mild when young, but aged Tilsit quickly develops a flavor and aroma similar to Limburger. If you like your cheese mild, eat Tilsit after two months of ripening. If you want cheese with a real punch, let it age up to six months.

Ingredients/Equipment:

4 gals whole milk

½ tsp thermophilic culture

Pinch *Brevibacterium linens* culture

¾ tsp calcium chloride

¾ tsp liquid rennet

Stainless steel cooking pot

Larger pot for hot water bath

18% cool brine solution

Colander

Cheesecloth

One large tomme mold

Cheese mats

Ripening container

Thermometer

Curd knife

Skimmer

Measuring cup

Distilled water

Directions:

1. Prepare a draining container by placing a rack inside.

2. Using sterile equipment, pour milk into cooking pot and place into larger pot partially filled with water. Under medium heat, slowly warm the milk to 95° Fahrenheit, stirring gently. Turn off heat.

3. Sprinkle culture and *Brevibacterium linens* bacteria over the milk and let it stand for five minutes. Using skimmer, work the additives into the milk with a gentle up-and-down motion, disturbing the surface of the milk as little as possible. Cover and let ripen for 30 minutes, keeping the pot covered and wrapped in a towel to retain warmth.

4. Dilute the calcium chloride in ¼ cup of cool distilled water. Add to milk mixture, again using gentle up-and-down motion.

5. Dilute the rennet in ¼ cup of cool distilled water and add to mixture in the same manner as previous additions. Return to heat. Cover pot and let it sit for 40 minutes at 95° Fahrenheit.

6. Check for a clean break. If clean break is not present, wait another five to ten minutes. If there is a clean break, use curd knife and skimmer to cut curd into ½-inch cubes. Let stand for five minutes.

7. Return heat to low and slowly warm the mixture to 110° Fahrenheit, stirring continuously. Adjust the heat as needed to make sure it takes 40 minutes for this step to occur. Do not heat mixture too quickly. Curds will shrink down to the size of peas.

8. Turn off heat and let curds settle.

9. Pour the contents of the pot into a cloth-lined colander. Fill the tomme mold with the soft curds. Put on lid.

10. Place mold on rack in draining container. Place the lid on draining container to keep cheese warm. Drain cheese. Flip cheese in mold every 15 minutes for the first hour, then every hour or two for the rest of the day.

11. When cheese is firm, remove the cheese from mold and place in an 18 percent brine solution for 12 hours, turning the cheese over once during this process.

12. Remove cheese from brine and place on a rack. Allow the cheese to dry at room temperature 24 hours, turning once during this time.

13. Place cheese on a cheese mat in a ripening container. Ripen at 55° Fahrenheit and 90 percent humidity for six weeks. Turn cheese daily for the first week.

14. After first week, twice a week with a cloth dipped in a brine solution, turning the cheese each time. Continue this for as long as you ripen the cheese. As the cheese continues to ripen, it will develop a reddish-brown color and a pronounced, pungent aroma.

15. After two months, cheese is ready to eat as a mild cheese. If you desire a pungent cheese, continue to ripen for up to six months. Wrap the finished cheese in foil or parchment paper and store in the refrigerator for up to four weeks while eating.

Gruyère

Prep time: 60 minutes
Cook time: 140 minutes
Rest time: 5 minutes
Pressing time: 12 hours
Brining time: 12 hours
Drying time: 2-3 days
Ripening time: 4 weeks
Aging time: 6 months

Gruyère is one of many famous European cheeses. It is made in both Switzerland and France, in the Alpine region between the two countries. Unlike some French mold-rind cheeses such as Brie or Camembert, which have a soft, almost runny texture, it is a semi-firm cheese with a washed rind. It has a sweet, faintly nutty taste, especially when it is young. It can be aged for up to two years, and the longer it is aged, the sharper and richer the flavor becomes. Gruyère is the cheese traditionally melted on the top of French onion soup, and due to its melting qualities, it is an ideal fondue cheese.

Ingredients/Equipment:

16 qts whole cow's milk

½ tsp thermophilic culture

¾ tsp calcium chloride

¾ tsp liquid rennet

18% brine solution

Non-reactive cooking pot

Large pot for hot water bath

Distilled water

Colander

Cheesecloth

Skimmer

Stainless steel whisk

Round mold

Cheese press

Cheese mat

Thermometer

Ripening container

Directions:

1. Start with sterilized equipment. Pour milk into a cooking pot that has been placed into a hot water bath. Over medium heat, warm milk to 90º Fahrenheit, stirring gently as the milk warms. Once milk reaches 90º Fahrenheit, remove from heat.

2. Sprinkle the culture over the surface of the milk and let stand for five minutes. Using skimmer, gently draw the culture down into the milk with an up-and-down motion, doing your best not to break the surface of the milk. Cover, return to heat, and let mixture ripen for ten minutes, maintaining temperature at 90º Fahrenheit.

3. Dilute calcium chloride in 1/4 cup of cool distilled water and add to milk, using the same up-and-down motion.

4. Dilute rennet in 1/4 cup of cool distilled water and add to the mixture, again using an up-and-down motion to disturb the surface as little as possible. Cover pot again and let it sit for 40 minutes, maintaining the 90° Fahrenheit temperature.

5. Check mixture for a clean break. If curds do not break clean, let them sit for another ten minutes. Once a clean break is achieved, use the skimmer and whisk to cut the curd into very small pieces, about the size of rice grains. Use the skimmer to lift the mixture and ensure that all curds are cut into very small pieces.

6. Return pot to low heat and slowly warm curds to 114° Fahrenheit, stirring mixture gently and continuously. Adjust the heat as needed so that it takes one hour for the mixture to reach 114° Fahrenheit. Do not heat mixture too quickly. Once curds are heated, let them rest for five minutes.

7. Drain off whey by pouring half of it through the cloth-lined mold to warm it. Discard the rest or save it for other recipes.

8. Fill the warmed mold with curds. Pull the cloth up over the curds and smooth it over the top of the bundle. Place lid on mold.

9. Place mold in press or put a 10-pound weight on top of mold. Press for one hour. Remove cheese from press and unwrap. Turn cheese, rewrap, and replace in press. Continue pressing at 15 pounds of pressure for 12 hours.

10. Remove cheese from press. Unwrap it and place it in a brine solution for 12 hours, turning it once during this process.

11. Remove cheese from brine and let dry on a cheese mat placed on a rack at room temperature for two to three days, until cheese is dry to the touch. Turn cheese daily during this process.

12. Place cheese on a clean mat in a ripening container and ripen at 50°-54° Fahrenheit and 85 percent humidity for one month. During this time,

wipe the cheese's rind with a brine-soaked cloth once every other day, turning the cheese each time.

13. After the first month, wash the rind once a week with brine solution. The rind will continue to develop, displaying different colors molds on its surface. After two months, discontinue the brine wash; rub the cheese once a week with a soft clean cloth or a cheese brush. This will help firm up the rind. Continue to ripen and turn the cheese once a week for a minimum of six months. The cheese can be ripened under these conditions for up to two years if desired. Once the cheese is cut, wrap and store the wedge in the refrigerator.

Piora

Prep time: 60 minutes
Cooking time: 2 hours, 25 minutes
Pressing time: 12 hours, 30 minutes
Brining time: 20 hours
Drying time: 2-3 days
Ripening time: 3-6 months

Piora was originally made in the region of northern Italy near the Swiss Alps. It is a firm cheese with small "eyes," or holes, and is similar in flavor to some of the Swiss cheeses. It can be made with either cow's milk or a mixture of cow's and goat's milk. The addition of goat's milk will give it a slightly sharper, tangier flavor. It is an excellent snack and sandwich cheese.

Ingredients/Equipment:

4 gals whole milk, either all cow's milk or a mixture of 3 gals cow's milk and 1 gal goat's milk
½ tsp thermophilic culture
¾ tsp calcium chloride
¾ tsp liquid rennet
18% salt brine solution
Stainless steel cooking pot

Larger pot for hot water bath

Colander

Cheesecloth

Large (3.5x7.5 in) tomme mold

Cheese press

Cheese mats

Ripening container

Stainless steel whisk

Skimmer

Measuring cup

Distilled water

Thermometer

Directions:

1. Using sterilized equipment, pour milk into cooking pot and place in a larger pot partially filled with water. Over medium heat, warm the milk to 92° Fahrenheit, stirring gently as the milk heats. Once the thermometer reads 92° Fahrenheit, turn off heat.

2. Add culture to milk and let stand for five minutes. Using a skimmer, work it gently into the milk using an up-and-down motion, disturbing the surface of the milk as little as possible.

3. Dilute calcium chloride in ¼ cup of cool distilled water and add it to the mixture with the same gentle motion.

4. Dilute rennet in ¼ cup of cool distilled water and add it to the mixture in the same manner as before.

5. Cover pot and let it sit for 40 minutes, maintaining the temperature at 92° Fahrenheit throughout.

6. Check for a clean break. If a clean break is not present, let mixture stand for five to ten minutes. If clean break occurs, use whisk and skimmer to cut the curd into very small pieces, about the size of grains of rice. Once curds are cut, let them stand for five minutes. Stir gently for

ten minutes. Let curds stand for five minutes more, and then stir gently for ten minutes more.

7. Return pot to low heat and begin to heat the curds to 120° Fahrenheit, stirring gently throughout this process. Adjust and monitor the heat to ensure that this step takes 40-45 minutes. Do not heat curds too quickly.

8. Once temperature reaches 120° Fahrenheit, stir the curds for another 30 minutes, maintaining temperature throughout. The curds should be quite firm and springy when squeezed.

9. Pour the curd mixture into a cheesecloth-lined colander. Fill the prepared mold with curds. Pull the cheesecloth up around the curd bundle, smoothing it over the top. Put on the lid.

10. Place mold in a cheese press and press at five pounds of pressure for 30 minutes. Remove cheese, unwrap, turn, and rewrap. Place mold back into cheese press and press at 25 pounds of pressure for 12 hours.

11. Remove the cheese from the press. Unwrap it and place it in the brine solution for 20 hours, turning it halfway through this process.

12. Remove the cheese from the brine and place it on a cheese mat placed on a rack. Dry the cheese for two to three days at room temperature, turning it once a day during the process. Cheese should be dry to the touch at the end of this step.

13. Place cheese on a clean cheese mat in a ripening container. Ripen at 50°-54° Fahrenheit and 80-90 percent humidity for three to six months. During this time, turn cheese twice a week and wipe with a clean cloth soaked in a brine solution. Once the rind has firmed up (usually after six weeks to two months of ripening), discontinue the brine wash and rub the cheese with a clean cloth instead. This will control the rate of mold growth but still allow it to grow on the rind.

Brick

Prep time: 60 minutes

Cooking time: 1 hour, 50 minutes

Resting time: 35 minutes

Draining time: 35 minutes

Pressing time: 6 hours

Brining time: 8 hours

Drying time: 24 hours

Ripening time: 2 weeks

Brick is Limburger's less pungent cousin. Like Limburger, brick gets its aroma from the addition of a specific bacteria, *Brevibacterium linens*. This ripening agent is available through cheese-making suppliers. Brick is an American cheese, and it takes its name from its shape. However, if you do not have a brick-shaped mold, you may use a standard round, 2-pound mold. Brick does have some aroma, but the flavor is usually quite mild. However, aging it longer gives it a greater punch.

Ingredients/Equipment:

4 gals whole cow's milk

½ tsp thermophilic culture

¾ tsp calcium chloride

¾ tsp liquid rennet

18% brine solution

Pinch of *Brevibacterium linens*

Non-reactive cooking pot

Larger pot for hot water bath

Colander

Cheesecloth

Skimmer

Curd knife

Brick-shaped mold or 2 lb round mold

Measuring cup

Stainless steel ladle

Cheese press

Cheese mat

Thermometer

Ripening container

Cutting board

Drying rack

Measuring cup

Directions:

1. Start with sterilized equipment. Prepare a draining container by placing a rack inside a food-grade plastic container. Place a cutting board on top of the rack and cover it with a cheese mat.

2. Pour the milk into a stainless steel or enameled cooking pot. Place the pot in a larger pot partly filled with water. Over medium heat, warm the milk to 90° Fahrenheit, stirring gently. Turn off heat.

3. Sprinkle the thermophilic culture and the *Brevibacterium linens* ripening agent over the surface of the milk. Let rest for five minutes. Using a skimmer, work the additives into the milk with a gentle up-and-down motion, disturbing the surface of the milk as little as possible. Cover pot and let rest for 15 minutes.

4. Dilute calcium chloride in ¼ cup of cool distilled water. Add to milk using the same up-and-down motion.

5. Dilute rennet in ¼ cup of cool distilled water. Add to milk mixture using the same motion as before. Cover and let sit for 40 minutes, maintaining mixture at 90° Fahrenheit throughout.

6. Check for a clean break. If curds are not breaking, let sit for another ten minutes. Using skimmer and a long-handled knife, cut mixture into ⅜-inch pieces, stirring gently. Let curds settle for five minutes.

7. Return heat to low and slowly warm curds to 104° Fahrenheit, stirring gently throughout the process. Do not heat the curds too quickly; this step should take 40 minutes, so adjust the heat as needed to remain in

that timeframe. Once mixture reaches 104° Fahrenheit, cover the pot and let it rest for five minutes.

8. Using a measuring cup, dip off whey until only one inch of whey remains to cover the curds. Replace the dipped whey with an equal amount of distilled water, heated to 104° Fahrenheit. Stir gently for ten minutes. Let curds settle and rest for five minutes.

9. Pour contents of pot into a cloth-lined colander. Using a ladle or your clean hands, fill the prepared mold with the warm curds, pulling the cheesecloth up around the curds and smoothing it over the top.

10. Cover the container and let the curds drain for 15 minutes. Turn the cheese over, cover the container again and let cheese drain for another 20 minutes.

11. Unwrap, turn, and rewrap cheese. Add the 5-pound weight (a regular brick will work). Press for six hours, turning cheese every two hours.

12. Remove cheese from the mold. Unwrap and place cheese in 18 percent salt brine solution. Let cheese soak for eight hours, turning once during the process.

13. Remove cheese from brine and place on a cheese mat on a rack in a ripening container. Let dry, uncovered, at room temperature for 24 hours.

14. Place cheese on a clean cheese mat in a clean ripening container. Ripen cheese at 60° Fahrenheit and 90 percent humidity for two weeks. Turn cheese daily and wash rind with a clothed dipped in brine once every other day. A reddish color will begin to develop on rind after 10-12 days.

15. Once the red color spreads (after about two weeks), wipe the surface of the cheese with a clean damp cloth. This will remove some of the red coating. Dry cheese with a clean paper towel.

16. You may eat the cheese at this point, or wrap cheese in foil and place in refrigerator at 45° Fahrenheit to continue the ripening process. Cheese will become stronger as it ripens further.

Handkäse

Prep time: 45 minutes

Cooking time: 1 hour, 15 minutes

Resting time: 2 hours, 5 minutes

Drying time: 2 days

Ripening time: 6-8 weeks

Also called "hand cheese," this German cheese is just that — one that is shaped by hand. Handkäse is also one of those rare cheeses made totally with skim milk, so it is lower in fat than many others. Handkäse has a firm yet creamy texture, but the use of both brine and ripening bacteria gives Handkäse a sharp and pungent flavor, not as potent as Limburger, but no one will ever mistake Handkäse for cream cheese. It is usually eaten as a snack cheese, often accompanied by beer and dark German bread.

Ingredients/Equipment:

8 qts skim milk

¼ tsp mesophilic culture

Pinch of *Brevibacterium linens* ripening bacteria

¼ tsp liquid rennet

2 tsps kosher or pickling salt

Simple brine solution

Non-reactive cooking pot

Colander

Cheesecloth

Ripening container

Thermometer

Skimmer

Cheese knife

Distilled water

Directions:

1. In a sterilized cooking pot, heat milk over low heat until it reaches 77° Fahrenheit, stirring gently during this process to prevent milk from scorching. Remove from heat.

2. Sprinkle culture and the ripening bacteria over the surface of the milk and allow it to stand for five minutes. Using the skimmer and an up-and-down motion, gently draw the culture and bacteria into the milk, breaking the surface as little as possible. Cover and let stand for 30 minutes.

3. Dilute rennet in ¼ cup of cool distilled water and add to the milk mixture using the same up-and-down motion. Cover and let stand for 30 minutes.

4. Check for a clean break. If clean break is not present, let stand for an additional five minutes. Once a clean break is present, use a skimmer and cheese knife to cut the curd into ½-inch cubes. Let stand for five minutes.

5. Return pot to low heat and slowly warm the curds to 120° Fahrenheit, adjusting heat as needed to ensure that it takes one hour to heat curds to this temperature. Do not heat curds too quickly. Turn off heat; cover pot and let stand for one hour.

6. Pour contents of pot into cloth-lined colander. Transfer curds to a bowl and break up curds with your hands. Work salt into curds.

7. Shape cheese by hand into six small cylinders or patties that fit into your hand.

8. Dry cheeses on a cheese mat placed on a rack in a ripening container for one to two days, turning several times until dry. Remove any collected whey from the container, wiping it with a paper towel.

9. Once cheeses are dry, place on a clean cheese mat in the ripening container. Ripen at 50° Fahrenheit and 85-90 percent humidity. Wipe cheeses every second day with a cloth soaked in a simple brine solution.

10. After about two weeks, a reddish smear will begin to develop on the rind of the cheese. Continue to wipe the cheese with the brine solution every second day for another four to six weeks. The longer the cheese is ripened, the more pungent and sharp the cheese will become. Once the cheese has ripened to your taste, wrap and store in the refrigerator.

Gammelost

Prep time: 45 minutes
Cooking time: 40 minutes
Resting time: 4 days, 7 hours
Pressing time: 12 hours
Drying time: 2-3 days
Ripening time: 3 weeks-7 months

Gammelost means "old cheese" in Norwegian, the culture that created this stinky masterpiece. Gammelost is made from soured skim milk, and it can be ripened for a mere three weeks — when it is only somewhat pungent — or for up to seven months, which is how many Norwegians prefer it. In addition to its sour milk base, gammelost is made with two types of mold powder, including the mold that creates Roquefort cheese. These molds, readily available through mail order, help the cheese develop a complex and varicolored mold. This cheese is for the true adventurer.

Ingredients/Equipment:

16 qts skim milk
½ tsp thermophilic culture
1/8 tsp *Penicillium roqueforti* mold powder
Pinch *Cylindrocarpon spp.* mold powder
1 tsp pickling or kosher salt
Non-reactive cooking pot
Thermometer
Colander
Cheesecloth

Large tome mold
Draining container
Cheese press
Cheese mat
Ripening container
Thin metal knitting needle or meat skewer
Skimmer

Directions:

1. Pour milk into a large non-reactive cooking pot and let come to room temperature.

2. Sprinkle culture over the surface of the milk and let stand for five minutes. Using a skimmer and a gentle up-and-down motion, work the culture into the milk, disturbing the surface of the milk as little as possible. Cover and let stand for 48 hours or until milk is very sour.

3. Place pot in a hot water bath and slowly warm milk to 145° Fahrenheit. Turn off heat and hold for 30 minutes. The solids will separate from the whey and form a stringy mass. Using the skimmer, dip the curd mass from the pot and ladle into a cloth-lined colander. Fold the cloth over the top of the mass and press curd through the cloth to expel as much whey as possible. Let drain for six to seven hours.

4. Remove curd from cloth. Using your hands, break into pieces and pack into the mold. Let drain on a rack in a draining container for two days at room temperature.

5. Remove cheese from mold and break up again into 1-inch pieces. Place in a bowl and sprinkle with both mold powders. Mix in salt. Pack cheese into a cloth-lined mold. Pull the cloth up around the curds and fold neatly, smoothing the cloth across the top of the bundle. Place mold in cheese press and press at light pressure for 12 hours.

6. Remove cheese from press and unwrap. Dry on a rack at room temperature for two to three days, turning daily. The cheese will begin to develop a yellowish color and a strong, yeasty odor.

7. Place cheese on a cheese mat in a ripening container. Ripen at 50°
    Fahrenheit and 90 percent humidity for three weeks to seven months.
    Mold will begin to grow on the surface. Turn cheese and rub mold into
    the rind by hand three times a week. After two weeks, pierce the cheese
    with the needle or skewer all the way through, both vertically and hori-
    zontally, to encourage blue veining in the cheese's interior.

Fontina

Prep time: 45 minutes
Cook time: 25-35 minutes
Rest time: 48 hours
Aging time: 90 days

Fontina was originally created in Italy, where several fine versions are still crafted
today. It is not necessary to buy a plane ticket to Italia to enjoy this cheese, but
it does require some work. It must be pressed, brine-washed, and carefully aged.
Once ready, it is delicious sliced on sandwiches or melted in recipes. Due to the
brine wash, it is slightly salty, but it also possesses a mild creaminess beneath the
briny flavor.

Ingredients/Equipment:

16 qts whole cow's milk
½ tsp mesophilic culture
¾ tsp calcium chloride
¾ tsp liquid rennet
18% brine solution
Cooking pot
Colander
Cheesecloth
13.5x7.5 in tomme mold
Cheesecloth
Cheese press
Cheese matting
Thermometer

Directions:

1. Take a sterile, non-reactive cooking pot. Place it in a larger pot for a hot water bath. Add milk and heat to 88° Fahrenheit, stirring gently throughout. Remove from heat.

2. Sprinkle the mesophilic culture over the milk's surface. Let stand for about five minutes. Using a skimmer, gently work culture into milk in an up-and-down motion. Cover pot and let ripen for one hour. Keep the temperature at 88° Fahrenheit throughout this step.

3. Dilute the calcium chloride in ¼ cup of cool distilled water. Add this mixture to the milk using the same up-and-down motion with the skimmer, disturbing the milk's surface as little as possible.

4. Dilute rennet in ¼ cup of cool distilled water. Add to milk mixture in the same manner as other ingredients. Cover the pot again and let rest 45-50 minutes, again maintaining the temperature.

5. Check the mixture for a clean break. If the mixture does not break clean, let it rest for ten more minutes.

6. Once the break is clean, cut the curd into pea-sized pieces. Let stand for five minutes and then stir for ten minutes.

7. Using a measuring cup, remove four quarts of whey from the pot. This will reduce the whey by about 25 percent. Replace the whey with four quarts of distilled water, heated to 145° Fahrenheit. Sift mixture gently for ten minutes. Let mixture rest for ten minutes.

8. Pour the mixture into a large colander and let drain for ten minutes.

9. Fill the cloth-lined mold with curd mixture. Pull the cloth up around the mixture and fold excess cloth over top. Put lid on mold.

10. Place mold in cheese press. Press lightly for 15 minutes. Remove cheese from press and redress, refolding cloth around it. Press at medium pressure for 12 hours.

11. Remove cheese from press. Unwrap and place in a cool, 18-percent brine solution for 12 hours, turning cheese once during the process.

12. Remove cheese from brine solution. Place cheese on a mat-covered rack and let dry for 24 hours at room temperature. Turn cheese once during process.

13. Transfer cheese to a clean mat and place in ripening container. Let ripen at 55° Fahrenheit and 90 percent humidity for three days.

14. At the end of three days, wash cheese with a brine solution. Continue to ripen, washing cheese in brine solution every other day for one month. After that, continue to ripen, and wash the cheese in brine solution twice a week, turning the cheese each time it is washed. Cheese is ready to eat after 90 days of ripening.

Buttermilk hand cheese

Prep time: 25 minutes
Cooking time: 1 hour, 5 minutes
Resting time: 1 day, 2 hours
Draining time: 6-7 hours
Drying time: 2-3 days
Ripening time: 6-8 weeks

This cheese is German in origin, and it is called hand cheese because the patties or logs are shaped by hand. Buttermilk gives this cheese a tangy punch, and the ripening process, which includes a weekly wipe down with brine, adds both saltiness and pungency to the final cheese, while the texture remains creamy. The addition of caraway seeds or dill adds another layer of flavor. Curds produced by buttermilk are very fine, so use tightly-woven muslin or a clean linen towel to drain the cheese.

Ingredients/Equipment:

4 qts buttermilk
Salt to taste
½ tsp caraway seeds or dried dill weed (optional)
Large glass or ceramic bowl
Non-reactive cooking pot

Larger pot for hot water bath
Thermometer
Tightly-woven muslin or linen towel
Colander
Ripening container
Cheese mats
Cheese rack

Directions:

1. Pour buttermilk into a bowl and cover with a clean towel. Let ripen at room temperature for 24 hours.

2. Put cooking pot into a larger pot filled with water to create a hot water bath. Pour ripened buttermilk into the cooking pot and heat to 125° Fahrenheit, stirring milk gently to prevent scorching. Turn off heat. Continue stirring gently for 20 minutes. Cover and let sit for two hours.

3. Pour contents of pot through cloth-lined colander. Tie the four corners of the cloth together to form a bag. Hang bag from a wooden spoon laid across the edge of the cooking pot. Let drain for six to seven hours.

4. Remove curds from cloth. Add salt to taste. Add caraway seeds or dill if desired. Mix well and shape curds into patties or small logs.

5. Dry cheeses on cheese mat placed on a rack at room temperature for two to three days or until dry to the touch. Turn cheeses twice a day during this process.

6. Place cheeses on a clean cheese mat in a ripening container. Cover and ripen at 50° Fahrenheit and 90 percent humidity. Keep lid on container to create a humid environment. Turn cheeses daily.

7. Wash surface of cheeses twice weekly with a clean cloth dipped in a brine solution to encourage the development of the rind. Ripen for six to eight weeks. Wrap ripened cheeses in plastic wrap and store in the refrigerator.

Monostorer

Prep time: 40 minutes

Cooking time: 35-40 minutes

Resting time: 1-2 hours

Draining time 10 minutes

Pressing time 8-10 hours

Brining time: 12 hours

Drying time: 2 days

Ripening time: 2-3 months

This sheep's milk cheese comes from the Transylvania region of what is now Romania. It is a fairly simple cheese with only a few basic ingredients. The sheep's milk produces a rich and creamy "paste," (the body of the cheese), while the brine wash adds a hint of saltiness to the rind. The flavor is mild, and the aroma is faintly earthy. The curds are crumbled and mixed twice during the cheese's production, which gives the finished cheese a very solid and silky texture.

Ingredients/Equipment:

8 qts sheep's milk

½ tsp liquid rennet

2 tsps pickling or kosher salt

Cool brine solution

Cooking pot

Colander

Cheesecloth

Large tome mold

Cheese press

Cheese matting

Cheese rack

Ripening container

Thermometer

Measuring cup

Distilled water

Directions:

1. Start with sterilized equipment. In a non-reactive cooking pot, warm milk over low heat to 88° Fahrenheit, stirring gently to prevent scorching. Remove from heat.

2. Dilute rennet in ¼ cup of cool distilled water. Using a skimmer, gently work culture into milk in an up-and-down motion. Cover pot and let ripen for one to two hours until a firm curd has formed.

3. Use a curd knife and skimmer to cut curd into ½-inch cubes. Let settle. Carefully pour contents of pot into cloth-lined colander. Let drain for ten minutes.

4. Press the curd down by gathering the cloth and pressing the curd down with your hands in the colander.

5. Once curd stops dripping, unwrap and use your hands to break curd up into small pieces. Blend in salt.

6. Sprinkle curd with ¼ cup of warm distilled water. Mix again with your hand, pressing the curd as you mix.

7. Crumble curd again.

8. Fill prepared mold with curd, pulling cloth up neatly around curd bundle and smoothing it across the top. Put on lid.

9. Place mold in cheese press and press at 20 pounds of pressure for eight to ten hours.

10. Remove cheese from press. Place in brine solution for 12 hours, turning once during this time.

11. Remove cheese from brine solution. Place on a clean rack and dry at room temperature for two days, turning cheese once during this time.

12. Place cheese on clean mat in ripening container. Ripen at 55° Fahrenheit and 90 percent humidity for two to three months. Every second day, turn cheese and wipe with a cloth dipped in brine solution. The rind will gradually become firm and turn a pale yellow, and the cheese will soften slightly.

13. Wrap finished cheese in foil or parchment paper and store in the refrigerator.

Cabra al vino

Prep time: 30 minutes

Cook time: 100 minutes

Resting time: 25 minutes

Pressing time: 24 hours, 20 minutes

Drying time: 6 hours

Soaking time: 48 hours

Ripening time: 3 months

This Spanish goat's milk cheese receives much of its flavor from the "bath" it takes in red wine, which has earned it the nickname "Drunken Goat." This wine bath gives the rind a rich red color and flavors it with the wine's aroma and taste. The cheese itself is semi-soft and slightly sweet. It is an excellent snack cheese. It pairs well with bread, salty meats such as prosciutto, and fruit.

Ingredients/Equipment:

2 gals whole goat's milk

½ tsp mesophilic culture

⅛ tsp calcium chloride

1 tsp liquid rennet or ¼ tablet dry rennet

1 ½ qts of red wine, either sweet or dry, depending on your taste

Distilled water

Cooking pot

2-qt glass or glazed ceramic mixing bowl

Colander

Cheesecloth

Curd knife

Skimmer

Measuring cup

2 lb mold, cheesecloth-lined

Cheese press

Drying rack

Ripening container

Cheese mat

Thermometer

Directions:

1. Use sterilized equipment. Pour milk into a cooking pot and place over medium heat. Heat milk until it reaches 90° Fahrenheit.

2. Stir in mesophilic culture and cover pot, letting it rest for ten minutes. If using homogenized milk, dilute the calcium chloride in ½ cup of distilled water and add to milk mixture.

3. Dilute rennet in ¼ cup of distilled water and add to mixture, maintaining temperature at 90° Fahrenheit throughout this process. Stir for one minute until rennet is thoroughly mixed into milk.

4. Cover pot and let it sit one hour, maintaining temperature at 90° Fahrenheit. Check for a clean break. If clean break is not present, wait another ten minutes.

5. If mixture breaks clean, cut curds into ½-inch cubes. Stir, remove from heat, and let rest for five minutes.

6. Using a measuring cup, draw off ⅓ of the whey. Gradually add about two and a half cups of distilled water, which should be pre-heated to 175° Fahrenheit. Stir and monitor the temperature until the mixture is 92° Fahrenheit. Once the curds reach this temperature, let them rest for ten minutes, stirring occasionally.

7. Drain off the whey to the level of the curds. Add the remaining 3 ¼ cups of water heated to 175° Fahrenheit, stirring constantly until the mixture reaches 100° Fahrenheit. Return the pot to the heat and maintain temperature at 100° Fahrenheit for 15 minutes, stirring frequently to prevent curds from matting.

8. Maintaining temperature at 100° Fahrenheit, allow curds to simmer for 30 minutes.

9. Pour mixture into a colander, reserving the whey if you wish for other cheese-making recipes such as ricotta. Return drained curds to pot and using a curd knife and skimmer, reduce the pieces to ¼-inch bits.

10. Pour the curds into a cheesecloth-lined 2-pound mold. Pull the cloth up around the bundle of curds and smooth it across the stop. Put on lid.

11. Place bundle in a cheese press and press at 20 pounds of pressure for 20 minutes.

12. Remove cheese from press, unwrap, turn, and rewrap it. Return cheese to press and press at 20 pounds for 12 hours.

13. Remove cheese from press, unwrap, turn, and rewrap it. Return cheese to press and press at 20 pounds for another 12 hours.

14. Remove cheese from press and unwrap it. Place cheese in a glass or glazed ceramic bowl containing one and a ½ quart of red wine. Allow cheese to soak in wine at room temperature for 24 hours.

15. Remove cheese from wine bath and pour wine into a sealed container, storing it in the refrigerator for the next bath.

16. Place cheese on a rack and allow it to dry at room temperature for six hours or until dry to the touch.

17. After bringing the stored wine back to room temperature, soak the cheese in the wine bath for another 24 hours.

18. Store the unwrapped cheese on a mat in the ripening container for three months at 50° Fahrenheit and 80-85 percent humidity. Turn the cheese daily for the first two weeks.

19. After the first two weeks, wipe cheese once a week with a clean cloth dipped in brine solution.

Caerphilly

Prep time: 40 minutes

Cook time: 1 hour, 50 minutes

Resting time: 30 minutes

Pressing time: 16 hours, 40 minutes

Drying time: 3-6 days

Ripening time: 3 weeks

Caerphilly is now made in England, but it originally came from Wales. Welsh miners often took this cheese with them as part of their lunch. It is a cow's milk cheese with a mild flavor, but a tangy after bite. Unlike some other cheese in this section, it has a fairly short ripening period, only about three weeks, so you can taste and enjoy it soon after making it. It is especially tasty with dark breads and good-quality ale.

Ingredients/Equipment:

2 gals whole cow's milk

¼ tsp mesophilic culture

⅛ tsp calcium chloride

½ tsp liquid rennet

2 tbsps cheese or kosher salt

Distilled water

Cooking pot

Larger pot for hot water bath

Colander

Cheesecloth

Curd knife

2-lb mold

Cheesecloth

Cheese press

Thermometer

Directions:

1. Use sterilized equipment. Pour milk into a cooking pot and place in a larger water-filled pot over medium heat. Heat milk until it reaches 90° Fahrenheit.

2. Stir in mesophilic culture and cover pot, letting it rest for 30 minutes at 90° Fahrenheit. If using homogenized milk, dilute the calcium chloride in ¼ cup of distilled water and add to milk mixture.

3. Dilute rennet in ¼ cup of distilled water and add to mixture, stirring for two minutes.

4. Cover pot and let it sit for 40 minutes, maintaining temperature at 90° Fahrenheit. Check for a clean break. If clean break is not present, wait another ten minutes.

5. If mixture breaks clean, cut curds into ¼-inch cubes.

6. Gradually begin to raise the temperature of the mixture to 92° Fahrenheit. Do not heat mixture too quickly; this step should take approximately ten minutes.

7. Once the target temperature of 92° Fahrenheit is reached, maintain this temperature for 40 minutes, stirring constantly.

8. Remove mixture from heat and let rest for five minutes.

9. Drain the curds into a cheesecloth-lined colander, and allow mixture to drain for five to ten minutes or until the whey no longer drips.

10. Cut the curds into 1-inch thick slabs and stack them one on top of another. Turn the stack over, top to bottom, twice in ten minutes.

11. Making sure your hands are clean, break the curds into thumbnail-sized pieces and blend in the salt.

12. Pour the curds into a cheesecloth-lined 2-pound mold. Pull the cloth up around the bundle of curds and smooth it across the stop. Put on lid.

13. Place bundle in a cheese press and press at ten pounds of pressure for ten minutes.

14. Remove cheese from press, unwrap, turn, and rewrap it. Return cheese to press and press at ten pounds for ten minutes.

15. Remove cheese from press, unwrap, turn, and rewrap it. Return cheese to press and press at 15 pounds for 20 minutes.

16. Remove cheese from press, unwrap, turn, and rewrap it. Return cheese to press and press at 15 pounds for 16 hours.

17. Remove cheese from press and unwrap it. Allow it to dry on a clean surface at room temperature until dry to the touch, usually three to six days. Turn the cheese twice daily during this process.

18. Ripen unwrapped cheese in the refrigerator at 55° Fahrenheit and 80-85 percent humidity for three weeks, turning every other day to ensure even ripening.

Halloumi

Prep time: 30 minutes
Cook time: 3 hours
Resting time: 2 hours, 20 minutes
Pressing time: 2 hours

Originally produced on the island of Cyprus, Halloumi is traditionally made with sheep's milk. However, since this is the hardest milk for the cheese maker to find, Halloumi can also be made with whole goat's milk. Halloumi is flavored with mint and sometimes served in slices that are broiled with lemon. It is also an excellent grilling cheese, as it is semi-firm but melts well.

Ingredients/Equipment:

2 gals whole goat's milk
¼ tsp mesophilic culture
½ tsp liquid rennet or ¼ tablet dry rennet
1 tsp dried mint leaves
¼ cup cheese salt
Distilled water

Cooking pot

Larger pot for hot water bath

Non-reactive cooking pan (stainless steel, Pyrex, or glass)

Stainless steel cooking spoon

Colander

Cheesecloth

Curd knife

2-lb mold

Thermometer

Directions:

1. Use sterilized equipment. Pour milk into a cooking pot and place in a larger, water-lined pot over medium heat. Heat milk until it reaches 86° Fahrenheit.

2. Stir in mesophilic culture and blend for two minutes.

3. Dilute rennet in 1/4 cup of distilled water and add to mixture, maintaining temperature at 86° Fahrenheit throughout this process. Stir for one minute until rennet is thoroughly mixed into milk.

4. Cover pot and let it sit for 40 minutes, maintaining temperature at 86° Fahrenheit. Check for a clean break. If clean break is not present, wait another ten minutes.

5. If mixture breaks clean, cut curds into 1/4-inch cubes, keeping them as uniform as possible.

6. Gradually begin to raise the temperature of the mixture to 104° Fahrenheit. Do not heat mixture too quickly; this step should take approximately 45 minutes.

7. Once the target temperature of 104° Fahrenheit is reached, maintain this temperature for 20 minutes, stirring constantly.

8. Line a colander with cheesecloth and place in a deep bowl. Pour the curds into the colander and drain for ten minutes or until the whey no longer drips into the bowl. Reserve the whey.

9. Rehydrate mint by placing it in a 1/2 cup of boiling distilled water for two minutes. Drain water and reserve mint leaves.

10. Blend mint leaves into curds with a spoon.

11. Pour the curds into a cheesecloth-lined 2-pound mold. Pull the cloth up around the bundle of curds and smooth it across the stop. Put on lid.

12. Place bundle in a cheese press and press at 30 pounds of pressure for one hour.

13. Remove cheese from press, unwrap, turn, and rewrap it. Return cheese to press and press at 40 pounds for one hour. Cheese should be firm, with a slightly spongy consistency.

14. Heat the reserved whey in a non-reactive pan to 190° Fahrenheit. Remove the cheese from the mold, unwrap, and cut into 2-inch thick strips. Place in hot whey for one hour, maintaining target temperature throughout.

15. Drain into a cloth-lined colander and let rest at room temperature for 20 minutes.

16. Sprinkle with salt and let mixture rest for two hours at room temperature. Wrap and store in refrigerator. Cheese will be good for up to two weeks.

Pyrenees

Prep time: 30 minutes
Cook time: 90 minutes
Resting time: 1 hour, 50 minutes
Pressing time: 24 hours, 45 minutes
Drying time: 3-5 days
Ripening time: 4-6 months

This cow's milk cheese is produced in both France and Spain in the regions surrounding the Pyrenees, a mountain range that separates the two countries. It has a creamy-white color and a fairly mild flavor, but the flavor does grow slightly sharper if the cheese is aged over four months. This version includes green peppercorns, which give the cheese a bit of spice. The peppercorns can be left out of the recipe if a milder taste is preferred. Pyrenees is often eaten with fruit and wine.

Ingredients/Equipment:

2 gals whole cow's milk

¼ tsp mesophilic culture

¼ tsp calcium chloride

½ tsp liquid rennet

1 tbsp salt

1 tbsp green peppercorns (optional, available in larger supermarkets and many gourmet stores)

Distilled water

Cooking pot

Large pot for hot water bath

Colander

Glass or glazed ceramic mixing bowl

Wooden spoon or dowel

Cheesecloth

Curd knife

2-lb mold

Wooden cheese board

Thermometer

Directions:

Note: Follow these steps if you are planning to use the peppercorns. If you do not wish to add the peppercorns, disregard these instructions and start with number one on the list below. Before you begin the recipe, boil the peppercorns in a ½ cup of water for 15 minutes. Strain the peppercorns and sit the water aside. Add the peppercorn water to the milk before adding the mesophilic culture. Add the boiled peppercorns to the curds when you add the salt.

1. Use sterilized equipment. Add milk to cooking pot and heat to 90° Fahrenheit. Add water from boiled peppercorns (see note above). Add the mesophilic culture, stir for one minute, and then cook the mixture at 90° Fahrenheit for 45 minutes.

2. Dilute calcium chloride in ¼ cup of cool distilled water and add to mixture. Stir for one minute.

3. Add rennet to the mixture and stir with an up-and-down motion to ensure even distribution. Remove mixture from heat. Cover and set aside for 45 minutes.

4. Check mixture. Curd should be quite firm. Check for a clean break. If one is not present, wait ten minutes.

5. Using curd knife, cut mixture into ½-inch cubes.

6. Place pot in larger hot water bath. Slowly raise temperature to 100° Fahrenheit. Do not heat mixture too quickly; this step should take approximately 30 minutes. The whey will rise to the top of the mixture, and the curds will shrink during this process.

7. Once target temperature is reached, cover pot and allow mixture to rest for five minutes.

8. Pour the curds into a colander lined with cheesecloth with a larger bowl underneath.

9. Pull up edges of the cheesecloth-lined bundle. Tie the edges to a wooden spoon resting on the edge of the colander or tie bundle to a kitchen faucet, allowing whey to continue to drain for one hour.

10. Empty the curds into a large bowl and crumble with your hands or a large spoon. The curds should be the size of large marbles. Add the boiled green peppercorns at this point if desired (see note above).

11. Sprinkle curds with salt and work salt into the curds evenly.

12. Pack the curds into a cheesecloth-lined mold. Curds will be fairly stiff, and you will have to push to pack them into the mold.

13. Place bundle in a cheese press and press at five pounds of pressure for 30 minutes.

14. Remove cheese from press, unwrap, turn, and rewrap it. Return cheese to press and press at ten pounds for 15 minutes.

15. Remove cheese from press, unwrap, turn, and rewrap it. Return cheese to press and press at 20 pounds of pressure for 12 hours.

16. Remove cheese from press, unwrap, turn, and rewrap it. Return cheese to press and press at 20 pounds for another 12 hours.

17. Remove the cheese from the press and unwrap it. Place cheese on a wooden cheese board and allow it to air-dry at room temperature for three to five days or until dry to the touch.

18. Once the cheese is dry and has formed a firm rind, ripen in the refrigerator at 55º Fahrenheit and 80-85 percent humidity for four to six months.

Bra Duro

Prep time: 60 minutes
Cooking time: 115 minutes
Pressing time: 44 hours and 40 minutes
Brining time: 24 hours
Aging time: 6 months

This cheese has nothing to do with ladies' lingerie. Bra is the name of a city in the Piedmont region of northern Italy — a town that has proclaimed itself as the "cheese capital of Europe." Bra cheese is made in two forms, *Bra Duro* and *Bra Tenero*. *Bra Duro* is slightly harder in texture and is aged longer than its milder cousin, *Bra Tenero*. Both cheeses are made from cow's milk and go well with fruit and wine. This version of *Bra Duro* requires long and careful aging for full flavor. Unlike many other cheeses, it must be made with low-fat milk.

Ingredients/Equipment:

2 gals 1 or 2% cow's milk
¼ tsp thermophilic culture

1 tsp liquid rennet

18% brine solution

Non-reactive cooking pot

Distilled water

Colander

Stainless steel curd knife

Stainless steel whisk

2-lb cheese mold

Cheese press

Wooden cheese board

Thermometer

Directions:

1. Use sterilized equipment. Pour milk into a cooking pot and heat milk until it reaches 90° Fahrenheit.

2. Stir in mesophilic culture and cover pot, letting it rest for 30 minutes at 90° Fahrenheit.

3. Dilute rennet in ¼ cup of distilled water and add to mixture, stirring for two minutes.

4. Cover pot and let it sit for 40 minutes, maintaining temperature at 90° Fahrenheit. Check for a clean break. If clean break is not present, wait another ten minutes.

5. If mixture breaks clean, cut curds into ¼-inch cubes.

6. Gradually begin to raise the temperature of the mixture to 100° Fahrenheit. Do not heat mixture too quickly; this step should take approximately 30 minutes. Stir curds frequently with a stainless steel whisk, using and up-and-down, twisting motion to break up all the curds.

7. Drain the curds into a cheesecloth-lined colander, and quickly transfer curds to a cheesecloth-lined 2-pound mold. Pull the cloth up around the bundle of curds and smooth it across the stop. Put on lid.

8. Place bundle in a cheese press and press at ten pounds of pressure for ten minutes.

9. Remove cheese from press and unwrap it. Making sure your hands are clean, break the cheese into small pieces in a mixing bowl. Repack the pieces into the cheesecloth and return the wrapped cloth to the press.

10. Press cheese at ten pounds for 15 minutes.

11. Remove cheese from press and unwrap it. Repeat the unwrapping, breaking cheese into pieces, and repacking cheese into mold.

12. Press cheese at 30 pounds of pressure for 15 minutes.

13. Remove cheese from press and unwrap it. Repeat the unwrapping, breaking cheese into pieces, and repacking cheese into mold.

14. Press cheese at 40 pounds of pressure for 20 hours.

15. Remove cheese from press and unwrap it. Repeat the unwrapping, breaking cheese into pieces, and repacking cheese into mold.

16. Press cheese at 50 pounds for 24 hours.

17. Remove the cheese from the mold. Unwrap it and place it in a brine solution for 24 hours, turning the cheese every six hours.

18. Remove the cheese from the brine solution, pat it dry with a clean paper towel, and place it on a cheese board.

19. Put the cheese in the refrigerator and age it at 55° Fahrenheit and 80-85 percent humidity for six months. Turn the cheese daily for the first two weeks, then once a week after that. Using a clean cloth dipped in a brine solution, wipe the cheese once a week during the aging process.

CASE STUDY: GOAT CHEESE SPECIALISTS

Split Creek Farm, LLC
3806 Centerville Road
Anderson, SC 29625
www.splitcreek.com
info@splitcreek.com
864-287-3921 (p)
864-287-3921 (f)

For 23 years, Split Creek Farm has created a variety of cheeses featuring milk from their own herd of registered Alpine and Nubian goats. These prized animals produce an average of 2,400 pounds of milk apiece per year. Split Creek produces yogurt, dessert cheeses (especially their customer favorite, the almond apricot cheese ball), and fromage blanc, feta, and chèvre, both plain and in such flavors as tomato-basil, garden garlic, pesto, pepper, dill, and chive.

Split Creek cheese makers produce more than 700 pounds of cheese each week, which is sold to fine restaurants, gourmet shops, and health food stores. Like many cheese makers, they also sell online. They are proud of their ability to create "a value added, artisan cheese that is wholesome and consistent in quality." Like many other cheese makers, they feel that the secret to quality control is to taste every batch of cheese they make. Their cheeses have won many awards, including a perfect score for their feta from the American Dairy Goat Association and a bronze medal at both the American Cheese Society and the Wisconsin Cheese Makers Association. They feel their cheeses compare favorably with their European cousins; although, they note that "a greater variety and range of flavors are accepted and allowed by European customers." However, Split Creek hopes to continue to educate American consumers about the qualities and taste of goat's milk cheese.

Chapter Eight

Firm Cheeses and Blue Cheese

Firm cheeses are very versatile and the texture makes them wonderful snack foods and sandwich fillings. These cheeses are popular with most people and can be sliced, grated, or crumbled. Many firm cheeses are important in cooking as well. For example, lasagna would not  be the same without a dusting of Parmesan, and without cheddar, could you really call it mac and cheese? Firm cheeses need extra drying and aging time, so they are not for the impulsive cheese maker. However, the results will please both you and the lucky people who get to sample your wares.

CASE STUDY: JUST TWO FRIENDS PLAYING AROUND IN THE KITCHEN

Orb Weaver Farm
3406 Lime Kiln Road
New Haven, VT 05472
(802) 877-3755 (p)
www.orbweaverfarm.com

Cheese makers Marjorie Susman and Marian Pollack started making cheese in 1981. As they said, "We are self-taught and played around in the kitchen until we came up with a cheese we wanted…a good cheese for cooking with and eating. The first was a ricotta, then paneer…" Their "playing around" led to the production of 7,000 pounds of cheese each year and a blue ribbon for their farmhouse cheddar from The American Cheese Society. The partners do all the work themselves, from milking the cows to making the cheese. They work "in a beautiful, sunlit room, making a great product. I enjoy it all; the magic of it never ceases to amaze me." Orb Weaver Farmhouse Cheese is sold to local co-ops, markets, and restaurants. Their cheese is also sold online. Susman and Pollack milk their own Jersey cows, and during the six months they are not making cheese, they operate their own market garden. Their advice to cheese makers is, "Realize that this is a very physical process…pick a cheese that reflects you and your farm. Start slow. Don't sell cheese before it's ready. Any handmade cheese is unique; what the cows eat, even how the water tastes all makes it unique."

Colby

Prep time: 60 minutes

Cook time: 1 hour, 40 minutes

Rest time: 2 hours

Pressing time: 13 hours

Brining time: 12 hours

Drying time: 2-3 days

Ripening time: 6 weeks-2 months

Colby cheese is a Wisconsin native. It is also a favorite of many people who do not like cheese that is too strong. Colby is somewhat like cheddar, but with a much milder flavor. It is usually eaten as a snack or in sandwiches. Some people also use it in recipes in place of cheddar when a milder flavor is desired. Colby does need to ripen, but unlike cheddar, it does not age well, so once ripe, it should be eaten within a month or so and kept tightly wrapped in the refrigerator between meals.

Ingredients/Equipment:

16 qts whole cow's milk
½ tsp mesophilic culture
¾ tsp calcium chloride
¾ tsp liquid rennet
Distilled water
18% brine solution
Cooking pot
Larger pot for hot water bath
Colander
Cheesecloth
1 large (3.5x7.5 in) tomme mold
Cheese press
Cheese matting
Drying rack
Cheese wax
Natural bristle brush
Thermometer

Directions:

1. Place a sterile, non-reactive cooking pot in a larger pot for a hot water bath. Add milk and heat to 86° Fahrenheit, stirring gently throughout. Remove from heat.

2. Sprinkle the mesophilic culture over the milk's surface. Let stand for about five minutes. Using a skimmer, gently work culture into milk in

an up-and-down motion. Cover pot and let ripen for one hour. Keep the temperature at 86° Fahrenheit throughout this step.

3.   Dilute the calcium chloride in ¼ cup of cool distilled water. Add this mixture to the milk using the same up-and-down motion with the skimmer, disturbing the milk's surface as little as possible.

4.   Dilute rennet in ¼ cup of cool distilled water. Add to milk mixture in the same manner as other ingredients. Cover the pot again and let it rest 30 minutes, again keeping the temperature at 86° Fahrenheit.

5.   Check the mixture for a clean break. If the mixture does not break clean, let it rest for ten more minutes.

6.   Once the break is clean, use a skimmer and curd knife cut the curd into ½-inch cubes. Let stand for five minutes.

7.   Return the pot to the heat and slowly warm the mixture to 104° Fahrenheit, stirring slowly throughout the process. Adjust the heat as needed so that it takes 45 minutes for the mixture to come to 104 ° Fahrenheit. It is very important not to heat the mixture too quickly. The curds will shrink to the size of navy beans. Once the temperature reaches 104° Fahrenheit, allow the mixture to rest for 15 minutes, maintaining temperature.

8.   Using a measuring cup, remove whey from the pot until you can see the surface of the curds. Replace the measured whey with the same amount of distilled water, pre-heated to 104° Fahrenheit, and stir for two minutes. Cover and let rest for ten minutes at the same temperature.

9.   Drain off whey and pack curds into prepared mold. Pull cheesecloth up around the bundle of curds and smooth it across the top of the package. Put lid on mold.

10.   Place mold in cheese press. Press at ten pounds of pressure for one hour. Remove cheese from press, unwrap, turn over, and rewrap. Place back in press and press at 15 pounds of pressure for 12 hours.

11. Remove cheese from press. Unwrap it and place it in brine solution for 12 hours, turning the cheese once during the process. Remove cheese from brine and place it on a mat laid on a rack. Let it air dry for two to three days, until cheese is dry to the touch.

12. Coat cheese with two coats of cheese wax, letting wax dry between coats.

13. Ripen cheese at 50°-54° Fahrenheit and 85 percent humidity for six weeks, turning the cheese once a week to help it ripen evenly. Cheese may be ripened for up to two months for slightly sharper flavor, but it is ready to eat at six weeks. Once cut, it will keep for nearly a month in the refrigerator if properly wrapped.

Cotswold

Prep time: 15 minutes
Cook time: 3 hours, 10 minutes
Resting time: 15 minutes
Pressing time: 26 hours, 25 minutes
Drying time: 2-5 days
Ripening time: 1-3 months

Cotswold is a firm-textured English cheese made from cow's milk. It was originally produced in the British county of Gloucestershire, where another famous cheese, Double Gloucester, is also produced. Cotswold is traditionally flavored with dried onions and chives, which gives it a distinct flavor that goes well in sandwiches or on cheese boards. If the herbs are not added, it has a very mild flavor, much like a farmer's cheese but with a firmer texture. This cheese can be waxed if you wish, or you can allow it to develop its natural rind during the ripening process.

Ingredients/Equipment:

2 gals whole cow's milk
¼ tsp mesophilic culture
⅛ tsp calcium chloride

1 tsp liquid rennet or ¼ tablet dry rennet

Distilled water

2 tbsps dried chives

2 tbsps dried onion

Cooking pot

Colander

Cheesecloth

Curd knife

Skimmer

Measuring cup

2-lb mold

Cheese press

Drying rack

Ripening container

Cheese mat

Thermometer

Cheese wax (optional)

Natural bristle brush (optional)

Directions:

1. Use sterilized equipment. Pour milk into a cooking pot and place over medium heat. Heat milk until it reaches 90º Fahrenheit.

2. Stir in mesophilic culture and cover pot, letting it rest for 45 minutes at 90º Fahrenheit. If using homogenized milk, dilute the calcium chloride in ½ cup of distilled water and add to milk mixture.

3. Dilute rennet in ¼ cup of distilled water and add to mixture, maintaining temperature at 90º Fahrenheit throughout this process. Stir for one minute until rennet is thoroughly mixed into milk. Add dried onions and chives.

4. Cover pot and let it sit 45 minutes, maintaining temperature at 90º Fahrenheit. Check for a clean break. If clean break is not present, wait another ten minutes.

5. If mixture breaks clean, cut curds into ¼-inch cubes. Maintaining the temperature at 90º Fahrenheit, stir the curds for 20 minutes. Then, gradually begin to raise the temperature of the mixture to 104º Fahrenheit. Do not heat mixture too quickly; this step should take about 35 minutes.

6. Once the target temperature of 104º Fahrenheit is reached, maintain this temperature for 30 minutes, stirring constantly.

7. Remove mixture from heat and let rest for five minutes.

8. Line a colander with cheesecloth and place in a deep bowl. Pour the curds into the colander and drain for ten minutes or until the whey no longer drips into the bowl.

9. Pour the curds into a cheesecloth-lined 2-pound mold. Pull the cloth up around the bundle of curds and smooth it across the stop. Put on lid.

10. Place bundle in a cheese press and press at ten pounds of pressure for 15 minutes.

11. Remove cheese from press, unwrap, turn, and rewrap it. Return cheese to press and press at 30 pounds for ten minutes.

12. Remove cheese from press, unwrap, turn, and rewrap it. Return cheese to press and press at 40 pounds of pressure for two hours.

13. Remove cheese from press, unwrap, turn, and rewrap it. Return cheese to press and press at 50 pounds of pressure for 24 hours.

14. Remove cheese from press and unwrap it. Allow it to dry on a clean surface at room temperature until dry to the touch, usually two to five days. Turn the cheese twice daily during this process.

15. If you wish to wax the cheese, coat it with two or three coats of wax, using a natural bristle brush and allowing the wax to dry between coats.

16. Place cheese in the refrigerator and ripen for one to three months at 55º Fahrenheit and 80-85 percent humidity. Turn cheese weekly during this

process. If cheese is unwaxed, brush weekly with a natural bristle brush to remove any mold on the rind.

Classic Swiss

Prep time: 25 minutes

Cooking time: 2 hours, 35 minutes

Resting time: 5 minutes

Pressing time: 14 hours, 45 minutes

Brining time: 12 hours

Ripening time in refrigerator: 1 week

Ripening time outside of refrigerator: 2-3 weeks

Aging time: 3 months

Swiss cheese, with its holes or "eyes," is perhaps the most recognizable cheese around. However, the Swiss do not call their cheeses "Swiss." While most Swiss cheeses are named after the region in which they are made, the term "Swiss cheese" was created in America to describe the firm, pale yellow, tangy cheeses with eyes that were being imported from Switzerland. Whoever named it, Swiss cheese is now known and loved all over the world. In order to make this cheese at home, you need a specific powder called *Probionic shermanil* powder. It is available through most cheese-making suppliers.

Ingredients/Equipment:

2 gals whole cow's milk

½ tsp thermophilic culture

½ tsp *Probionic shermanil* powder

¾ tsp calcium chloride

2 lbs of cheese salt or kosher salt

1 gal distilled water

Non-reactive cooking pot

Colander

Cheesecloth

2-lb mold

Cheese press

Thermometer

Directions:

1. Place sterilized cooking pot over medium heat. Add milk and heat to 90° Fahrenheit, stirring gently throughout. Add thermophilic starter culture and mix well.

2. Remove ¼ cup of milk from the pot and add the probotic powder. Mix thoroughly to dissolve the powder. Return milk to the rest of the mixture and mix thoroughly. Cover and allow the milk to ripen for ten minutes, maintaining the 90° temperature.

3. Dilute rennet in ¼ cup of cool distilled water. Add to milk mixture using a gentle up-and-down motion. Cover and let sit for 30 minutes, maintaining mixture at 90° Fahrenheit throughout.

4. Using a curd knife and a stainless steel whisk, cut mixture into ¼-inch cubes, stirring gently.

5. Once the mixture is cut into curds, continue gentle stirring for another 40 minutes, maintaining mixture at 90° Fahrenheit throughout the process. This step, called fore working, helps expel the whey from the curds before they are heated further.

6. Heat the curds by one degree every minute until the mixture reaches 120° Fahrenheit. This will take 30 minutes. Once the mixture reaches 120° Fahrenheit, cook for 20 minutes at this temperature, stirring frequently.

7. Wearing protective gloves, pick up a handful of the curds and rub them together gently. If they break apart, the curds are sufficiently cooked. If they stick together, return them to the mixture and cook mixture at 120° Fahrenheit for another ten minutes.

8. Once curds are cooked, let mixture rest for five minutes.

9.   Pour off the whey, reserving it if desired for other recipes.

10. Ladle curds to cloth-lined mold. Work quickly; you do not want the curds to cool. Pull the cheesecloth up around the curds and smooth the cloth across the top. Place lid on mold.

11. Place mold in cheese press and press at ten pounds of pressure for 15 minutes.

12. Remove from press and unwrap, turn, and rewrap cheese. Replace in press and press at 14 pounds of pressure for 30 minutes.

13. Repeat the process but press at 14 pounds of pressure for two hours.

14. Repeat the process but press at 14 pounds of pressure for 12 hours.

15. Remove cheese from press and unwrap. Place cheese in a non-reactive bowl with the brine solution and place the bowl in the refrigerator for 12 hours.

16. Remove cheese from brine mixture and pat it dry with clean paper towels.

17. Place cheese on a clean cheese board and store at 50-55° Fahrenheit and 85 percent humidity for one week. Turn cheese once a day, wiping it each time with a clean cloth dipped in brine solution.

18. Place the cheese in a warm, humid room, such as the kitchen. Maintain the temperature between 68-74° Fahrenheit. Allow the cheese to age, turning it and wiping it with a clean cloth dipped in salt brine daily. Continue this process for two to three weeks or until cheese starts to swell and becomes slightly rounded. This is an indication that the eyes are forming within the cheese.

19. Return the cheese to the refrigerator or cheese cave and age at 45° Fahrenheit and 80 percent humidity for a minimum of three months. Turn the cheese three times a week and remove any surface mold by wiping it with a clean cloth dipped in salt brine. A reddish color on the rind of the cheese is normal and should be left alone.

Jarlsberg

Prep time: 40 minutes

Cooking time: 70 minutes

Resting time: 72 hours

Aging time: 8 weeks

A variation on the Emmental, or Swiss, variety of cheese, Jarlsberg was first crafted in Norway. Jarlsberg has a slightly sweet taste and a firm, almost rubbery texture. The large "eyes" are produced through careful ripening and cooling. Jarlsberg is a wonderful snack cheese. Like many Swiss-style cheeses, it has a faintly nutty flavor. It also goes well in many sandwiches, including the classic ham and cheese.

Ingredients/Equipment:

14 qts whole cow's milk

2 qts 1% milk

½ tsp thermophilic culture

½ tsp propionic bacteria powder

¾ tsp calcium chloride

¾ tsp liquid rennet

18% cool brine solution

Non-reactive cooking pot

Large pot for water bath

Colander

Cheesecloth

Large (3.5x7.5 in) tomme mold

Cheese press

Cheese mats

Skimmer

Thermometer

Directions:

1. Place sterilized cooking pot into hot water bath. Add milk and heat to 92° Fahrenheit, stirring gently throughout. Remove from heat.

2. Sprinkle the culture and propionic bacteria over the surface of the milk and let stand for five minutes. Using a skimmer and an up-and-down motion, draw the culture and bacteria down into the milk, disturbing the surface as little as possible. Cover and let ripen for 45 minutes. Maintain temperature at 92° Fahrenheit throughout.

3. Dilute calcium chloride in ¼ cup of cool distilled water. Add to milk using the same up-and-down motion.

4. Dilute rennet in ¼ cup of cool distilled water. Add to milk mixture using the same motion as before. Cover and let sit for 40 minutes, maintaining mixture at 92° Fahrenheit throughout.

5. Check for a clean break. If curds are not breaking, let sit for another ten minutes.

6. Using skimmer and a long-handled knife, cut mixture into bean-sized pieces, stirring gently. Once the mixture is cut into curds, continue gentle stirring for another 20 minutes. Let curds settle for five minutes.

7. Using a measuring cup, remove about 30 percent of the whey, until you can see the surface of the curds. Add the equivalent amount of distilled water, warming the water to 140° Fahrenheit before adding it to the mixture.

8. Return the pot to low heat, slowly warming curd to 108° Fahrenheit, stirring gently and constantly. Keep the heat low so that the process takes 30 minutes total. Then remove from heat and let curds settle.

9. Pour pot into a cloth-lined colander and let drain for ten minutes.

10. Transfer curds to cloth-lined mold. Pull the cheesecloth up around the curds and smooth the cloth across the top. Place lid on mold.

11. Place mold in cheese press or put a brick on top of the mold. Press for 30 minutes. Remove from press and redress cheese. Replace in press and keeping pressing at firm pressure for 12 hours.

12. Remove cheese from press and unwrap. Place cheese in brine solution for two hours, turning cheese once during the process.

13. Remove cheese from brine mixture. Place cheese on a mat-lined rack. Dry at room temperature for two to three days, turning once a day to aid drying.

14. Coat cheese with two thin layers of cheese wax, allowing wax to dry between coats.

15. Ripen at 50° Fahrenheit for two weeks, turning cheese once daily.

16. After two weeks, continue to ripen cheese at 65° Fahrenheit for four to six weeks. Turn cheese twice a week during this process. After the ripening has occurred, the cheese is ready to eat.

Leerdammer

Prep time: 65 minutes
Cooking time: 2 hours, 10 minutes
Resting time: 35 minutes
Draining time: 10 minutes
Pressing time: 24 hours, 15 minutes
Brining time: 20 hours
Drying time: 2 days
Ripening time: 6 weeks

Leerdammer is a Dutch Emmental, or Swiss-style, cheese. It is a relatively new cheese, created by a Dutch company in 1976 and first marketed in 1984. It is named for the city of Leerdam where its factory is located. Like most Swiss cheeses, Leerdammer is firm-textured, cream or pale yellow in color, with small holes or eyes and a faintly sweet, nutty flavor. It is an excellent snack or sandwich cheese.

Ingredients/Equipment:

14 qts whole cow's milk

2 qts 1% milk

½ tsp thermophilic culture

¼ tsp propionic bacteria powder

¾ tsp calcium chloride

¾ tsp liquid rennet

18% cool brine solution

Non-reactive cooking pot

Large pot for water bath

Colander

Cheesecloth

Large (3.5x7.5 in) tomme mold

Cheese press

Cheese mats

Skimmer

Thermometer

Directions:

1. Place sterilized cooking pot into hot water bath. Add milk and heat to 88º Fahrenheit, stirring gently throughout. Remove from heat.

2. Sprinkle the culture and propionic bacteria over the surface of the milk and let stand for five minutes. Using a skimmer and an up-and-down motion, draw the culture and bacteria down into the milk, disturbing the surface as little as possible. Cover and let ripen for 30 minutes. Maintain temperature at 88º Fahrenheit throughout.

3. Dilute calcium chloride in ¼ cup of cool distilled water. Add to milk using the same up-and-down motion.

4. Dilute rennet in ¼ cup of cool distilled water. Add to milk mixture using the same motion as before. Cover and let sit for 40 minutes, maintaining mixture at 88º Fahrenheit throughout.

5. Check for a clean break. If curds are not breaking, let sit for another ten minutes.

6. Using skimmer and a long-handled knife, cut mixture into bean-sized pieces, stirring gently. Once the mixture is cut into curds, continue gentle stirring for another 20 minutes. Let curds settle for five minutes.

7. Using a measuring cup, remove about 25 percent of the whey, until you can see the surface of the curds. Add the equivalent amount of distilled water, warming the water to 88° Fahrenheit before adding it to the mixture.

8. Return the pot to low heat, slowly warming curd to 102° Fahrenheit, stirring gently and constantly. Keep the heat low so that the process takes 30 minutes total. When the mixture reaches this temperature, maintain it and stir pot for an additional 30 minutes.

9. Using a measuring cup, remove three cups of whey. Add enough cool water to lower the temperature to 97° Fahrenheit. Let curds settle and hold for ten minutes.

10. Pour pot into a cloth-lined colander and let drain for ten minutes.

11. Pour contents of pot into cloth-lined colander and let drain for ten minutes.

12. Transfer curds to cloth-lined mold. Pull the cheesecloth up around the curds and smooth the cloth across the top. Place lid on mold.

13. Place mold in cheese press or put a brick on top of the mold. Press for 15 minutes. Remove from press and redress cheese. Replace in press and keeping pressing at firm pressure for four hours.

14. Remove cheese from press and unwrap. Place cheese in brine solution for 20 hours at 54° Fahrenheit, turning cheese once during the process.

15. Remove cheese from brine mixture. Place cheese on a mat-lined rack. Dry at room temperature for two days, turning once a day to aid drying.

16. Coat cheese with two thin layers of cheese wax, allowing wax to dry between coats.

17. Ripen at 40º Fahrenheit for two weeks, turning cheese once daily.

18. After two weeks, continue to ripen cheese at 65º Fahrenheit for four more weeks. Turn cheese twice a week during this process. After the ripening has occurred, the cheese is ready to eat.

Manchego

Prep time: 70 minutes

Cooking time: 95 minutes

Resting time: 5 minutes

Pressing time: 6 hours and 30 minutes

Brining time: 6 hours

Aging time: from 5 days-1 year, depending on taste

This famous Spanish cheese is made from sheep's milk in the La Mancha region of Spain, the setting for Don Quixote's famous windmill tilting. Because sheep's milk is hard to obtain, most home versions of Manchego are made from cow's milk. By adding lipase powder, an additive available from cheese-making suppliers, your milk will have a tangier flavor, which in turn will give the cheese greater richness and depth. *Manchego fresco* is aged for five days; *Manchego curado* is aged for three to 12 weeks; *Manchego virejo* is aged for up to 12 months, and *Manchego aceite* is aged for over a year. As is true of most cheeses, the longer it is aged, the sharper, deeper, and richer the flavors will be.

Ingredients/Equipment:

2 gals whole milk (sheep's milk if available, but cow's milk will work)

½ tsp mesophilic culture

½ tsp thermophilic culture

½ tsp lipase powder (optional)

1 tsp calcium chloride

½ tsp liquid rennet

18% brine solution

Non-reactive cooking pot

Distilled water

Colander

Cheesecloth

Stainless steel curd knife

Stainless steel whisk

2-lb cheese mold

Cheese press

Wooden cheese board

Thermometer

Directions:

1. Begin with sterilized equipment. A cooking pot over low heat, add milk and warm to 86° Fahrenheit. Add mesophilic and thermophilic starters and mix well. Cover and allow milk to ripen for 45 minutes, maintaining 86° Fahrenheit throughout.

2. Add lipase if desired.

3. Dilute rennet in one-fourth cup of distilled water and add to mixture with a gentle up-and-down motion, stirring for one minute.

4. Cover pot and let it sit 30 minutes, maintaining temperature at 86° Fahrenheit. Check for a clean break. If clean break is not present, wait another ten minutes.

5. If mixture breaks clean, cut curds into one-fourth inch cubes. Let sit for five minutes.

6. Cut cubes into rice-sized pieces by slowly stirring them with a stainless steel whisk for 30 minutes.

7. Gradually begin to raise the temperature of the mixture by two degrees every five minutes, to a target temperature of 104° Fahrenheit. Do not heat mixture too quickly; this step should take approximately 45 minutes. Stir gently to prevent matting.

8. Let curd sit for five minutes and then drain off whey.

9. Transfer curds to a cheesecloth-lined 2-pound mold. Pull the cloth up around the bundle of curds and smooth it across the stop. Put on lid.

10. Place bundle in a cheese press and press at 15 pounds of pressure for 15 minutes.

11. Remove cheese from press and unwrap it. Turn cheese, rewrap it, and place it back into the mold.

12. Press cheese again at 15 pounds for 15 minutes.

13. Remove cheese from press and unwrap it. Turn cheese, rewrap it, and place it back into the mold.

14. Press cheese at 15 pounds for 15 minutes.

15. Remove cheese from press and unwrap it. Turn cheese, rewrap it, and place it back into the mold.

16. Press cheese at 30 pounds for six hours.

17. Remove cheese from press and unwrap it. Repeat the unwrapping, breaking cheese into pieces, and repacking cheese into mold.

18. Remove the cheese from the mold. Unwrap it and place it in a brine solution chilled to 55° Fahrenheit. Place in the refrigerator for six hours.

19. Remove the cheese from the brine solution, pat it dry with a clean paper towel, and place it on a cheese board.

20. Return cheese to refrigerator or cheese cave, aging it at 55° Fahrenheit, turning daily. You may age the cheese for any length of time, depending on how sharp you want the finished cheese to be. Turn the cheese daily for the first two weeks, then once a week after that. Wipe the cheese with a clean cloth dipped in brine to remove any visible mold. If you age the cheese longer than five days, wipe the aging cheese with a clean cloth soaked in olive oil once a week to keep the cheese from drying out during the aging process.

CASE STUDY: GRAFTON CHEESE RISES AGAIN

Grafton Village Cheese Co.
Grafton Village Cheese Company
P.O. Box 1200
Battleboro, VT 05301
www.graftonvillagecheese.com
802-246-2221 (p)
802-246-2210 (f)

Grafton Village Cheese rose from the ashes — literally. Founded in 1892 as the Grafton Cooperative Cheese Company, the business closed in 1912 after a fire destroyed the factory. However, 50 years later, a historical foundation restored many of the old buildings in the village of Grafton, and Grafton Village Cheese began. Today, the company produces more than 2 million pounds of fine cheddar each year, including their 4 Star four-year-old cheddar and Classic Reserve two-year-old cheddar, as well as Cave-Aged Truckle, a washed-rind cheese bathed in beer, and Grafton Duet, a succulent layering of Grafton cheddar and St. Pete's Select blue cheese. They also offer a smoked cheddar with a unique Vermont twist — the cheese is smoked over maple wood chips for six hours.

The cheese makers at Grafton Village believe that fine cheese starts with the best milk. They contract with small dairy cooperatives throughout the state. They believe that Jersey cows, with milk that is especially high in protein and butterfat, provide some of the best milk for cheese making. In addition, Grafton Village cheese makers use milk that is free of antibiotics and growth hormones. Their greatest challenge is "realizing that all milk is not created equal. Every vat of cheese we make performs differently because of the milk; therefore, we must be artists, not button-pushers based on a stop-watch."

Grafton Village imposes strict quality control on its cheese; any worker can place a quality hold on a product, and each cheese in storage is graded three times before it is cut and packaged for retail sale. Grafton Village cheeses are sold through their online store, two retail stores, and to many gourmet shop and natural food stores across the United States.

(The cheese makers admit they also eat a good bit of the cheese before it makes it to a store!) Their advice to beginning cheese makers? "The learning curve is very steep. Don't expect to be an expert in a week, or even a month. Beginning cheese makers tend to get frustrated after the first week. Most do not realize how much there is to learn before they get started. If you want to make cheese for sale, have a plan, everything from knowledge of your equipment to the quality of milk. It's a lot of work and dedication. Also, make sure you have a marketing plan. You can make good cheese, but you must have a market for it. Good luck future cheese makers!"

Farmhouse cheddar

Prep time: 60 minutes

Cooking time: 1 hour, 15 minutes

Resting time: 5 minutes

Draining time: 1 hour

Pressing time: 12 hours, 20 minutes

Drying time: 2-4 days

Aging time: 4 weeks

Just as Brie is the pride of France, cheddar is the king of English cheeses. Thanks in part to Englishmen who immigrated to America in the 17th century, the United States has also enjoyed a thriving cheddar industry. Today, quality cheddar cheeses are made in several states, including Vermont, Wisconsin, Oregon, Washington, and California. Every cheddar cheese recipe includes a step known as "cheddaring," where the curds are broken up and salt is worked into them. This step is part of what gives cheddar its distinctive texture and flavor. This recipe is an excellent one for less-experienced cheese makers; the cheese needs to age for only a month before it is ready to eat. Please note that if you want cheddar to be yellow just add annatto dye, a natural coloring made from the seeds of the annatto plant. However, white cheddars are prized as well.

Ingredients/Equipment:

2 gals whole cow's milk

½ tsp mesophilic culture

½ tsp liquid rennet

¼ tsp annatto coloring (optional)

1 tbsp cheese or kosher salt

Distilled water

Cooking pot

Colander

Large draining bowl

Cheesecloth

Curd knife

2-lb mold

Wooden cheese board

Cheese wax (optional)

Natural bristle brush (optional)

Thermometer

Directions:

1. Start with sterilized equipment. Pour milk into non-reactive cooking pot and place over medium heat. Warm milk to 90° Fahrenheit. Add starter and mix well. Cover and allow milk to ripen at 90° for 30 minutes.

2. Optional: Dilute annatto in ¼ cup of cool distilled water and add to milk mixture. Turn off heat and let rest for 15 minutes.

3. Dilute rennet in ½ cup of cool distilled water. Add to milk mixture; stir gently but thoroughly to ensure rennet is mixed throughout the milk. Cover and allow milk to ripen for 45 minutes, maintaining temperature at 90° Fahrenheit.

4. Check for a clean break. If there is no clean break, allow mixture to sit for an additional ten minutes.

5. When clean break is present, use curd knife to curd mixture into ½-inch cubes. Allow curds to rest for ten minutes at room temperature.

6. Place the pot in a larger pot filled with hot water and gradually heat the curds to 100° Fahrenheit, raising the temperature no more than two degrees every five minutes. Stir gently to keep the curds from matting together. The curds will shrink noticeably during this step.

7. Once the mixture reaches 100° Fahrenheit, remove the pot from the hot water bath, cover it, and allow the curds to sit for five minutes.

8. Pour the curds into a cheesecloth-lined colander. Tie the corners of the cheesecloth into a knot and hang the bundle to drain for an hour. Make sure the curds are not in a drafty spot.

9. Place the drained curds into a bowl and break them apart with your fingers, first making sure that your hands are clean. The pieces should be walnut-sized when you are done. Add the salt and mix well.

10. Pack the curds into a 2-pound, cheesecloth-lined mold. Pull the cloth up over the curd bundle, smooth the cloth, and put on the lid.

11. Place mold in a cheese press and press for ten minutes at ten pounds of pressure.

12. Remove cheese from mold, unwrap it, turn it over, and rewrap it. Place mold back into cheese press and press for ten minutes at 20 pounds of pressure.

13. Remove cheese from mold, unwrap it, turn it over, and rewrap it. Place mold back into cheese press and press for 12 hours at 50 pounds of pressure.

14. Remove cheese from press and unwrap. Place cheese on a clean wooden cheese board.

15. Let cheese dry at room temperature for two to four days. When cheese is dry to the touch, you may wax it if you wish, coating it with two coats of cheese wax, allowing each coat to dry before applying the next layer.

16. Age cheese at 50-55° Fahrenheit for four weeks.

Goat's milk cheddar

Prep time: 60 minutes
Cooking time: 3 hours, 5 minutes
Resting time: 10 minutes
Pressing time: 13 hours, 15 minutes
Drying time: 2 days
Aging time: 4-12 weeks

While cheddar is traditionally a cow's milk cheese, goat's milk also makes delicious cheddar. This recipe requires a minimum of four weeks' aging, but as with all cheddars, the longer you age the cheese, the sharper the final flavor will be. You can wax this cheese or leave it unwaxed. If you plan to age it longer than four weeks, a protective coating of wax will reduce the likelihood of mold developing. As with other cheddars, you may add annatto coloring or leave the cheese its natural white color.

Ingredients/Equipment:

2 gals whole goat's milk
½ tsp mesophilic culture
¼ tsp calcium chloride
½ tsp liquid rennet
¼ tsp annatto coloring (optional)
Cheese or kosher salt
Distilled water
Cooking pot
Cheesecloth
Curd knife
2-lb mold
Wooden cheese board
Cheese wax (optional)
Natural bristle brush (optional)
Thermometer

Directions:

1. Start with sterilized equipment. Pour milk into non-reactive cooking pot and place over medium heat. Warm milk to 85° Fahrenheit. Add starter and mix well. Cover and allow milk to ripen at 85° Fahrenheit for 30 minutes.

2. Optional: Dilute annatto in ¼ cup of cool distilled water and add to milk mixture. Turn off heat and let rest for 15 minutes.

3. Dilute rennet in ½ cup of cool distilled water. Add to milk mixture; stir gently but thoroughly to ensure rennet is mixed throughout the milk. Cover and allow milk to ripen for one hour, maintaining temperature at 85° Fahrenheit.

4. Check for a clean break. If there is no clean break, allow mixture to sit for an additional ten minutes.

5. When clean break is present, use curd knife to curd mixture into ½-inch cubes. Allow curds to rest for ten minutes at room temperature.

6. Return pot to heat and gradually heat the curds to 98° Fahrenheit, raising the temperature no more than two degrees every five minutes. Stir gently to keep the curds from matting together.

7. Once the mixture reaches 98° Fahrenheit, maintain that temperature for 45 minutes, stirring occasionally throughout this process.

8. Drain whey and add two tablespoons of salt to the curds, mixing well.

9. Pack the curds into a 2-pound, cheesecloth-lined mold. Pull the cloth up over the curd bundle, smooth the cloth, and put on the lid.

10. Place mold in a cheese press and press for 15 minutes at 20 pounds of pressure.

11. Remove cheese from mold, unwrap it, turn it over, and rewrap it. Place mold back into cheese press and press for one hour at 30 pounds of pressure.

12. Remove cheese from mold, unwrap it, turn it over, and rewrap it. Place mold back into cheese press and press for 12 hours at 50 pounds of pressure.

13. Remove cheese from press and unwrap. Turning the cheese over as you work, rub the surface with cheese salt. Place cheese on a clean wooden cheese board.

14. Let cheese dry at room temperature for two to three days, rubbing it with salt once a day during this process. When cheese is dry to the touch, you may wax it if you wish, coating it with two coats of cheese wax, allowing each coat to dry before applying the next layer.

15. Age cheese at 50-55° Fahrenheit for 4-12 weeks.

Sage Derby

Prep time: 1 hour, 10 minutes
Cooking time: 3 hours
Resting time: 1 hour, 25 minutes
Pressing time: 12 hours
Drying time: 30 days
Aging time: 1 to 3 months

Derby is a hard English cheese, similar to cheddar in its preparation and flavor. This version, Sage Derby is colored and flavored with an infusion of fresh sage leaves, which gives the finished cheese a very distinctive herb flavor and a delicate green tinge. If you wish, you can skip the sage and just make the cheese without it, but Sage Derby is a taste experience well worth the extra time and effort.

Ingredients/Equipment:

4 gals whole cow's milk
½ tsp mesophilic culture
¾ tsp liquid rennet
¼ tsp annatto coloring (optional)
¾ tsp calcium chloride

3 tbsps pickling or kosher salt

Distilled water

1 cup fresh sage leaves (optional)

Cooking pot

Larger pot for hot water bath

Colander

Large draining bowl

Cheesecloth

Curd knife

Skimmer

Large (3.5x7.5 in) tomme mold

Cheese mat

Cheese wax (optional)

Natural bristle brush (optional)

Thermometer

Directions:

1. Start with sterilized equipment. Pour milk into non-reactive cooking pot and place pot of milk in a larger pot filled with water. Warm milk to 90º Fahrenheit. Turn off heat.

2. Sprinkle starter on the surface of the milk and allow it to rest for five minutes. Using a skimmer, work the culture into the milk with a gentle up-and-down motion, disturbing the surface of the milk as little as possible. Cover and turn on heat again. Allow milk to ripen at 90º Fahrenheit for one hour.

3. Optional: Dilute annatto in ¼ cup of cool distilled water and add to milk mixture. Turn off heat and let rest for 15 minutes.

4. Dilute calcium chloride in ¼ cup of cool distilled water. Using a skimmer, work the culture into the milk with a gentle up-and-down motion, disturbing the surface of the milk as little as possible.

5. Dilute rennet in ¼ cup of cool distilled water. Add to milk mixture; stir gently but thoroughly to ensure rennet is mixed throughout the milk.

Cover and allow milk to ripen for 45 minutes, maintaining temperature at 90° Fahrenheit.

6. Check for a clean break. If there is no clean break, allow mixture to sit for an additional ten minutes. When clean break is present, use curd knife to curd mixture into ⅜-inch cubes, using the skimmer to lift and move the curds to ensure all are cut.

7. Place the pot in a larger pot filled with hot water and gradually heat the curds to 96° Fahrenheit. Do not raise heat too soon; this step should take approximately 45 minutes. Let curds settle.

8. Wash one cup of fresh sage leaves. Chop roughly and place in small bowl. Boil two cups of water and pour over the leaves. Let mixture infuse for 30 minutes or until cool.

9. Carefully pour off whey, leaving the curds in the bottom of the pot. Press the curds down lightly with your hand to help them knit together. Put the lid back on the pot and let stand for 15 minutes. Turn the curd mass over in the pot and press firmly to help expel more whey and knit curds. Drain off collected whey. Continue turning the curd mass in the pot every 15 minutes for one hour, pressing curds each time.

10. Remove the mass from the pot. Cut the mass into 1-inch by ½-inch pieces. Pour cooled sage water over pieces. Mix thoroughly and allow pieces to soak for 15 minutes. Drain liquid. Place pieces into a bowl and toss them with salt.

11. Pack the curds into a prepared mold and press them down firmly as you fill the mold. Pull the cloth up around the mass and smooth the cloth across the top. Put on lid.

12. Place mold in a cheese press and press for 30 minutes at 15 pounds of pressure.

13. Remove cheese from mold, unwrap it, turn it over, and rewrap it. Place mold back into cheese press and press for 12 hours at 20 pounds of pressure.

14. Remove cheese from press and unwrap. Place cheese on a clean cheese mat. Let cheese dry at room temperature for three days. When cheese is dry to the touch, you may wax it if you wish, coating it with two coats of cheese wax, allowing each coat to dry before applying the next layer.

15. Ripen cheese at 54-60° Fahrenheit for at least one month but up to three months. Turn cheese weekly to ensure even ripening. Once cheese is ripe, wrap and store in the refrigerator.

Classic cheddar

Prep time: 75 minutes
Cooking time: 3 hours, 55 minutes
Resting time: 25 minutes
Pressing time: 13 hours
Drying time: 1-2 days
Aging time: 3 months-2 years

This, of course, is the classic preparation for cheddar cheese. It is time-consuming, but much of the time involved is in the aging process. Some very high-quality cheddars are aged for up to 12 years. This cheese will be mild and tasty at three months, rich and full-bodied at six months, sharp and piquant to the tongue at a year, and after that, the flavor will increasingly become stronger. As with other cheddar recipes, add the annatto coloring if you want yellow cheddar instead of white. The finished cheese will make a terrific sandwich or snack. Shredded, it will add a tasty element to any recipe.

Ingredients/Equipment:

4 gals whole cow's milk
½ tsp mesophilic culture
¾ tsp liquid rennet
¼ tsp annatto coloring (optional)
¾ tsp calcium chloride
2 ½ tbsps pickling or kosher salt

Distilled water

Cooking pot

Larger pot for hot water bath

Colander

Large draining bowl

Cheesecloth

Curd knife

Skimmer

Large (3.5x7.5 in.) tomme mold

Cheese mat

Cheese wax (optional)

Natural bristle brush (optional)

Thermometer

Directions:

1. Start with sterilized equipment. Pour milk into non-reactive cooking pot and place pot of milk in a larger pot filled with water. Warm milk to 88° Fahrenheit. Turn off heat.

2. Sprinkle starter on the surface of the milk and allow it to rest for five minutes. Using a skimmer, work the culture into the milk with a gentle up-and-down motion, disturbing the surface of the milk as little as possible. Cover and turn on heat again. Allow milk to ripen at 88° Fahrenheit for 40 minutes.

3. Optional: Dilute annatto in ¼ cup of cool distilled water and add to milk mixture. Turn off heat and let rest for 15 minutes.

4. Dilute calcium chloride in ¼ cup of cool distilled water. Using a skimmer, work the culture into the milk with a gentle up-and-down motion, disturbing the surface of the milk as little as possible.

5. Dilute rennet in ¼ cup of cool distilled water. Add to milk mixture; stir gently but thoroughly to ensure rennet is mixed throughout the milk.

Cover and allow milk to ripen for 30 minutes, maintaining temperature at 88° Fahrenheit.

6. Check for a clean break. If there is no clean break, allow mixture to sit for an additional ten minutes.

7. When clean break is present, use curd knife to curd mixture into ½-inch cubes. Allow curds to rest for five minutes at room temperature.

8. Place the pot in a larger pot filled with hot water and gradually heat the curds to 102° Fahrenheit. Do not raise heat too soon; this step should take about 45 minutes. Stir gently to keep the curds from matting together. The curds will shrink noticeably during this step.

9. Once the mixture reaches 102°, turn the heat very low and cover the pot. Allow the curds to ripen for 30 to 40 minutes, maintaining the temperature at 102° Fahrenheit throughout.

10. Pour the whey curds into a cheesecloth-lined colander. Reserve the whey if you wish to make ricotta, but remember that the whey must be used within two hours.

11. Return the curds to the pot and place the pot back in the hot water bath, maintaining temperature at 102° Fahrenheit. Cover pot and let stand for ten minutes. The curds will form a spongy mass. After ten minutes, turn the mass over and allow it to stand another ten minutes. Then turn the mass on its side for ten minutes, and turn the mass on its other side for an additional ten minutes, covering the pot each time you turn the mass.

12. Remove the mass from the pot. Cut the mass into 2-inch long, ½-inch wide strips like French fries. Place pieces in a bowl and toss them with salt.

13. Pack the curds into a prepared mold and press down firmly as you fill the mold. Pull the cloth up around the mass and smooth the cloth across the top. Put on lid.

14. Place mold in a cheese press and press for one hour at 15 pounds of pressure.

15. Remove cheese from mold, unwrap it, turn it over, and rewrap it. Place mold back into cheese press and press for 24 hours at 25 pounds of pressure.

16. Remove cheese from press and unwrap. Place cheese on a clean cheese mat.

17. Let cheese dry at room temperature for one to two days. When cheese is dry to the touch, you may wax it if you wish, coating it with two coats of cheese wax, allowing each coat to dry before applying the next layer.

18. Age cheese at 50° Fahrenheit for three months for mild cheddar, six months for medium cheddar, or a year or more for sharp cheddar.

Stirred curd cheddar

Prep time: 70 minutes
Cooking time: 2 hours, 25 minutes
Resting time: 60 minutes
Pressing time: 26 hours, 20 minutes
Drying time: 2-5 days
Aging time: 2-6 months

This cheddar requires less aging time than others. It can be made with either cow's or goat's milk, but you must use whole milk to get the right texture and flavor. If you prefer white cheddar, skip the annatto coloring; it will not affect the taste of the finished cheese. As is true of most cheddar recipes, this cheese requires very careful and fairly long cooking at different temperatures at various stages. Be sure you have enough time to devote to the process, or enlist someone else to take a turn over the stove.

Ingredients/Equipment:

2 gals whole cow's milk
½ tsp mesophilic culture
½ tsp liquid rennet
¼ tsp annatto coloring (optional)
¾ tsp calcium chloride

2 tbsps pickling or kosher salt

Distilled water

Cooking pot

Larger pot for hot water bath

Colander

Large draining bowl

Cheesecloth

Curd knife

Skimmer

Large (3.5x7.5 in) mold

Cheese mat

Cheese wax (optional)

Natural bristle brush (optional)

Thermometer

Directions:

1. Begin with sterilized equipment. Pour milk into non-reactive cooking pot and place pot of milk in a larger pot filled with water. Warm milk to 90° Fahrenheit. Turn off heat.

2. Sprinkle starter on the surface of the milk and allow it to rest for five minutes. Using a skimmer, work the culture into the milk with a gentle up-and-down motion, disturbing the surface of the milk as little as possible. Dilute the annatto coloring, if desired, in ¼ cup of cool distilled water and add to mixture.

3. Dilute rennet in ¼ cup of cool distilled water. Add to milk mixture; stir gently but thoroughly to ensure rennet is mixed throughout the milk. Return pot to heat. Cover and allow milk to ripen for 45 minutes, maintaining temperature at 90° Fahrenheit.

4. Check for a clean break. If there is no clean break, allow mixture to sit for an additional ten minutes.

5. When clean break is present, use curd knife to curd mixture into ½-inch cubes. Allow curds to rest for 15 minutes at room temperature.

6. Place the pot in a larger pot filled with hot water and gradually heat the curds to 100° Fahrenheit. Do not raise heat too soon; this step should take about 30 minutes. Stir gently to keep the curds from matting together.

7. Once the mixture reaches 100° Fahrenheit, turn the heat very low. Allow the curds to ripen for 30 minutes, maintaining the temperature at 100° Fahrenheit throughout. Stir gently throughout this step.

8. Pour the whey and curds into a cheesecloth-lined colander. Drain for several minutes, but do not allow the curds to mat, which will happen if draining takes too long.

9. Return the curds to the pot stir them with your fingers, separating any curd particles that have matted.

10. Add salt and blend well. Do not squeeze or press the curds; keep them separated as much as possible.

11. Return the curds to the heat and maintain the curds at 100° Fahrenheit for one hour, stirring every five minutes to avoid matting. Monitor heat carefully.

12. Line a 2-pound mold with cheesecloth. Pack the curds into a prepared mold and press them down firmly as you fill the mold. Pull the cloth up around the mass and smooth the cloth across the top. Put on lid.

13. Place mold in a cheese press and press for 10 minutes at 15 pounds of pressure.

14. Remove cheese from mold, unwrap it, turn it over, and rewrap it. Place mold back into cheese press and press for 10 minutes at 30 pounds of pressure.

15. Repeat the process but press at 40 pounds of pressure for two hours.

16. Repeat the process but press at 50 pounds of pressure for 24 hours.

17. Remove cheese from press and unwrap. Place cheese on a clean cheese mat.

18. Let cheese dry at room temperature for two to five days. When cheese is dry to the touch, you may wax it if you wish, coating it with two coats of cheese wax, allowing each coat to dry before applying the next layer.

19. Age cheese at 55° Fahrenheit for two to six months. This will produce a mild to medium cheddar cheese, depending on the length of time it is aged.

Jalapeño cheddar

Prep time: 70 minutes

Cooking time: 2 hours, 40 minutes

Resting time: 60 minutes

Pressing time: 26 hours, 20 minutes

Drying time: 2-5 days

Aging time: 2-6 months

This recipe pairs a medium cheddar cheese with the zippy flavor and texture of minced jalapeño peppers. Be sure to thoroughly boil the peppers before chopping and adding them to the cheese recipe. Also, be sure to add the boiled water to the recipe, as much of the flavor of the peppers is in the water. The finished cheese is fairly spicy but not overwhelmingly hot. If you are concerned about too much heat, use the smaller amount of peppers listed.

Ingredients/Equipment:

2 gals whole cow's milk

½ tsp mesophilic culture

½ tsp liquid rennet

¼ tsp annatto coloring (optional)

¾ tsp calcium chloride

2 tbsps pickling or kosher salt

1-4 tbsps chopped jalapeño peppers

Distilled water

Cooking pot

Larger pot for hot water bath

Colander

Large draining bowl

Cheesecloth

Curd knife

Skimmer

Large (3.5x7.5 in) mold, cheesecloth-lined

Cheese mat

Cheese wax (optional)

Natural bristle brush (optional)

Thermometer

Directions:

1. Start with sterilized equipment. Boil peppers for 15 minutes, making sure you use enough water to cover the peppers throughout the cooking process.

2. Strain the flavored water into a small bowl and let cool. Cool and chop the peppers and reserve them in another bowl.

3. Pour milk into non-reactive cooking pot and place pot of milk in a larger pot filled with water. Add reserved water from boiled chilies. Warm milk to 90° Fahrenheit. Turn off heat.

4. Sprinkle starter on the surface of the milk and allow it to rest for five minutes. Using a skimmer, work the culture into the milk with a gentle up-and-down motion, disturbing the surface of the milk as little as possible. Dilute the annatto coloring, if desired, in ¼ cup of cool distilled water and add to mixture.

5. Dilute rennet in ¼ cup of cool distilled water. Add to milk mixture; stir gently but thoroughly to ensure rennet is mixed throughout the milk. Return pot to heat. Cover and allow milk to ripen for 45 minutes, maintaining temperature at 90° Fahrenheit.

6. Check for a clean break. If there is no clean break, allow mixture to sit for an additional ten minutes.

7. When clean break is present, use curd knife to curd mixture into ½-inch cubes. Allow curds to rest for 15 minutes at room temperature.

8. Place the pot in a larger pot filled with hot water and gradually heat the curds to 100° Fahrenheit. Do not raise heat too soon; this step should take about 30 minutes. Stir gently to keep the curds from matting together.

9. Once the mixture reaches 100° Fahrenheit, turn the heat very low. Allow the curds to ripen for 30 minutes, maintaining the temperature at 100° Fahrenheit throughout, adjusting heat if necessary. Stir gently throughout this step.

10. Pour the whey and curds into a cheesecloth-lined colander. Drain for several minutes, but do not allow the curds to mat, which will happen if draining takes too long.

11. Return the curds to the pot stir them with your fingers, separating any curd particles that have matted.

12. Add salt and blend well. Do not squeeze or press the curds; keep them separated as much as possible.

13. Gently stir in chopped boiled peppers.

14. Return the curds to the heat and maintain the curds at 100° Fahrenheit for one hour, stirring every five minutes to avoid matting. Monitor heat carefully.

15. Line a 2-pound mold with cheesecloth. Pack the curds into a prepared mold and press them down firmly as you fill the mold. Pull the cloth up around the mass and smooth the cloth across the top. Put on lid.

16. Place mold in a cheese press and press for 10 minutes at 15 pounds of pressure.

17. Remove cheese from mold, unwrap it, turn it over, and rewrap it. Place mold back into cheese press and press for 10 minutes at 30 pounds of pressure.

18. Repeat the process but press at 40 pounds of pressure for two hours.

19. Repeat the process but press at 50 pounds of pressure for 24 hours.

20. Remove cheese from press and unwrap. Place cheese on a clean cheese mat.

21. Let cheese dry at room temperature for two to five days. When cheese is dry to the touch, you may wax it if you wish, coating it with two coats of cheese wax, allowing each coat to dry before applying the next layer.

22. Age cheese at 55° Fahrenheit for two to six months. This will produce a mild to medium cheddar cheese, depending on the length of aging time.

CASE STUDY: NOTHING BUT CHEDDAR

Shelburne Farms
1611 Harbor Road
Shelburne, VT 05482
(802) 985-3210 (p)
(802) 985-8123 (f)
www.shelburnefarms.org

Sometimes specialization is the way to go. As part of Shelburne Farms, a National Historic Landmark, Shelburne Farms Cheese has been making delicious farmhouse, raw milk, aged, and smoked cheddar cheese, as well as cheddar spread, for more than 25 years. All of these cheeses start with milk from a herd of 100 Brown Swiss dairy cows. The 600 gallons of milk produced each day enable Shelburne Farms to produce 140,000 pounds of cheese each year. These cheeses are sold online and to cheese shops and grocery stores. Shelburne Farms cheddars have won numerous awards, including a 2009 first place honor from the American Cheese Society for their smoked cheddar. Cheese making Manager Nat Bacon is rightfully proud of his company's cheeses: "I consider our cheese unique because we follow the traditions of English cheddar by using our own raw milk, and cheddaring by hand to give a distinctive flavor — a true farmhouse cheddar." Shelburne Farms also offers an educational video, "From Sun to Cheese," which discusses their philosophy as well as many of the steps involved in making artisan cheese. It can be viewed through a link at their Web site.

Lancashire

Prep time: 1 hour, 15 minutes

Cooking time: 2 hours

Resting time: 55 minutes

Draining time: 12 hours

Pressing time: 7 hours

Ripening time: 4-8 weeks

Lancashire is a British cheese. It is similar to cheddar, but it contains more moisture and has a stronger flavor than many cheddar cheeses. Traditionally, Lancashire is called "Crumbly Lancashire" when it has been aged for six to eight weeks, because these relatively young cheeses are moist and crumbly with almost a vinegary bite to them. If it is aged longer, for up to eight months, it becomes "Creamy Lancashire," a drier, firmer-bodied cheese with a deeper, almost nutty flavor. The British sometimes call Lancashire "Toasty" because it is a favorite cheese to use in such recipes as Welsh rarebit or other toasted/melted cheese recipes. The "stacking" of the curd in this recipe also contributes to the crumbly texture of the finished cheese.

Ingredients/Equipment:

14 qts whole milk

2 qts 2% milk

½ tsp mesophilic culture

½ tsp calcium chloride

½ tsp liquid rennet

3 tbsps kosher or pickling salt

Glass or ceramic mixing bowl

Non-reactive cooking pot

Larger pot for hot water bath

Colander

Large tome mold

Cheesecloth

Skimmer

Curd knife

Draining container

Cheese press

Cheese mats

Ripening container

Distilled water

Cutting board

Thermometer

Directions:

1. Begin with sterilized equipment. In a large non-reactive cooking pot, place in a hot water bath and warm milk over medium heat to 88° Fahrenheit, stirring gently. Turn off heat.

2. Sprinkle culture over surface of milk and let stand for five minutes. Using skimmer and a gentle up-and-down motion, gently draw culture into the milk while disturbing the surface as little as possible. Cover and let ripen for 45 minutes, maintaining temperature at 88° Fahrenheit.

3. Dilute calcium chloride in ¼ cup of cool distilled water and add to milk using the same gentle motion.

4. Dilute rennet in ¼ cup of cool distilled water and add to milk using the same gentle motion. Cover pot and let stand for 50 minutes, maintaining temperature at 88° Fahrenheit.

5. Check for a clean break. If necessary, wait another five to ten minutes. If clean break is present, use curd knife and skimmer to cut curds into

⅜-inch pieces, using the skimmer to gently lift and move the curds to ensure that all are cut. Let curds stand for five minutes.

6. Stir curds for ten minutes until they release more whey, become firmer, and float freely in the whey. Let curds settle.

7. Pour contents of pot into a cloth-lined colander. Return curds to pot and press down with your clean hands to knit them together. Put the lid back on the pot to keep the curds warm. Let stand for 15 minutes. Turn cake of curds over and let stand for 15 minutes more.

8. Cut cake of curd in half and pile one piece on top of the other in the pot. Cover and hold for another 15 minutes. The two halves will knit together into one piece.

9. Place curd on cutting board and cut into 1x½-inch pieces. Place in a bowl and toss with salt.

10. Fill prepared mold with curds. Pull cloth up around curds and smooth out over top of bundle. Put on the lid. Place mold on a rack in a draining container and let it drain overnight.

11. Place mold in cheese press. Press at medium pressure (12-15 pounds) for one hour. Remove from press, unwrap, flip, and redress cheese. Place back in the press and press at firm pressure (20 pounds) for six hours.

12. Remove cheese from press. Unwrap and place on a cheese mat in a ripening container. Ripen at 54-60° Fahrenheit and 85-90 percent humidity for four to eight weeks, depending on your taste. Turn cheese daily for the first week, then twice weekly thereafter. If mold appears, wipe rind with a cloth dipped in vinegar.

Cantal

Prep time: 55 minutes
Cooking time: 1 hour, 45 minutes
Resting time: 10 minutes
Pressing time: 3 days

Drying time: 2 days

Ripening time: 3-6 months

Cantal is sometimes called "the French cheddar" because it is the only French cheese that is made in a similar fashion as cheddar, using the "cheddaring" process of salting the curds. In this version, the curds are pressed, broken up and salted, and then packed into a mold for a second pressing. Like cheddar, Cantal can be mild-flavored with an almost tender texture, or it can be sharp to the palate and have a dry, flaky texture. Both flavor and texture are controlled by ripening. If you like a milder cheese with more moisture, age Cantal for three months. For a more full-bodied flavor and a flaky texture, age it a full six months.

Ingredients/Equipment:

16 qts whole milk (Cow's milk is traditional, but a blend of cow's and goat's milk will produce a cheese with a sharper, tangier flavor)

½ tsp thermophilic culture

¾ tsp liquid rennet

¾ tsp calcium chloride

Distilled water

Cooking pot

Larger pot for hot water bath

Large bowl

Colander

Cheesecloth

Curd knife

Large tome mold, cheesecloth-lined

Thermometer

Directions:

1. Start with sterilized equipment. Pour milk into non-reactive cooking pot and place over medium heat. Warm milk to 90° Fahrenheit, stirring gently. Turn off heat.

2. Sprinkle culture over surface of milk and let stand for five minutes. Using skimmer and a gentle up-and-down motion, draw culture down into the milk, disturbing the milk's surface as little as possible. Cover and hold for 15 minutes, maintaining temperature at to 90° Fahrenheit.

3. Dilute calcium chloride in ¼ cup of cool distilled water. Add to milk using the same gentle up-and-down motion.

4. Dilute rennet in ¼ cup of cool distilled water. Add to milk mixture using the same gentle up-and-down motion. Cover and allow milk to ripen for 30 minutes, maintaining temperature at 90° Fahrenheit.

5. Check for a clean break. If there is no clean break, allow mixture to sit for an additional ten minutes.

6. When clean break is present, use curd knife and skimmer to cut curd into pea-sized pieces. Use skimmer to lift curd and ensure that all curd is cut. Allow curds to rest for five minutes at room temperature.

7. Pour the curds into a cheesecloth-lined colander. Let the curds mat and form a spongy mass in the colander. Cut the curd mass into several large pieces.

8. Fill prepared mold with curds. Pull cloth up around curd bundle and smooth out over top. Place lid on mold.

9. Place mold in cheese press and press at light pressure (five to eight pounds) for 12 hours. Remove from press, unwrap and rewrap cheese, and replace in press. Press at light pressure another 12 hours.

10. Remove cheese from press and unwrap. Place in bowl and break mass apart into 1-inch chunks. Add the salt and mix well.

11. Wash and rinse mold and used cloth. Pack the salted curds back into the cloth-lined mold. Pull the cloth up over the curd bundle, smooth the cloth, and put on the lid.

12. Place mold in a cheese press and press for 36-48 hours at 30 pounds of pressure, removing, unwrapping, and rewrapping the cheese three times during the first 24 hours.

13. Remove cheese from press and unwrap. Place cheese on a clean cheese mat.

14. Let cheese dry at room temperature for two days or until fairly dry to the touch.

15. Place cheese on a clean cheese mat in a ripening container. Ripen cheese at 50° Fahrenheit and 85 percent humidity for three to six months. Twice a week, wash the rind with a clean cloth dipped in a saltwater solution and turn the cheese to ensure even ripening and development of the rind.

Montasio

Prep time: 55 minutes
Cooking time: 2 hours, 25 minutes
Resting time: 10 minutes
Pressing time: 19 hours
Brining time: 18 hours
Drying time: 1-2 days
Ripening time: up to 2 months
Aging time: up to 1 year

Montasio is an Italian cheese. Like so many other cheeses, it was originally made by monks. It is classified three ways — fresh, middle, and aged — depending, of course, on how long it has been aged before it is sold. Fresh Montasio, aged around 60 days, is white and sweet. Middle Montasio, aged for three to ten months, is firmer with a drier rind, a creamy color, and a slightly fruity flavor. Aged Montasio, aged for ten months to a year, is crumbly and pale yellow in color. Its flavor is almost wine-like in its intensity. Montasio is also a favorite cheese used to make frico — fried cheese. Small strips or shreds of Montasio are fried in olive oil and flipped like a pancake until both sides are crisp. Traditional Montasio is made from cow's milk, but this version uses a mixture of cow's and goat's milk for a tangier finished cheese.

Ingredients/Equipment:

8 qts goat's milk

8 qts whole cow's milk

½ tsp thermophilic culture

¾ tsp calcium chloride

¾ tsp liquid rennet

Cool brine solution

Non-reactive cooking pot

Larger pot for hot water bath

Colander

Large tome mold

Cheesecloth

Skimmer

Curd knife

Cheese press

Cheese mats

Ripening container

Distilled water

Cutting board

Thermometer

Directions:

1. Begin with sterilized equipment. In a large non-reactive cooking pot, place in a hot water bath and warm both types of milk over medium heat to 95° Fahrenheit, stirring gently. Turn off heat.

2. Sprinkle culture over surface of milk and let stand for five minutes. Using skimmer and a gentle up-and-down motion, gently draw culture into the milk while disturbing the surface as little as possible. Cover and let ripen for 30 minutes, maintaining temperature at 95° Fahrenheit.

3. Dilute calcium chloride in ¼ cup of cool distilled water and add to milk using the same gentle motion.

4. Dilute rennet in ¼ cup of cool distilled water and add to milk using the same gentle motion. Cover pot and let stand for 30 to 40 minutes, maintaining temperature at 95° Fahrenheit.

5. Check for a clean break. If necessary, wait another five to ten minutes. If clean break is present, use curd knife and skimmer to cut curds into pea-sized pieces, using the skimmer to gently lift and move the curds to ensure that all are cut. Let curds stand for five minutes.

6. Return heat to low and slowly warm curds to 110° Fahrenheit, stirring gently and continuously, adjusting heat as needed to make sure it takes 40 minutes to warm curds to this temperature. Do not warm curds too quickly. Turn off heat and continue to stir curds for another 30 minutes. Let curds settle.

7. Pour contents of pot into a cloth-lined colander. Fill prepared mold with curds. Pull cloth up around curds and smooth out over top of bundle. Put on the lid. Place mold on a rack in a draining container and let it drain overnight.

8. Place mold in cheese press. Press at firm pressure (20 pounds) for one hour. Remove from press, unwrap, flip, and redress cheese. Place back in the press and press at firm pressure (20 pounds) for 18 hours, removing and redressing cheese twice during this time.

9. Remove cheese from press. Unwrap and place in brine solution for 18 hours, turning once.

10. Remove cheese from brine. Dry cheese on a cheese mat placed on a rack at room temperature for one to two days, turning once or twice, until fairly dry to the touch.

11. Unwrap and place on a cheese mat in a ripening container. Ripen at 54° Fahrenheit and 85 percent humidity. Turn cheese daily for two weeks,

removing any collected whey and wiping container with a clean paper towel. If mold appears, wipe rind with a cloth dipped in brine solution.

12. After two weeks, turn cheese weekly. When the rind is fairly dry and has begun to develop, after about two months, rub it with a cloth dipped in olive oil once or twice a month. Continue aging for up to a year for a piquant cheese. Once cheese is ripened to your taste, wrap and store in the refrigerator.

Chihuahua

Prep time: 45 minutes
Cooking time: 2 hours
Resting time: 1 hour, 10 minutes
Pressing time: 12 hours
Drying time: 2 days
Ripening time 1-6 months

Despite the name, this cheese has no connection to small, yapping dogs. Chihuahua was first made by Mennonites who immigrated to the state of Chihuahua in northern Mexico. When fresh, this cheese is milky and slightly salty, with a satiny texture. With aging, it becomes more like cheddar, with a sharper flavor and a slightly dried, flakier feel in the mouth. Like cheddar, Chihuahua is an excellent snacking and sandwich cheese. If you like your cheese mild, it can be eaten after one month of aging. Otherwise, let it age up to six months in its wax coating.

Ingredients/Equipment:

16 qts whole milk
½ tsp mesophilic culture
¾ tsp calcium chloride
¾ tsp liquid rennet
3 tbsps kosher or pickling salt
Cheese wax
Waxing brush
Non-reactive cooking pot

Larger pot for hot water bath
Colander
Large tome mold
Cheesecloth
Skimmer
Curd knife
Cheese press
Cheese mats
Ripening container
Distilled water
Cutting board
Thermometer

Directions:

1. Begin with sterilized equipment. In a large non-reactive cooking pot, place in a hot water bath and warm milk over medium heat to 90° Fahrenheit, stirring gently. Turn off heat.

2. Sprinkle culture over surface of milk and let stand for five minutes. Using skimmer and a gentle up-and-down motion, gently draw culture into the milk, disturbing the surface as little as possible. Cover and let ripen for 40 minutes, maintaining temperature at 90° Fahrenheit.

3. Dilute calcium chloride in ¼ cup of cool distilled water and add to milk using the same gentle motion.

4. Dilute rennet in ¼ cup of cool distilled water and add to milk using the same gentle motion. Cover pot and let stand for 30 to 40 minutes, maintaining temperature at 90° Fahrenheit.

5. Check for a clean break. If necessary, wait another five to ten minutes. If clean break is present, use curd knife and skimmer to cut curds into ¼- to ½ -inch cubes, using the skimmer to gently lift and move the curds to ensure that all are cut. Let curds stand for five minutes.

6. Return heat to low and slowly warm curds to 102° Fahrenheit, stirring gently and continuously, adjusting the heat as needed to ensure that this step takes 40 minutes. Do not heat curds too quickly. Curds will shrink to about the size of peas or beans. Turn off heat and let curds settle. Hold for 15 minutes.

7. Pour contents of pot into a cloth-lined colander. Return curds to pot and press down with your clean hands to knit them together. Put the lid back on the pot to keep the curds warm. Let stand for 15 minutes.

8. Turn cake of curds over and let stand for 15 minutes more.

9. Cut cake of curd into four pieces and pile the pieces on top of one another in the pot. Cover and hold for another 15 minutes.

10. Place curd on cutting board and cut into 1x½-inch pieces. Place in a bowl and toss with salt.

11. Fill prepared mold with curds. Pull cloth up around curds and smooth out over top of bundle. Put on the lid.

12. Place mold in cheese press. Press at medium pressure (12-15 pounds) for 30 minutes. Remove from press, unwrap, flip, and redress cheese. Place back in the press and press at firm pressure (20 pounds) for overnight.

13. Remove cheese from press. Unwrap and dry on a mat placed on a rack at room temperature for two days, turning once or twice a day, until cheese is fairly dry to the touch.

14. Unwrap and coat with two or three layers of cheese wax. Ripen at 50° Fahrenheit for four weeks to six months. Turn cheese daily for the first four weeks.

Romano

Prep time: 40 minutes
Cooking time: 2 hours, 25 minutes
Resting time: 40 minutes

Pressing time: 13 hours, 30 minutes
Brining time: 20 hours
Drying time: 2-3 days
Ripening time: 5 months
Aging time: Up to 2 years

Along with its close cousin Parmesan, Romano is one of the indispensable cheeses of Italian cuisine. Like Parmesan, true Romano is only made in one region of Italy, but again like many other cheeses, Romano has been adapted by cheese makers all over the world. It is a hard grating cheese, wonderful in soups, on pizza, over pasta, and in many recipes. This version takes a great deal of time and care, but the result is a taste beyond any powder in the plastic shakers found in most grocery stores. This cheese is usually made with cow's milk, but a mixture of cow and goat's milk will give the finished cheese a more pronounced flavor. As is true for most cheeses, the longer you age it, the sharper it will taste. You may want to sample the cheese after seven or eight months to judge whether it is sharp enough for your palate or needs further aging and ripening.

Ingredients/Equipment:

4 gals whole milk, either cow's milk or a mixture of cow's and goat's
½ tsp thermophilic culture
¾ tsp calcium chloride
¾ tsp liquid rennet
18% brine solution
Olive oil
Distilled water
Stainless steel cooking pot
Larger pot for hot water bath
Large (3.5x7.5 in) tomme mold
Colander
Skimmer
Curd knife
Cheesecloth

Cheese press
Cheese mats
Ripening container
Thermometer

Directions:

1. Start with sterilized equipment. Pour milk into cooking pot and place that pot in a larger pot partially filled with water. Put pot on medium heat and warm milk to 90° Fahrenheit. Stir gently as the milk warms. Turn off heat.

2. Sprinkle the culture over the milk and let stand for five minutes. Then using a skimmer and an up-and-down motion, work the culture into the milk, mixing thoroughly, disturbing the surface of the milk as little as possible. Cover and let mixture sit for 15 minutes, maintaining temperature at 90° Fahrenheit.

3. Dilute the calcium chloride in ¼ cup of cool distilled water. Add this mixture to the milk using the same up-and-down motion.

4. Dilute rennet in ¼ cup of cool distilled water and add to milk mixture, once again using the up-and-down motion. Cover pot and let it sit for one hour, maintaining temperature at 90° Fahrenheit throughout.

5. Check for a clean break. If clean break is not present, let mixture sit another five to ten minutes. When clean break is present, use a curd knife and skimmer to cut the curd into ¼-inch pieces, using the skimmer to lift and gently move the curds, ensuring that all curds are cut. Let curds rest for five minutes.

6. Return the pot to the heat. Slowly warm the curds to 117° Fahrenheit, stirring gently and continuously. Adjust the heat as needed to ensure that it takes 45-50 minutes to raise the heat to 117° Fahrenheit. Once the mixture reaches the desired temperature, remove the pot from the heat, cover, and let rest for 30 minutes.

7. Place the cheesecloth-lined mold under the cloth-lined colander and drain off the whey through the mold, which will warm the mold as it drains. Fill the mold with curds, piling them higher in the center than at the edges of the mold. Pull cheesecloth up around the curds and fold and smooth it across the top. Put on the lid.

8. Place mold in cheese press and press at 15 pounds for 30 minutes. Remove cheese from press, unwrap, turn, and rewrap it. Then return to press and press at 15 pounds for one hour. Remove and redress, then place in mold and press at 20 pounds for 12 hours.

9. Remove cheese from press. Unwrap and place in brine solution. Allow cheese to soak for 20 hours, turning once during this process.

10. Remove the cheese from the brine. Unwrap and allow it to dry on a clean cheese mat for two to three days, turning it once a day, until the cheese is fairly dry to the touch.

11. Place cheese on a clean cheese mat in a ripening container. Ripen at 54° Fahrenheit and 85 percent humidity for at least five months, adjusting the lid of the ripening container and/or adding a bowl of water to maintain humidity. Turn cheese daily during the first two weeks, then twice a week for the next six weeks. After two months, turn the cheese once a week. If mold appears, wipe the cheese with a clean cloth dipped in a solution of vinegar and salt.

12. After three months, rub the cheese with olive oil to help develop the rind. Repeat the oil rub once a month. Continue to age cheese at 54° Fahrenheit for up to two years. The longer the cheese ages, the sharper the taste.

Parmesan

Prep time: 1 hour, 20 minutes
Cooking time: 3 hours
Resting time: 15 minutes
Pressing time: 12 hours, 30 minutes

Brining time: 20 hours

Drying time: 2-3 days

Ripening time: up to 1 year

Named for Parma region in Italy where it was first produced, Parmesan is the ubiquitous grating cheese usually found in shakers on pizza parlor tables. Parmesan is a delicious cheese to eat, especially shaved from the block and served with fruit and crackers. Of course, it adds a special flavor to nearly any Italian dish. Parmesan should be made with low-fat milk, and for best flavor, it should be ripened for at least six months. For supreme flavor, be patient and let this noble cheese ripen for up to a year. It will grow sharper as it ages. Many people also find that both Parmesan and Romano taste salty on the tongue.

Ingredients/Equipment:

4 gals of 2% cow's milk

½ tsp thermophilic culture

¾ tsp calcium chloride

¾ tsp liquid rennet

18% brine solution

Large stainless steel pot

Larger pot for hot water bath

Large (3.5x7.5 in) tomme mold

Cheesecloth

Colander

Skimmer

Whisk

Cheese press

Cheese mats

Ripening container

Thermometer

Distilled water

Measuring cup

Directions:

1. Using sterile equipment, pour milk into a large stainless steel pot. Place pot in a larger pot partially filled with water. Warm milk to 94º Fahrenheit, stirring gently. Turn off heat.

2. Sprinkle culture over the surface of the milk and let it stand for five minutes. Using a skimmer and a gentle up-and-down motion, draw culture down into the milk, disturbing the surface as little as possible. Cover the pot and let it sit for 45 minutes, keeping the temperature at 94º Fahrenheit throughout.

3. Dilute the calcium chloride in ¼ cup of cool distilled water. Add to milk mixture with the same gentle up-and-down motion, disturbing the surface of the milk as little as possible.

4. Dilute rennet in ¼ cup of cool distilled water. Add to milk mixture as before. Cover the pot and let stand for 45 minutes, maintaining temperature at 94º throughout.

5. Check for a clean break. As always, if clean break is not present, let mixture sit for five to ten minutes. Once clean break appears, use a whisk and a skimmer to cut curd into lentil-sized pieces, using the skimmer to life the curds and ensure that all are cut evenly. Let curds rest for ten minutes.

6. Under low heat, begin to slowly warm the curds to 124º Fahrenheit, stirring gently and continuously. Adjust the heat as needed to ensure that this process takes one hour. Do not heat mixture too quickly. Once the temperature of 124º Fahrenheit has been achieved, let the curds settle. Curds should mat together.

7. Place the prepared mold under a cheesecloth-lined colander and drain the whey through the mold, warming it. Fill the prepared mold with curds. Pull the cheesecloth up around the curds and smooth over the top of the curd bundle. Put on lid.

8. Place mold in a cheese press. Press at 15 pounds of pressure for 30 minutes. Remove cheese from press, unwrap, turn, and rewrap. Replace it in the press and press at 25 pounds of pressure for 12 hours.

9. Remove cheese from press. Unwrap and place in brine solution for 20 hours, turning cheese once halfway through this process.

10. Remove cheese from brine. Place cheese on a clean cheese mat on a rack, and allow it to dry for two to three days or until dry to the touch, turning the cheese once a day during this time.

11. Place cheese on a clean cheese mat in a ripening container. Ripen at 50° Fahrenheit and 85-90 percent humidity for a minimum of six months, turning daily for the first two weeks, then once a week thereafter. If mold appears on the rind, wipe cheese with a clean cloth dipped in a vinegar and salt solution.

12. After three months, rub the cheese once a week with a clean cloth soaked in olive oil. This will help the rind develop.

13. Cheese can be eaten after six months, but as noted, the best flavor comes after a year of ripening.

Kefalotyri

Prep time: 50 minutes
Cooking time: 2 hours, 45 minutes
Resting time: 25 minutes
Pressing time: 12 hours
Brining time: 12 hours
Drying time: 2-3 days
Ripening time: 6-14 weeks

Kefalotyri, which means "hat-shaped cheese," is a hard, sharp grating cheese, originally made in Greece. It could be called the Parmesan of the Greek Isles, as it bears a distinct resemblance to its Italian counterpart. Both cheeses are dry, sharp, and salty, ranging from pale cream to pale yellow in color. Both are used primarily as grating cheeses. Kefalotyri is usually grated over vegetables or pasta; it is also used in sauces. Like Parmesan, Kefalotyri becomes sharper and harder as it ages.

Ingredients/Equipment:

16 qts whole milk, either cow's milk or a blend of cow and goat's milk
½ tsp thermophilic culture
¾ tsp calcium chloride
¾ tsp liquid rennet
Cool brine solution
White vinegar
Large stainless steel pot
Larger pot for hot water bath
Large (3.5x7.5 in) tomme mold
Cheesecloth
Colander
Skimmer
Whisk
Cheese press
Cheese mats
Ripening container
Thermometer
Distilled water
Measuring cup

Directions:

1. Using sterile equipment, pour milk into a large stainless steel pot. Place pot in a larger pot partially filled with water. Warm milk to 92° Fahrenheit, stirring gently. Turn off heat.

2. Sprinkle culture over the surface of the milk and let it stand for five minutes. Using a skimmer and a gentle up-and-down motion, draw culture down into the milk, disturbing the surface as little as possible. Cover the pot and let it sit for 40 minutes, keeping the temperature at 92° Fahrenheit throughout.

3. Dilute the calcium chloride in ¼ cup of cool distilled water. Add to milk mixture with the same gentle up-and-down motion, again disturbing the surface of the milk as little as possible.

4. Dilute rennet in ¼ cup of cool distilled water. Add to milk mixture as before. Cover the pot and let stand for 45 minutes, maintaining temperature at 92° throughout.

5. Check for a clean break. As always, if clean break is not present, let mixture sit for five to ten minutes. Once clean break appears, use a whisk and a skimmer to cut curd into very small pieces, about the size of rice grains, using the skimmer to life the curds and ensure that all are cut evenly. Let curds rest for five minutes.

6. Under low heat, begin to slowly warm the curds to 113° Fahrenheit, stirring gently and continuously. Adjust the heat as needed to ensure that this process takes 40 minutes. Do not heat mixture too quickly. Once the temperature of 113° Fahrenheit has been achieved, turn off heat. Let stand 15 minutes.

7. Place the prepared mold under a cheesecloth-lined colander and drain the whey through the mold, warming it. Fill the prepared mold with curds. Pull the cheesecloth up around the curds and smooth over the top of the curd bundle. Put on lid.

8. Place mold in a cheese press. Press at 20 pounds of pressure for 30 minutes. Remove cheese from press, unwrap, turn, and rewrap. Replace it in the press and press at 25 pounds of pressure for 12 hours.

9. Remove cheese from press. Unwrap and place in brine solution for 12 hours, turning cheese once halfway through this process.

10. Remove cheese from brine. Place cheese on a clean cheese mat on a rack, and allow it to dry for two to three days or until dry to the touch, turning the cheese once a day during this time.

11. Place cheese on a clean cheese mat in a ripening container. Ripen at 54° Fahrenheit and 90 percent humidity for six weeks, turning daily. Wipe up any accumulated whey with a clean paper towel.

12. After six weeks, reduce temperature to 48° Fahrenheit and 90 percent humidity. Continue ripening cheese for another four to eight weeks, turning weekly. If mold appears, wipe cheese with a damp cloth dipped in vinegar.

13. Cheese can be eaten after six weeks, but as noted, the best flavor comes with continued ripening. Wrap and store ripened cheese in the refrigerator. It will keep a very long time, growing harder as it is stored.

Gjetost

Prep time: 20 to 30 minutes
Cooking time: 2-6 hours

Gjetost, pronounced "YET-oast," is a much-loved Norwegian cheese made from the whey of goat's milk. It is an excellent recipe to use up whey from another goat cheese production. Because of the high lactose content of the whey, gjetost is quite sweet. It is a rich caramel brown in color and has somewhat the same faintly salty, faintly nutty, sweet flavor. Gjetost is cooked and cooled until it is quite firm, and slivers of the cheese are usually served on breakfast toast. This cheese requires few ingredients, and it is not a complicated recipe, but it does require continuous monitoring, which makes it a good choice for a family cheese-making project.

Ingredients/Equipment:

1 gal of fresh whey from goat's milk
2 tsps cinnamon (optional)
Non-reactive cooking pot
Stainless steel spoon
Stainless steel whisk
13x9-in cake pan, buttered

Directions:

1. In a large, stainless steel cooking pot, bring the whey to a boil. Reduce heat to low and cook, stirring frequently, until the mixture is half its original volume. This can take anywhere from two to six hours. Be careful to stir frequently and monitor the heat to prevent scorching, especially toward the end of the cooking time.

2. Place pot in a sink full of cold water and whisk until mixture has cooled. This will prevent the mixture from becoming crystallized.

3. Stir in cinnamon if desired. Pour mass into prepared baking dish and let sit at room temperature until firm.

4. Unmold and store in refrigerator for four to six weeks while eating.

The Big Blues

Many cheeses have fans but not fanatics. The average cheese sampler might like a nibble of mild cheddar, a slice of Jarlsberg, or a pinch of Parmesan without getting passionate about any of these. However, those who love blue cheese are seldom lukewarm in their affection. Conversely, people who hate blue cheese usually *really* hate it. They hate the very idea of it. They cannot understand why anyone would willingly eat moldy cheese. Ah, but what a delicious mold it is.

All blue cheeses are made to be moldy. During the cheese-making process, a particular strain of mold — usually a little something called *Penicillium roqueforti* — is introduced into the curds and encouraged to spread throughout the cheese during the ripening and aging process. Cheese makers actually bore holes in the cheese in order to allow the mold to spread evenly throughout the body of the cheese or what is called the **paste**. These veins of mold, often blue, green, or gray, give an earthy aroma and a sharp, piquant taste to blue cheeses.

As discussed in the Introduction, blue cheese was probably an accident. Today, however, the noble blues are carefully crafted and widely appreciated. While

Roquefort is probably the best-known blue cheese, there are many other varieties made in many other countries. Excellent blue cheese can also be made at home. Each recipe requires time, patience, and the right mold powder, but the result is a divinely moldy delight.

CASE STUDY: CALIFORNIA BLUE

Point Reyes Farmstead Cheese Company
P.O. Box 9
Point Reyes, CA 94956
www.pointreyescheese.com
415-663-8880 (p)
415-663-8881 (f)

Bathed in the fresh breezes of the Pacific Ocean, Point Reyes Farmstead cheeses are hand-crafted from milk produced by 330 hard-working Holstein and Brown Swiss cows, which produce about 3,300 gallons of milk each day. This raw milk is used to make 600,000 pounds of cheese each year, sold nationally to specialty and gourmet shops, as well as through their online store. They make California's only classic-style blue cheese, their Point Reyes Original Blue. This fine blue cheese is aged for six months and has won multiple awards. Point Reyes also makes hand-pulled mozzarella. With such varied cheeses, they believe that it is important to maintain a variety of curing and aging facilities, each one set to certain temperature and humidity levels. Their advice to new cheese makers is: "There are many challenges as a farmstead producer. Forecasting demand when you produce an aged cheese is certainly one of the biggest. In addition to forecasting demand, achieving consistency with quality in every batch is certainly more difficult than it sounds. Go slow and methodically — do your research first and get networked in the specialty cheese community. You can avoid a lot of pitfalls and potential mistakes by talking to others that have been there!"

British blue (Stilton)

Prep time: 65 minutes

Cooking time: 20 minutes

Resting time: 4 hours

Draining time: 40 minutes

Pressing time: 12 hours

Ripening time: 4 months, 1 week

Like its European cousins Roquefort and Gorgonzola, Stilton is a much-beloved blue cheese. Strictly speaking, Stilton, which is protected under the European Union's trade policies, can only be made in three counties in England: Derbyshire, Nottinghamshire, and Leicestershire. For the sake of international harmony, we will call this recipe British blue, but it is a traditional Stilton-type cheese. Often in competition with cheddar for the title of "the king of English cheeses," Stilton is a semi-firm cheese with a rich and mellow flavor, shot through with sharper-flavored blue veining. Like all blue cheeses, this recipe requires the right mold powder (available through online cheese supply houses) and careful aging in order to come to full flavor.

Ingredients/Equipment:

15 qts whole milk

4 cups whipping cream

½ tsp mesophilic culture

⅛ tsp *Penicillium roqueforti* mold powder

½ tsp calcium chloride

½ tsp liquid rennet

4 tbsps pickling (canning) or kosher salt

Stainless steel cooking pot

Larger pot for hot water bath

Large (3.5x7.5 in) tomme mold

Colander

Skimmer

Curd knife

Cheesecloth

Cheese press
Cheese mats
Draining container
Ripening container
Thermometer
Thin knitting needle or metal skewer
Draining bowl
Cutting board

Directions:

1. Using sterile equipment, pour milk and cream into a large stainless steel pot. Place pot in a larger pot partially filled with water. Warm mixture to 86° Fahrenheit, stirring gently. Turn off heat.

2. Sprinkle culture and mold powder over the surface of the milk and let it stand for five minutes. Using a skimmer and a gentle up-and-down motion, draw culture down into the milk, disturbing the surface as little as possible. Cover and let ripen for one hour.

3. Dilute the calcium chloride in ¼ cup of cool distilled water. Add to milk mixture with the same gentle up-and-down motion, again disturbing the surface of the milk as little as possible.

4. Dilute rennet in ¼ cup of cool distilled water. Add to milk mixture as before. Cover the pot and let stand for 90 minutes at room temperature.

5. Check for a clean break. As always, if clean break is not present, let mixture sit for five to ten minutes. Once clean break appears, use skimmer to ladle thin slices of curd into the cloth-lined colander over a larger draining bowl. As they drain, the curds will be sitting the whey as it drains into the bowl. Cover the colander during the draining process to help maintain the temperature. Let drain for 90 minutes.

6. As the curd drains, lift and turn it with the skimmer to help break it up into smaller pieces, which facilitates acidification and firming.

7. Lift the cloth bundle out of the colander and tie the corners to form a bag. Suspend the bag and let it drain for 30-40 minutes or until the bundle no longer drips.

8. Place the bundle of curds in a cutting board in a draining container and place a second board on top of it. Weigh down the upper board with a large bowl full of water, a few bricks, or anything that weighs eight to ten pounds. Press overnight at room temperature.

9. Remove curd from bundle and break up into coarse pieces. Toss gently with salt. Fill mold with curd. Place lid on the mold and place on a rack in a clean draining container. Turn cheese every two or three hours for one day, then once a day for four more days, removing any collected whey from the container as it drains.

10. Remove cheese from mold. If cheese is still too soft to maintain its shape, replace it in the mold and let it drain for one more day. Prepare a clean cheese mat in a ripening container. Place the cheese on the mat. Cover and place container in ripening area.

11. Ripen at 53° Fahrenheit and 85 percent humidity. Turn cheese once daily for one week, draining off any collected whey during the process and wiping the container dry with a paper towel. Wipe the rind daily with a cloth soaked in salted water for the first week.

12. After two weeks, the cheese will have developed a moldy coating, and the blue mold should be growing inside the cheese. To ensure this process, pierce the cheese several times both vertically and horizontally with the needle or sewer. Turn the cheese once or twice a week for four more months. Once cheese has ripened, wrap in foil and store in refrigerator for two to three months.

White Stilton

Prep time: 60 minutes

Cooking time: 20 minutes

Resting time: 4 hours

Draining time: 40 minutes

Pressing time: 12 hours

Ripening time: 4 months, 1 week

This might be called blue cheese without the blue. White Stilton is very similar in composition to traditional Stilton, but it lacks the mold-created veins that give Stilton its sharpness. Minus the veins, white Stilton becomes a firm yet creamy cheese with a soft, rich flavor and tangy undertones. The whipping cream in the recipe gives this cheese a "fresh cream" taste. White Stilton is particularly tasty with fresh fruit or fruitcake.

Ingredients/Equipment:

15 qts whole milk

4 cups whipping cream

½ tsp mesophilic culture

½ tsp calcium chloride

½ tsp liquid rennet

4 tbsps pickling (canning) or kosher salt

Stainless steel cooking pot

Larger pot for hot water bath

Large (3.5x7.5 in) tomme mold

Colander

Skimmer

Curd knife

Cheesecloth

Cheese press

Cheese mats

Draining container

Ripening container

Thermometer

Directions:

1. Using sterile equipment, pour milk and cream into a large stainless steel pot. Place pot in a larger pot partially filled with water. Warm mixture to 86° Fahrenheit, stirring gently. Turn off heat.

2. Sprinkle culture over the surface of the milk and let it stand for five minutes. Using a skimmer and a gentle up-and-down motion, draw culture down into the milk, disturbing the surface as little as possible. Cover and let ripen for one hour.

3. Dilute the calcium chloride in ¼ cup of cool distilled water. Add to milk mixture with the same gentle up-and-down motion, again disturbing the surface of the milk as little as possible.

4. Dilute rennet in ¼ cup of cool distilled water. Add to milk mixture as before. Cover the pot and let stand for 90 minutes at room temperature.

5. Check for a clean break. If clean break is not present, let mixture sit for five to ten minutes. Once clean break appears, use skimmer to ladle thin slices of curd into the cloth-lined colander over a larger draining bowl. As they drain, the curds will be sitting the whey as it drains into the bowl. Cover the colander during the draining process to help maintain the temperature. Let drain for 90 minutes.

6. As the curd drains, lift and turn it with the skimmer to help break it up into smaller pieces, which facilitates acidification and firming.

7. Lift the cloth bundle out of the colander and tie the corners to form a bag. Suspend the bag and let it drain for 30-40 minutes or until the bundle no longer drips.

8. Place the bundle of curds in a cutting board in a draining container and place a second board on top of it. Weigh down the upper board with a large bowl full of water, a few bricks, or anything that weighs eight to ten pounds. Press overnight at room temperature.

9. Remove curd from bundle and break up into coarse pieces. Toss gently with salt. Fill mold with curd. Place lid on the mold and place on a rack

in a clean draining container. Turn cheese every two or three hours for one day, then once a day for four more days, removing any collected whey from the container as it drains.

10. Remove cheese from mold. If cheese is still too soft to maintain its shape, replace it in the mold and let it drain for one more day. Prepare a clean cheese mat in a ripening container. Place the cheese on the mat. Cover and place container in ripening area.

11. Ripen at 53° Fahrenheit and 85 percent humidity. Turn cheese once daily for one week, draining off any collected whey during the process and wiping the container dry with a paper towel. Wipe the rind daily with a cloth soaked in salted water for the first week.

12. After the first week, turn the cheese twice a week for the next four months, wiping cheese with a cloth soaked in salted water to keep the rind clean. Once cheese has ripened, wrap in foil and store in refrigerator for two to three months.

Roquefort-style French blue cheese

Prep time: 2 hours
Cooking time: 2 hours
Resting time: 15 minutes
Draining time: 48 hours, 30 minutes
Ripening time: 2-5 months

Since 1666, the name "Roquefort" has been protected under French law. Even today, any cheese labeled Roquefort must come from one of 13 producers who still make and age their cheese in the same limestone caves that have been producing Roquefort since it graced the table of French kings. Unless you wish to move to France and buy a limestone cave, your blue cheese will not be the true Roquefort. However, just as a recipe for British blue produces an excellent Stilton-style cheese, this recipe will yield a delicious French-style blue. The main ingredient in this cheese, apart from the traditional mold, is sheep's milk. As noted, this is a scarce commodity, so make certain you have a reliable supplier before you attempt this recipe. The finished cheese is incredibly rich due to the high fat content of the milk. The paste is creamy with a slightly buttery tang, and the veins, of course, give it that true pungent blue cheese flavor and aroma.

Ingredients/Equipment:

8 qts sheep's milk

½ tsp mesophilic culture

⅛ tsp *Penicullium roqueforti* mold powder

¼ tsp calcium chloride

¼ tsp liquid rennet

Stainless steel cooking pot

Larger pot for hot water bath

Thermometer

4 4-inch Camembert molds

Cheesecloth

Skimmer

Cheese knife

Metal knitting needle or meat skewer

Cheese press

Cheese matting

Cutting board

Cheese rack

Ripening container

Measuring cup

Distilled water

Directions:

1. Begin by sterilizing all equipment. Prepare a draining container by placing a rack inside. Place a cutting board on top of the rack. Cover the rack with matting. Place molds on top of all.

2. Pour milk into non-reactive cooking pot and place in larger pot partially filled with water. Warm milk over medium heat to 90° Fahrenheit, stirring gently. Turn off heat.

3. Sprinkle culture over the surface of the milk and let stand for five minutes. Using the skimmer and a gentle up-and-down motion, work the culture into the milk as gently as possible.

4. Dilute calcium chloride in ¼ cup of cool distilled water and work into milk mixture in the same manner.

5. Dilute rennet in ¼ cup of cool distilled water and work into milk mixture in the same manner. Cover pot and return to heat. Let sit for 90 minutes, maintaining temperature at 90° Fahrenheit throughout this time.

6. Check for a clean break. If clean break is not present, wait an additional five to ten minutes. Once clean break is present, use a long-bladed knife and skimmer to cut curd into ½-inch cubes. Let stand for five minutes to firm up curds.

7. Using a measuring cup, dip off whey until you see the surface of the curds.

8. Using a skimmer, carefully ladle curds into a cloth-lined colander and let drain for 30 minutes, lifting curds gently from time to time.

9. Ladle one scoop of curds into each prepared mold and let drain for ten minutes. Sprinkle a pinch of mold powder into each mold, and then add another layer of curd. Add another pinch of mold powder, then more curd. Continue until all the curds and mold powder are used.

10. Cover container and let cheeses drain at room temperature for two days, flipping every few hours to aid draining. After two days, remove cheese from the molds. Sprinkle ¾ teaspoon of salt over each side of the cheeses. Prepare a clean cheese mat in a ripening container.

11. Place cheese on mat. Cover and place in the ripening container. Let cheese ripen at 50-55° Fahrenheit and 85-90 percent humidity. Leave the container's lid slightly ajar to allow for air movement and to aid in drying. Turn cheeses daily, removing any collected whey from the bottom of the container and wiping with a clean paper towel.

12. One week after production, pierce cheeses all the way through both horizontally and vertically, approximately 12 times per cheese. This will allow air to penetrate to the center of the cheeses, aiding mold growth. Continue to ripen and turn cheeses daily.

13. Approximately ten days after production, blue mold should be visible on the outside of the cheeses.

14. Pierce cheese again at two weeks. Continue to ripen until a bluish-gray mold forms. You must carefully monitor humidity throughout this process. Too much moisture will cause the cheese to become soft, and the rind will not develop. Too little moisture will cause the cheese to dry out. Keep humidity constant at 85-90 percent.

15. Ripen cheese for two to five months. When ready, wrap cheeses in foil and store in the refrigerator for two to three months.

Fourme d'Ambert

Prep time: 60 minutes
Cooking time: 3 hours
Resting time: 10 minutes
Pressing time: 7 to 8 hours
Brining time: 12 hours
Drying time: 2 days
Ripening time: 1 month

This is another French blue cheese. It was originally made in south central France. Unlike Roquefort, it is made with cow's milk, but it uses the same type of mold powder to produce the blue veins. While the veins are sharp in flavor, the surrounding cheese or "paste" is firm yet creamy and moist, with a much softer impact on the palate. Like many blue cheeses, Fourme d'Ambert is particularly delicious with fruit and sweet dessert wines. It is also tasty in a salad, cut into small pieces and mixed with baby greens and sweet grape tomatoes. Be sure to use whole milk in this recipe in order to achieve the moist and creamy texture in the finished cheese.

Ingredients/Equipment:

16 qts whole milk
½ tsp mesophilic culture
⅛ tsp *Penicullium roqueforti* mold powder
½ tsp calcium chloride
½ tsp liquid rennet
Cool brine solution
Stainless steel cooking pot
Larger pot for hot water bath
Thermometer
Large tomme mold
Cheesecloth
Skimmer
Cheese knife
Metal knitting needle or meat skewer
Cheese press
Cheese matting
Cheese rack
Ripening container
Measuring cup
Distilled water

Directions:

1. Begin with sterilized equipment. Pour milk into non-reactive cooking pot and place in larger pot partially filled with water. Warm milk over medium heat to 90° Fahrenheit, stirring gently. Turn off heat.

2. Sprinkle culture and mold powder over the surface of the milk and let stand for five minutes. Using the skimmer and a gentle up-and-down motion, work the culture and mold powder into the milk as gently as possible.

3. Dilute calcium chloride in ¼ cup of cool distilled water and work into milk mixture in the same manner.

4. Dilute rennet in ¼ cup of cool distilled water and work into milk mixture in the same manner. Cover pot and return to heat. Let sit for 90

minutes, maintaining temperature at 90° Fahrenheit throughout this time.

5. Check for a clean break. If clean break is not present, wait an additional five to ten minutes. Once clean break is present, use a long-bladed knife and skimmer to cut curd into ½-inch cubes. Let stand for five minutes to firm up curds.

6. Using a skimmer, gently stir curds constantly for one hour, maintaining temperature at 90° Fahrenheit throughout this time. By the end of this process, curds will be small and firm.

7. Using a measuring cup, dip off whey until you can see the surface of the curds. Ladle curds into cheesecloth-lined mold. Pull the cloth up and around the curd bundle, smoothing it out over the top. Put on the lid.

8. Place mold in cheese press. Press cheese at light pressure (five to eight pounds) for one hour. Remove cheese from press, unwrap, turn and re-wrap. Place cheese back in mold and put mold back in press. Continue pressing at light pressure for six to seven hours.

9. Remove cheese from press and unwrap it. Place cheese in brining solution for 12 hours, turning once during this time.

10. Dry cheese on a rack for two days at room temperature. Pierce cheese all the way through several times both vertically and horizontally, using the needle or skewer. This will assist in the development of the blue veins.

11. Place cheese on a clean mat in a ripening container. Let cheese ripen at 50° Fahrenheit and 90 percent humidity. Turn cheese daily, removing any collected whey from the container and wiping container with a clean paper towel. A blue-gray moldy crust will begin to form in about two weeks. Continue ripening for one month. Cheese is now ready to eat. Wrap and foil and store in the refrigerator for up to three months.

Gorgonzola

Prep time: 55 minutes (per batch)

Cooking time: 30-40 minutes (per batch)

Resting time: 30 minutes

Draining time 6-7 hours

Pressing time: 10 hours

Drying time: 4 days

Ripening time: 3 months-one year

Gorgonzola is Italy's entry into the Blue Cheese Sweepstakes. Like other blue cheese, much of Gorgonzola's bite comes from the veining. However, there are traditionally two types of Gorgonzola. These are Gorgonzola Dolce, or sweet Gorgonzola, and Gorgonzola Piccante, or Mountain Gorgonzola. Gorgonzola Dolce, which is aged for about three months, has a creamy texture and a much milder flavor. It also tends to be less odorous than older Gorgonzola. Gorgonzola Piccante, on the other hand, is more flaky and crumbly in texture with a much more aggressive flavor, almost spicy. Traditionally, both types are made with the milk from two different milking sessions, one in the evening and one the next morning. This recipe is adapted to mimic that process, which is why some steps are "per batch." You will be making two batches of cheese and combining them into the final wheel.

Ingredients/Equipment:

16 qts whole milk, divided

½ tsp mesophilic culture, divided

½ tsp calcium chloride, divided

½ tsp liquid rennet, divided

⅛ tsp *Penicullium roqueforti* mold powder

Pickling (canning) or kosher salt

Larger pot for hot water bath

Thermometer

Large tomme mold

Cheesecloth

Draining bag

Skimmer

Cheese knife

Metal knitting needle or meat skewer

Cheese press

Cheese matting

Cheese rack

Ripening container

Measuring cup

Distilled water

Directions:

1. Begin with sterilized equipment. Pour eight quarts of milk into non-reactive cooking pot and place in larger pot partially filled with water. Warm milk over medium heat to 90° Fahrenheit, stirring gently. Turn off heat.

2. Sprinkle ¼ teaspoon of culture over the surface of the milk and let stand for five minutes. Using the skimmer and a gentle up-and-down motion, work the culture into the milk as gently as possible.

3. Dilute ¼ teaspoon of calcium chloride in ¼ cup of cool distilled water and work into milk mixture in the same manner.

4. Dilute ¼ teaspoon of rennet in ¼ cup of cool distilled water and work into milk mixture in the same manner. Cover pot let it sit for 20 minutes.

5. Check for a clean break. If clean break is not present, wait an additional five to ten minutes. Once clean break is present, use a long-bladed knife and skimmer to cut curd into ¾-inch cubes. Let stand for five minutes to firm up curds.

6. Using a skimmer, gently stir curd constantly for about 20 minutes or until curd size is reduced to about ½ inch. Let settle.

7. Using a measuring cup, dip off whey until you can see the surface of the curds. Ladle curds into a draining bag and let drain overnight at around 60° Fahrenheit.

8. The next morning, make a second batch of cheese following the same instructions as the previous batch, draining the new batch for six hour but not cooling it.

9. Keeping the two batches of curds separate, break up or cut the curds into 1- to 2-inch chunks or slices.

10. Fill a prepared mold with cheese chunks, placing warm curds at the bottom and sides of the mold and filling the center with the firmer, cooler curds from the previous day's batch. Reserve some warm curds for the top of the mold. As you fill the mold, sprinkle the mold powder on the cool curds in the middle. Top with the reserved warm curds. Pull cloth up around the curds and fold excess over the stop, smoothing out bundle. Put on lid.

11. Place mold in cheese press. Press cheese at light pressure (five to eight pounds) for two hours. Remove cheese from press, unwrap, turn, and rewrap. Place cheese back in mold and put mold back in press. Press for another two hours. Continue to unwrap, rewrap, and repress at two-hour intervals for the next six hours, pressing the cheese for 10 hours total. Remove cheese from press and unwrap.

12. Place cheese on a clean mat in a ripening container at room temperature. Sprinkle top of cheese with one teaspoon of salt and place upturned mold on cheese to help cheese retain its shape. After six to seven hours, turn cheese over and salt the other side. Replace the upturned mold and let cheese drain again. Let cheese drain for three more days. Turn cheese daily, removing any collected whey from the container and wiping container with a clean paper towel. Each time you turn the cheese, sprinkle it with ¼ teaspoon of salt.

13. Remove the upturned mold and place lid on ripening container. Let cheese ripen at 50° Fahrenheit and 75 percent humidity. Turn cheese daily for another two weeks.

14. Once cheese has ceased to lose whey, pierce cheese all the way through several times both vertically and horizontally, using a needle or skewer. This will assist in the development of the blue veins.

15. Increase ripening humidity to 90 percent and decrease the temperature to 48° Fahrenheit. Pierce cheese again. Wipe or scrape the surface of the cheese daily.

16. After two months, increase ripening humidity to 90 percent and decrease the temperature to 45° Fahrenheit. Let cheese ripen for another 30 days. After this time, the cheese is ready to eat, but if you want a sharper taste, it can be ripened for up to a year.

Cambozola

Prep time: 65 minutes
Cooking time: 35 minutes
Resting time: 1 hour, 35 minutes
Draining time: 18 hours
Ripening time: 4 weeks

This cheese is a delicious blend of Camembert and Gorgonzola. The addition of cream gives a milder, softer flavor to the "paste" of the cheese, and this helps reduce the impact of the sharp and acid veins. Cambozoloa also ripens more quickly than many other blue cheeses, so you can enjoy it sooner. Like all blue cheeses, it works well in salads, omelets, and with fresh fruit, especially pears, grapes, and sweet melons such as cantaloupe.

Ingredients/Equipment:

4 qts whole milk
4 qts whipping cream (35% fat)
¼ tsp mesophilic culture

⅛ tsp *Penicullium roqueforti* mold powder

⅛ tsp *Penicillium candidum* mold powder

¼ tsp calcium chloride

¼ tsp liquid rennet

Pickling or kosher salt

Stainless steel cooking pot

Larger pot for hot water bath

Thermometer

2 8-inch half-Brie molds

Cheesecloth

Skimmer

Cheese knife

Metal knitting needle or meat skewer

Cheese ripening paper

Cheese matting

Cheese rack

Ripening container

Distilled water

Directions:

1. Begin by sterilizing all equipment. Prepare a draining container by placing a rack inside. Place a cutting board on top of the rack. Cover the rack with matting. Place molds on top of all.

2. Pour milk and cream into non-reactive cooking pot and place in larger pot partially filled with water. Warm milk over medium heat to 86° Fahrenheit, stirring gently. Turn off heat.

3. Sprinkle culture and *Penicillium candidum* mold powder over the surface of the milk and let stand for five minutes. Using the skimmer and a gentle up-and-down motion, work the culture into the milk as gently as possible. Cover and let ripen for 15 minutes.

4. Dilute calcium chloride in ¼ cup of cool distilled water and work into milk mixture in the same manner.

5. Dilute rennet in ¼ cup of cool distilled water and work into milk mixture in the same manner. Cover pot and let sit for one hour at room temperature.

6. Check for a clean break. If clean break is not present, wait an additional five to ten minutes. Once clean break is present, use a long-bladed knife and skimmer to cut curd into ½-inch cubes. Let stand for five minutes to firm up curds.

7. Using the skimmer, stir curd very gently in a lifting motion, moving curd from the bottom and sides of the pot for ten minutes or until the pieces of curd begin to shrink in size and become rounded.

8. Using a measuring cup, dip off whey until you see the surface of the curds.

9. Using a skimmer, carefully ladle curds into a cloth-lined colander and let drain for ten minutes.

10. Fill each prepared mold half full of curds. Let stand for 15 minutes, covering colander with pot lid to keep remaining curds warm.

11. Sprinkle a pinch of *Penicillium roqueforti* mold powder into each mold and add another layer of curd. Waiting 15 minutes between each layer, continue to add another pinch of mold powder, then more curd until all the curds and mold powder are used.

12. Cover container and let cheeses drain at room temperature for six hours at room temperature. Flip cheeses over and let them drain overnight.

13. Remove cheeses from the molds. Sprinkle ½ teaspoon of salt over each side of the cheeses. Prepare a clean cheese mat in a ripening container.

14. Place cheeses on mat. Cover and place in the ripening container. Let cheese ripen at 50-55° Fahrenheit and 85-90 percent humidity. Turn cheeses daily, removing any collected whey from the bottom of the container and wiping with a clean paper towel. Once the cheeses are fairly dry, pierce cheeses all the way through both horizontally and vertically with a clean steel knitting needle or meat skewer.

15. After 10-12 days, a white fuzzy mold should begin to develop on the cheeses. At this point, wrap cheeses in cheese ripening paper and return to the ripening container.

16. Cheeses should be ready to eat four weeks after production. When ready, store wrapped cheeses in the refrigerator.

Bleu du Queyras

Prep time: 60 minutes
Cooking time: 35 minutes
Resting time: 1 hour, 45 minutes
Draining time: 1 week, 4 hours
Drying time: 1 week
Ripening time: 4 weeks

This French blue cheese was originally made by small farmers in the Alpine area of eastern France, near the Italian border. Unlike many other blue cheeses, it is made specifically with low-fat milk. It is also traditionally made with a blend of cow's and goat's milk. As always, use the freshest milk you can find. This is a fairly fast-ripening cheese; it can be enjoyed after only one month of ripening.

Ingredients/Equipment:

4 qts of 2% cow's milk
4 qts of goat's milk
¼ tsp mesophilic culture
¼ tsp liquid rennet
¼ tsp calcium chloride
Pinch of *Penicillium roqueforti* mold powder
Pickling or kosher salt
Stainless steel cooking pot
Thermometer
3 4-inch Camembert molds
Cheesecloth
Skimmer

Cheese knife

Metal knitting needle or meat skewer

Cheese matting

Cheese rack

Ripening container

Distilled water

Measuring cup

Directions:

1. Begin by sterilizing all equipment. Prepare a draining container by placing a rack inside. Place a cutting board on top of the rack. Cover the rack with matting. Place molds on top of all.

2. Pour both types of milk into non-reactive cooking pot. Warm milk mixture over medium heat to 86° Fahrenheit, stirring gently. Turn off heat.

3. Sprinkle culture over the surface of the milk and let stand for five minutes. Using the skimmer and a gentle up-and-down motion, work the culture into the milk as gently as possible. Cover and let ripen for 30 minutes.

4. Dilute calcium chloride in ¼ cup of cool distilled water and work into milk mixture in the same manner.

5. Dilute rennet in ¼ cup of cool distilled water and work into milk mixture in the same manner. Cover pot and let sit for 45 minutes at room temperature. If the room is cool, keep pot warm by wrapping it in a towel or sitting it in a larger pot of warm water.

6. Check for a clean break. If clean break is not present, wait an additional five to ten minutes. Once clean break is present, use a long-bladed knife and skimmer to cut curd into ¾-inch cubes. Let stand for 15 minutes to firm up curds.

7. Using a measuring cup, dip off whey until you see the surface of the curds.

8. Using a skimmer, carefully ladle curds into a cloth-lined colander and let drain for four hours, flipping after two hours.

9. Using your hands, gently break up and mix the curds. Let drain for ten minutes, and then break up again.

10. Using your hands, gently mix in two teaspoons of salt and the pinch of mold powder.

11. Fill each prepared mold with curds, letting them drain and refilling with more curd as the curds drain down. Do not press down on the curds. Place molds on rack in draining container.

12. Cover container and let cheeses drain at room temperature for one week at cool room temperature (65° Fahrenheit). Remove collected whey daily. Flip cheeses six or seven times a day, leaving them in their molds throughout this process.

13. Remove cheeses from the molds. Sprinkle ½ teaspoon of salt over each side of the cheeses. Prepare a clean cheese mat in a ripening container. Place cheeses on mat. Dry uncovered for one week at 65° Fahrenheit, turning cheeses daily.

14. Once the cheeses are fairly dry, pierce cheeses all the way through both horizontally and vertically with a clean steel knitting needle or meat skewer.

15. Replace cheeses in container and cover. Let cheeses ripen at 42-44° Fahrenheit and 85 percent humidity. Turn twice a week. After the first week, pierce cheeses again.

16. Cheeses should be ready to eat four weeks after production. When ready, wrap cheeses in foil and store in the refrigerator.

Blue Gouda

Prep time: 60 minutes

Cook time: 90 minutes

Rest time: 25 minutes

Pressing time: 8 to 12 hours

Brining time: 12 hours

Drying time: 2-3 days

Ripening time: 6 weeks-3 months

This might be an unexpected combination, but part of the fun of home cheese making is to discover new and different types of cheese that are not normally sold in your local grocery store. Because Gouda is a washed-curd cheese, it has a tighter texture and lower moisture content than most blue cheeses. Therefore, the veins in blue Gouda will be not as plentiful or pronounced as in some of the other blues. However, the veins will develop, and the combination of Gouda's creamy, buttery flavor and the sharp bite of blue cheese are delightful.

Ingredients/Equipment:

16 qts whole cow's milk

½ tsp mesophilic culture

¾ tsp calcium chloride

⅛ tsp *Penicillium roqueforti* mold powder

¾ tsp liquid rennet

18% brine solution

Non-reactive cooking pot

Large pot for hot water bath

Distilled water

Colander

Cheesecloth

Skimmer

Curd knife

Large round mold

Cheese press

Cheese mat
Thermometer
Ripening container
Stainless steel knitting needle or meat skewer
Cheese wax
Natural bristle brush

Directions:

1. Start with sterilized equipment. Pour milk into a cooking pot that has been placed into a hot water bath. Over medium heat, warm milk to 85° Fahrenheit, stirring gently as the milk warms. Once milk reaches 85° Fahrenheit, remove from heat.

2. Add the mold powder to the milk and stir in gently.

3. Sprinkle the culture over the surface of the milk and let stand for five minutes. Using skimmer, gently draw the culture down into the milk with an up-and-down motion, doing your best not to break the surface of the milk.

4. Dilute calcium chloride in ¼ cup of cool distilled water and add to milk, using the same up-and-down motion.

5. Dilute rennet in ¼ cup of cool distilled water and add to the mixture, again using an up-and-down motion to disturb the surface as little as possible. Cover pot again and let it sit for 30 minutes, maintaining the 85° Fahrenheit temperature.

6. Check mixture for a clean break. If curds do not break clean, let them sit for another ten minutes. Once a clean break is achieved, use the skimmer and curd knife to cut curd into 1/2-inch cubes. Let curds settle to the bottom of the pot and rest for five minutes. Gently stir curds for five minutes, and then let them settle for five minutes again.

7. Using a measuring cup, remove six cups of whey from the pot, taking care not to disturb the curds at the bottom of the pot.

8. Replace the drained whey with an equivalent amount of distilled water heated to 140° Fahrenheit to bring the curds to 92° Fahrenheit. Stir curds gently for ten minutes, maintaining the temperature at 92° Fahrenheit.

9. Let curds settle and begin to mat together. Drain off whey until curds are just exposed and replace with an equal amount of distilled water heated to 110° Fahrenheit, which will bring the temperature of the pot to about 98° Fahrenheit. Stir continuously for 20 minutes. The curds will shrink to the size of navy beans. Once they shrink, let them stand for ten minutes.

10. Drain whey, pouring it through the prepared mold to warm it. The curds will knit together at this point. Using your washed hands, break off chunks of curd and place them in the prepared mold, mounding them up in a cone shape. Curds will continue to drain and will lose volume. Pull up cheesecloth around the curd bundle and fold cloth neatly over the top of the bundle. Put on the mold lid.

11. Place mold in cheese press or put a 5-pound weight on the mold. Press at five pounds of pressure for 30 minutes.

12. Remove cheese from press and unwrap it. Turn cheese over, rewrap it, and return it to the press or place a ten to 12-pound weight on it. Press at 10-12 pounds of pressure for 12 hours.

13. Remove cheese from press and unwrap. Pierce cheese approximately 25 times with the knitting needle or skewer. Be sure to pierce cheese all over, both horizontally and vertically.

14. Place cheese in a brine solution for 12 hours, turning it once during this process.

15. Remove cheese from brine and let dry on a cheese mat placed on a rack at room temperature for two to three days, until cheese is dry to the touch. Turn cheese daily during this process.

16. Place cheese on a clean mat in a ripening container and ripen at 50° Fahrenheit and 85 percent humidity for one week.

17. Coat cheese with two or three coats of wax, using a natural bristle brush and letting each coat of wax dry. Then ripen cheese at 50º Fahrenheit and 85 percent humidity for five weeks to three months. Turn cheese once a week to ensure even ripening.

CASE STUDY: GOOD CHEESE FROM THE DEEP SOUTH

Flat Creek Lodge Dairy and Farm
Swainsboro, GA
www.flatcreeklodge.com/dairy-and-farm.htm

Part of the Flat Creek Lodge resort, this dairy farm and cheese-making operation uses the milk from their own herd of Jersey cows and dairy sheep. This milk is turned into approximately 25,000 pounds of fine cheeses each year, including Aztec Cheddar, flavored with cocoa and guajillo chilies; Blue Farmhouse, a firm blue cheese; and Colbaa, made from a blend of cow and sheep's milk, flavored with scallions and ginger. Their quality control is of the most basic kind — they taste everything before it is offered for sale. Flat Creek Lodge cheeses and their makers are the proud recipients of awards from the U.S. Cheese Championships, The North American Jersey Cheese Contest, and the American Cheese Society. Flat Creek Lodge cheeses are available online and at specialty cheese shops. While they are passionate fans of American cheeses, the Flat Creek cheese makers are truly international in their scope. As one cheese maker put it, "Good cheese is good cheese." Their advice for beginning cheese makers is simple, "Use good ingredients, and stay clean."

Quick Guide to Troubleshooting

It is a sad truth that every new venture has its share of problems. Cheese making is no exception to this rule. However, many difficulties can be avoided, and others can be fixed. This section will help you determine what is wrong with your cheese and if it can be salvaged. Remember, this is food. If the problem is bad enough, it is better to toss out a batch of cheese than to risk poisoning everyone at the family picnic. Fortunately, very few cheese-related troubles are that bad.

Obviously, the best way to fix a problem is to avoid it in the first place. A bit of planning will help you steer clear of many of the most common issues. First, make sure you have everything you need before you start on your recipe. 10 p.m. on a Saturday night is the wrong time to start a batch of blue cheese and discover that you are fresh out of *Penicillium roqueforti* powder. Make sure you have all the necessary ingredients and equipment before you pour the first cup of milk. Use good-quality equipment. The right pan will help prevent scorching and other accidents, and a superior thermometer will enable you to make sure everything is cooked at exactly the right temperature.

Second, follow the directions exactly, especially when you first start making cheese. Master cheese makers can tweak a recipe here and there and end up with a new and exciting creation. The new cheese maker who does this will probably end up with a lump of soggy curds. Measure every ingredient carefully, monitor temperatures exactly, and follow all directions for pressing, drying, and aging.

Finally, start small. Try making a fresh cheese or a batch of yogurt before you tackle Brie and Stilton. Use the cheese journal, as described in Chapter 5, and record your progress when trying a new recipe. Most importantly, do not get discouraged. Even the most expert cheese maker occasionally has a bad batch, just as the best cook occasionally burns the roast. Work through the recipe one step at a time and have fun learning new skills. When problems do occur, consult the information below for possible solutions:

I. My fresh cheeses are not developing proper texture or flavor:

- If the curd is too soft, you may not have used enough rennet. Add another drop or two to the next batch.

- Soft curd may also mean the activity of the rennet was destroyed because you mixed it with warm instead of cool water. Always mix rennet with cool water before adding it to the milk mixture.

- Soft curd can indicate that the quality of the rennet may have been damaged by improper storage. Store liquid rennet in the refrigerator and store powdered rennet in the freezer.

- If the curd is too hard, too much rennet was added. Make sure you measure rennet carefully.

- Curd that is too hard may also be caused by cheese that is too acidic. Ripen it for a shorter period of time, or add a bit less starter culture (reduce by a couple of drops) to the milk mixture.

II. Cheese has little or no flavor or a sour taste:

- The cheese may need to be aged longer.

- The cheese may need higher acidity. Add a couple of extra drops of starter culture to the recipe.

- If the cheese is sour, it may have too high an acid level. Use a bit less culture in the next batch.

III. The finished cheese is too dry:

- Too little rennet was used. Add a few drops more to the next batch.

- The curd was cut too small. Be sure to cut the curd as described in the recipe.

- The cooking temperature was too high. Be sure to monitor temperature carefully and use a trustworthy thermometer.

- The curds were worked too hard. Handle the curds gently and follow the recipe exactly as to how much pounding, squeezing, or agitating they need.

IV. The wrong kind of mold is growing on my cheese:

- Cleanliness is everything. Always use clean cheese mats, ripening containers, molds, and racks.

- Cheese was aged at too high a humidity. Check the recipe and lower humidity in the aging container if needed.

- Surface mold can usually be removed by wiping cheese with a cloth that has been dampened in white vinegar.

V. My "stretchable" cheeses will not stretch:

- Mozzarella will not stretch if the pH balance is wrong. Be sure to check pH balance. It should be at 5.0 to 5.2. If it is below 5.0, the curd needs to ripen longer before stretching. If it is above 5.2, shorten the ripening time.

VI. My mold-ripened cheeses are going bad:

- Pink, brown, or black mold on mold-ripened cheeses indicate either bad bacteria or too high humidity. Reduce humidity in the ripening area. Clean the ripening container, racks, and other equipment with a mild bleach solution. Be sure to rinse thoroughly, as bleach residue will also cause problems. Pink mold is safe to eat; black or brown mold should be gently scrubbed away with a mixture of ¼ cup of white vinegar and one teaspoon of coarse salt.

- If the crust on the mold-ripened cheese is thick and gritty, instead of white and fuzzy, too much mold has developed. Reduce the amount of mold powder in the next batch. Also, make sure to wrap cheese in ripening paper as soon as white fuzzy mold covers the cheese.

- If the cheese ripens too quickly and has an unpleasant ammonia scent or taste, slow down the ripening process by reducing the temperature in the ripening area.

- If the ripened cheese is too runny, there was too much moisture in the curd. Stir the next batch of curd for an additional five minutes.

- If the mold-ripened cheese is too firm, it was stirred too long during the curd-making process.

- If mold does not cover the cheese in 12 to 14 days, raise the temperature in the ripening area and increase the humidity as well. The cheese may also have been over-salted; reduce salt in the next batch.

VII. My blue cheeses are making me blue:

- Pink, brown, or black mold blue cheeses also indicate either bad bacteria or too high humidity. Reduce humidity in the ripening area. Clean the ripening container, racks, and other equipment with a mild bleach solution. Be sure to rinse thoroughly, as bleach residue will also cause problems. Pink mold is safe to eat; black or brown mold should be gently scrubbed away with a mixture of ¼ cup of white vinegar and one teaspoon of coarse salt.

- If the veins of blue mold are not developing in the cheese, the cheese is too solid and air is not getting in to encourage mold growth. Pierce the cheese several more times with the steel knitting needle or skewer.

- If the cheese becomes very strong-smelling before the ripening period is over, reduce humidity in the ripening container.

- If the blue mold is developing too slowly, increase the humidity in the ripening area. The cheese may also be too dry; cook or stir the next batch a bit less to maintain moisture in the curd.

VIII. My hard cheeses are giving me a hard time:

- If the cheese cracks during pressing or is too dry and crumbly when finished, the curd may have been cooked at too high a temperature or stirred too long. Cook at a slightly lower temperature and do not stir as long in the next batch.

- If the finished texture is rubbery, reduce the amount of rennet in the next batch. For a washed-curd cheese, do not wash as much, thereby leaving more whey in the curds to increase moisture.

- If the cheese puffs up and splits open, it has been contaminated with bad bacteria and must be thrown out. Always maintain strict hygiene standards.

- If the rind on an older cheese seems dusty and almost rotted, you may have cheese mites, tiny insects that will attack your cheese. Be sure to wash down and sanitize your ripening area. The cheese is still safe to eat.

- If the rind seems greasy, use lower-fat milk in the next batch of cheese. You can also reduce the temperature in the ripening area, which will help somewhat.

- If a waxed cheese develops "bruised" spots, there are moisture pockets under the wax that will allow bacteria to develop and damage the cheese. Make sure your cheese is completely dry before waxing. If the bruised spots appear, cut them away and use the cheese right away. You can try to re-wax the cheese and continue the aging process, but watch such cheeses carefully for any indication of more rot.

Chapter Nine

Man (and Woman) Cannot Live by Cheese Alone

While a few people probably scoop Cheez Whiz straight from the jar, most of us want some companions to accompany our cheese on its journey across the palate. In other words, who wants to eat cheese by itself? Many of us are intimidated by all of the "rules" created by the foodies of the world, especially those that cover cheese and wine. You have probably heard some of them: pears with port, red wine with cheddar, white wine with Brie, Boone's Farm with Velveeta, etc. Now, these rules are not wrong; they are simply narrow. Yes, certain cheeses taste especially good with certain wines. At the same time, it is a big world out there, and not everyone enjoys the same flavors. Also, not everyone likes wine, and cheese is such a versatile food, it seems a shame to only let it mingle with the grapey group. So here are some ideas to help your cheeses make new friends, so to speak, and provide you with a variety of taste sensations.

Cheese and Wine: The Basics

As noted above, the rules about wine and cheese exist for a reason. Before breaking the rules, it is always a good idea to understand them, and rules about which wine to serve with a particular type of cheese are almost as old as the foods themselves. Cheese and wine are often associated with each other because they actually have a great deal in common. Both are agricultural products, of course, and

both have been made by almost every civilization on earth. Both are made from items that can be eaten fresh: people enjoy grapes and milk almost as much as they like wine and cheese. Fermentation works on the ingredients of both cheese and wine, combining the elements into a more flavorful whole. Finally, both wine and cheese can be consumed when they are young, bright, and light on the palate, or they can be aged until their flavors are deep and complex. When pairing cheeses and wines, most experts try to match their characteristics; in other words, if a wine has a powerful flavor and aroma, it is usually paired with a cheese that can stand up to its strength. In contrast, light, sweet wines are usually paired with creamy cheeses that are less aged and gentle on the tongue. The following are some classic couples in the romance of wine and cheese:

- **Soft, fresh cheeses:** These are often matched with light and fruity wines such as Sauvignon blanc or new Beaujolais.

- **Soft, ripened cheeses:** Such French favorites as Brie and Camembert are excellent with sparkling wines, especially Champagne. They also go well with a Chardonnay or other full-flavored white wine.

- **Tangy cheeses such as goat cheese:** These work well with a wine that has an assertive flavor, such as a Burgundy.

- **Blue cheeses:** The famous blues, such as Stilton or Roquefort, pair beautifully with sweet dessert wines such as port, Riesling, or Asti Spumante.

- **Aged cheeses:** From Gouda to cheddar, most aged cheeses need an assertive wine that can complement their flavors without being overpowered by them. The best wines for these cheeses include some vintage Burgundies, Cabernet Sauvignon, and White Zinfandel.

Of course, this guide only scratches the surface. The most important consideration is this: Do you like the wine you have chosen to go with your cheese? Every cheese is different, and even the same type of wine can vary from one producer to another or even one year to another. For example, a wheel of cheddar aged for three months will have a mild flavor and might taste just right with a semi-dry Champagne or Chardonnay. The same cheese, if it has spent two years ripening in a cheese cave, would completely overpower the Champagne you once thought was so delightful. Now the sharp, pungent flavor demands a full-bodied, fruity Cabernet to accompany it. Therefore, the best way to discover which wines and cheeses are harmonious partners is to taste your favorites and let your palate be the final judge.

Matching Cheese and Beer

While wine is viewed as cheese's natural partner, beer is often left on the sidelines, looking on wistfully as Brie and Champagne dance away together. This is both unfair and unnecessary. After all, many fine beers and ales are brewed with just as much care and attention as the best wines. Like wine, beer can be found in almost every culture and in flavors ranging from very mild to quite assertive. In addition, most beers are less acidic than wines, so they "fight" less with many cheeses. So if wine is not your "thing," try matching a good-quality beer with your cheese selection. As with wine, there are basic guidelines for this process, but the final result is a matter of personal preference. The following are some suggestions:

- Young, fresh cheeses (fromage blanc, some goat's cheeses, farmer's cheese) go well with light, golden beers. Think pale ale or golden Belgian beers.

- Sharp cheeses (cheddar, aged Parmesan, smoked Gouda) match well with beers rich in hops and bitters. These include such favorites as pilsners and pale ale with lots of hops.

- Aged, nutty cheeses (Asiago or Gruyère) taste best with rich, malty beers. These include porter, stout, brown ale, and Oktoberfest beers.

- Blue cheeses (Stilton, Roquefort, Gorgonzola) are offset by sweeter, fruity beers. These include wheat and cherry beers.

Showing Off Your Wares: The Cheese Board

Whether hand-crafted or purchased at the local gourmet house, cheeses are great partners when you entertain, and one of the simplest ways to serve them is the cheese board. As with other aspects of entertaining, there is no one right way to build a cheese board; however, these tips will help you create a cheese board that will dazzle and nourish your guests with a minimum of fuss.

How much cheese will you need? If there are plenty of other snacks available or if the cheeses serve as an appetizer before dinner, plan on one to two ounces of cheese per guest. However, if the cheese is going to be the focus of the evening — or if your friends are big eaters — plan to have four to six ounces per person. It is always better to have plenty than not enough.

Cheeses taste better when they are not ice-cold. Remove all of your cheeses from the refrigerator 30 minutes to one hour before serving to allow them to warm and soften for maximum aroma, texture, and taste.

Mix it up but do not overwhelm the palate. Offer a variety of cheese with different tastes and textures, from soft and mild to sharp and crumbly. However, too many cheeses can crowd the board and confuse the taster. Try four to six cheeses on your board. A good selection would include soft (Brie), mild (Gouda), classic (sharp cheddar), strong (Gorgonzola), and unexpected (a sweet dessert cheese like mascarpone or lemon cheese). Obviously, the combinations are only limited by your imagination and the availability of the different cheeses.

Choose accompaniments that do not distract from the cheeses. Plain crackers or breadsticks and simple breads are good choices. Dried fruits such as figs, cherries, and apricots go well with most cheeses, as do nuts such as almonds and walnuts, and fresh fruits, including apples, pears, grapes, and sweet melons. Depending on the type of cheese, chutneys and fruit preserves can also be good partners.

Be sure that the cheeses are easy to eat. While huge wedges of cheddar or whole wheels of Brie are dramatic, they are hard to manage. Slice the cheeses before serving, using the right knife. Soft cheese should be cut into pieces or wedges with a butter knife or small paring knife. Hard cheese should be sliced with a chef's knife or a cheese wire. Very soft, runny cheeses should be presented in small individual ramekins or serving dishes.

Do the Fondue

Back in the 1970s, every "hip" home had two elements in common — at least one avocado-green appliance and a fondue pot balanced over a Sterno-fueled burner. There was nothing more fashionable than inviting six friends to come over, sit on sofa cushions on the floor, and drop hot cheese sauce in their laps. Today, fondue is making a comeback, as the easy recipes and bite-size nibbles fit well into the modern family's routine. Electric fondue pots (no need for open flames!) are readily available, but you can also use a 1-quart slow cooker to heat your cheesy dips. Long-handled forks can be purchased at any kitchen store or in the house wares section of most major stores.

When making fondue, be sure to use good-quality cheeses that melt well. These include cheddar, Fontina, havarti, provolone, and many more. Adding a teaspoon or two of cornstarch to the melted cheese will help it blend more smoothly and prevent separation or lumps in the sauce. When using bread as your dipping material, be sure to purchase firm and chewy-textured loaves that will stand up to being dunked. Pre-sliced white bread is just too soft. French or Italian loaves are a much better choice. Cut the loaves into bite-sized chunks instead of neat slices. Many fondue recipes call for wine to be added to give a bit of acidity and blend the flavors together. Use a dry, crisp white wine, not a sweet wine. If you do not wish to use wine, a splash of lemon juice will add the same acidic balance.

Here are a few basic fondue recipes to use with your homemade cheeses. Feel free to experiment with blends of cheeses, herbs, additions such as beer or wine, and other flavors including Worcestershire or hot sauces. All of these make a delicious difference in the quality of your fondue.

Cheesy cheddar fondue

Prep time: 10 minutes
Cooking time: 20 minutes

Because cheddar is such a favorite with cheese lovers, this fondue is ideal for any group. Once the mixture is melted, keep the fondue or slow cooker on a "low" heat setting in order to maintain the melted texture without scorching the cheese. Serve with cubed ham, bread, or crunchy raw vegetables such as bite-sized pieces of cauliflower and broccoli florets. For best results, open the beer an hour or so before adding it to the recipe; flat beer works better for this dish than beer with a great deal of foam.

Ingredients/Equipment:

1 lb of shredded aged cheddar cheese

1 tbsp cornstarch

½ tsp powdered mustard

1 tbsp unsalted butter

1 cup beer

½ tsp Worcestershire sauce

Large mixing bowl

Large saucepan

Fondue pot or slow cooker

Long forks

Directions:

1. In a large bowl, toss the cheese with the cornstarch and mustard powdered until coated.

2. In a large saucepan, melt the butter into the beer over medium to high heat. Bring this mixture to a boil. Reduce the heat to low and gradually add the cheese mixture, stirring continuously and adding more cheese as the first batch melts. Stir in the Worcestershire and hot sauce.

3. Transfer mixture to a fondue pot or slow cooker set on low heat. Using long-handled forks, dip the bread, ham, and other items into the mixture and eat. This recipe serves six as an appetizer.

Parmesan-pesto fondue

Prep time: 5 minutes

Cooking time: 20 minutes

This dish uses both cream cheese and Parmesan, along with pesto sauce, either homemade or store-bought. The combination of ingredients makes a fondue with a definite Italian flair. Make your own pesto for this dish or use a prepared pesto available at delicatessens, gourmet food stores, and large supermarkets. Serve this with hearty Italian bread, bread sticks, or raw vegetables.

Ingredients/Equipment:

1 lb cream cheese

2 cups light cream or half-and-half

1 ½ cups freshly grated Parmesan cheese (about 6 ounces)

Salt to taste

Pinch of cayenne pepper

½ cup basil pesto

Double boiler or saucepan set in hot water bath

Fondue pot or slow cooker

Long forks

Directions:

1. Melt the cream cheese in a double boiler over low to medium heat. Gradually stir in the cream until mixed and heated throughout. Add the Parmesan and stir until cheese is melted and fondue begins to thicken. Season with salt and cayenne pepper.

2. Transfer the mixture to a fondue or slow cooker on low heat. Drop teaspoons of pesto sauce onto the surface of the cheese mixture. Using a knife or skewer, swirl the pesto gently through the cheese mixture.

Kickin' Jack fondue with Tequila

Prep time: 5 minutes
Cooking time: 20 minutes

The use of pepper Jack cheese and Tequila gives this fondue real Tex-Mex appeal. Cooking the cheese mixture burns off some of the alcohol, but this particular fondue may still be considered more of an adult indulgence due to the "spirited" flavor. It is perfect for the guys at a Super Bowl party or as part of a Tex-Mex buffet. You can adjust the heat by adding crushed red pepper or extra cayenne to the mixture. Instead of serving with bread cubes, try tortilla or corn chips.

Ingredients/Equipment:

2 lbs pepper Jack cheese, shredded

2 tbsps cornstarch

2 12-oz bottle of beer, preferably Mexican

1 large clove of garlic, minced

¼-½ tsp cayenne pepper

⅓ cup Tequila

⅓ cup diced fresh jalapeños (optional)

Large mixing bowl

Saucepan

Fondue pot or slow cooker

Long forks

Directions:

1. In a large bowl, toss cheese with cornstarch until coated.

2. In a large saucepan, combine beer, garlic, and cayenne pepper. Cook over medium heat until the beer is heated thoroughly and the mixture begins to bubble around the edges. Reduce heat to low and gradually stir in the cheese mixture, letting each addition melt before adding more. Stir in the tequila and let cook for approximately one minute. Add jalapeños if desired.

3. Transfer to fondue or slow cooker set on low heat.

Gouda and cheddar fondue

Prep time: 5 minutes

Cooking time: 20 minutes

This fondue gets its flavor from combining the sharp bite of cheddar cheese with the smooth creaminess of Gouda. It also uses apple cider and lemon juice instead of beer or wine, so it is a G-rated fondue, suitable for families. Serve this fondue with pita triangles, cubes of dark bread, pretzels, bread sticks, or bite-sized broccoli and cauliflower pieces.

Ingredients/Equipment:

1 lb Gouda cheese, shredded

8 oz cheddar cheese, shredded

1 ½ tbsps cornstarch

1 ½ tsps powdered mustard

1 ½ cups unsweetened apple cider or apple juice

1 ½ tbsps fresh lemon juice

Large mixing bowl

Fondue pot or slow cooker

Long forks

Directions:

1. In a large bowl, toss the cheese with the cornstarch and mustard until coated.

2. In a medium saucepan, heat the apple cider and lemon juice until hot but not boiling. Reduce heat to low and gradually add the cheese mixture, letting each addition melt before adding the next.

3. Transfer to fondue or slow cooker set on low heat.

Cooking with Cheese

Cheese, of course, is delicious all by itself or paired with bread, fruit, crackers, wine, or ale. However, cheese is also one of the most versatile ingredients to use in recipes. From breakfast to late night snacks, cheese can be used in a nearly endless parade of appetizers, salads, dips, entrees, and desserts. The following are just a few of the many recipes that you can create using the delicious cheeses you produced.

Tangy mustard sauce

This sauce, which uses crème fraîche to give it a tangy creaminess, is delicious with fish or chicken. It can also be thinned with additional olive oil and used as a salad dressing or marinade for chicken, fish, or pork.

Prep time: 5 minutes
Resting time: 1 hour

Ingredients/Equipment:

½ cup coarse country-style mustard
2 tbsps crème fraîche
4 tsps light brown sugar
1 tbsp cider or white wine vinegar
½ tsp salt
½ tsp black or white ground pepper
½ cup light olive or vegetable oil
Medium mixing bowl
Whisk or fork

Directions:

1. In a medium bowl, use a whisk or fork to beat together the mustard, crème fraîche, sugar, vinegar, salt, and pepper. Gradually add the oil, blending thoroughly.

2.   Cover and refrigerate for at least one hour or until flavors are blended. Whisk again and spoon into a serving bowl. Serve as a dipping sauce next to the meat or fish or drizzled over the top for more intense flavor.

Pepper Parmesan dressing

Prep time: 20 minutes
Resting time: 24 hours

While there are many fine salad dressings on the market, nothing can compare to homemade for freshness. Handcrafted salad dressings are also lower in sodium and preservatives than their bottled cousins, and you can flavor them to exactly suit your palate or the greens they accompany. This dressing, with its creamy Parmesan taste, is wonderful over a simple wedge of iceberg lettuce or a bowl of mixed baby greens. Once made, it keeps in the refrigerator for up to two weeks.

Ingredients/Equipment:

¾ cup mayonnaise
¼ cup sour cream
2 tsps white vinegar
¼ tsp dried basil
⅛ tsp garlic powder
3 tbsps grated Parmesan cheese
1 tsp cracked black peppercorns
2 tbsps milk
Covered jar or bottle

Directions:

Mix together all ingredients and place in covered jar, bottle, or other container in the refrigerator for 24 hours, to allow flavors to mix.

Buffalo chicken dip

Prep time: 10 minutes
Cooking time: 20 minutes

This tasty dip combines all the elements of buffalo wings except the bones. It can be made in the oven, slow cooker, or microwave. You can use canned chicken or shredded chicken from a deli rotisserie bird. It makes a great tailgate snack. Serve this dip with crackers or celery sticks.

Ingredients/Equipment:

8 oz cream cheese, softened at room temperature
½ cup ranch salad dressing
½ cup bottled hot sauce, such as Tabasco® or Frank's RedHot® Sauce
½ cup crumbled blue cheese
2 cans (9.75 oz each) of chuck chicken breast in water, drained, or 2 cups shredded cooked chicken
9x9 baking dish or
Glass microwavable baking dish or
2-quart slow cooker

Oven directions: Heat oven to 350° Fahrenheit. Place cream cheese into a 9x9 inch heatproof baking dish. Mix in ranch dressing, hot sauce, and cheese. Stir in shredded chicken. Bake 20 minutes or until mixture is heated through.

Microwave directions: Prepare as listed above. Place in microwave-safe dish and microwave on high, uncovered, for five minutes or until hot, stirring once halfway through.

Slow cooker directions: Combine ingredients as directed above. Place mixture into a 2-quart slow cooker and add cover. Cook on a high setting for 90 minutes or low setting for 2 ½ hours until hot and bubbly.

Goat cheese "super balls"

Prep Time: 30 minutes

Resting Time: 1 hour

What is more fun than super balls, those brightly colored, high-bouncing balls that can be found in every arcade prize machine? This delicious appetizer will remind you of those toys. The finished bite-sized morsels are colorful and easy to serve and eat. They make great finger food at parties where you want to go beyond cheddar and saltines.

Ingredients/Equipment:

8 oz of goat's milk cream cheese

Assorted coatings for the cheese balls. Consider some of the following: fresh herbs such as chopped chives, minced dill, parsley, or cilantro; finely chopped white onion; toasted and finely chopped almonds, walnuts, or pecans; poppy or sesame seeds; spices such as curry powder, cayenne pepper, paprika, or crushed red pepper; crisp fried, drained, and crumbled bacon; crushed garlic croutons; dry French onion soup mix or ranch dressing mix.

Melon scoop or teaspoon

Cookie sheet

Paper towels

Small bowls or saucers

Serving plate

1. Cut the goat cheese into 16 squares. Using a melon scoop or a plastic teaspoon, shape each piece of cheese into a ball, rather like a ball of cookie dough. Put the balls on a paper towel-lined cookie sheet and cover with several more paper towels. Let the balls rest on the countertop for about one hour. This allows any excess moisture to drain.

2. Place each coating in a small shallow bowl or saucer. Take each cheese ball and roll it into the coating, making sure the ball is thoroughly coated. Put the finished balls on a clean serving plate and place a toothpick or cocktail stick into each ball.

3. Serve immediately or cover with plastic wrap and store in the refrigerator for up to six hours before serving.

Fried cream cheese wontons

Prep time: 15 minutes
Cooking time: 10 minutes

Wontons, those tasty Chinese dumplings, are a favorite snack around the world. This version, using your homemade cream cheese, also features crab meat and green onions. If you want to make a more economical wonton, you can substitute mock crab meat for the real thing. Finely diced shrimp would also be delicious in this recipe.

Ingredients/Equipment:

8 oz of softened cream cheese

2 green onions, finely chopped

½ tsp garlic powder

½ tbsp sugar

¾ cup chopped lump crab meat, mock crab, or cooked chopped shrimp

1 package of wonton wrappers

2 cups vegetable oil

Mixing bowl

Wok or deep fry pan

Slotted spoon

Paper towels

Directions:

1. Combine ingredients in mixing bowl and mix well.

2. Lay out ten wonton wrappers. Moistening the edge of each wrapper, place approximately one teaspoon of the crab and cream cheese mixture in the center of each wonton.

3. Fold the edges of the wonton wrapper, pressing each one along the dampened edges to seal it firmly.

4. In a wok or a deep fry pan, heat the oil until it is just smoking. Fry the wontons until golden brown. Remove and drain onto paper towels.

Mushroom, tomato, and Gruyère breakfast casserole

Prep time: 30 minutes

Resting time: 12-13 hours

Cooking time: 45-50 minutes

Unfamiliar cheeses can sometime be intimidating. If your mother cooked with Swiss, cheddar, and Velveeta, finding the right recipe for an "exotic" cheese may seem daunting. To steal from Rogers and Hammerstein, "How Do You Solve a Problem Like Gruyère?" This terrific breakfast casserole is the answer to that question. You should assemble it the night before and let it rest in the refrigerator before cooking. In the morning, simply sit it out and let it warm up on the counter, then bake and serve.

Ingredients/Equipment:

4 whole wheat English muffins, split

1 tbsp olive oil

2 medium tomatoes, chopped

1 lb button mushrooms, washed and diced

8 eggs

½ cup low-fat milk

½ tsp garlic powder

½ tsp onion powder

2 tsps dried basil

1 cup grated Gruyère

Salt and pepper to taste

9x13 baking dish

Skillet

Large spoon

Mixing bowl
Whisk

Directions:

1. Arrange English muffin halves in the bottom of a greased 9x13 inch baking dish.

2. Heat oil in a large skillet over medium heat. Add tomatoes, mushrooms, salt, and pepper. Cook, stirring occasionally, until mixture is tender and liquid has thickened — about ten minutes. Spoon tomato mixture over the English muffin halves, set aside to cool.

3. In a large bowl, whisk together the eggs, milk, garlic powder, and onion powder. Pour evenly over the tomato and muffin mixture, and then sprinkle with basil. Cover and chill overnight.

4. Set aside dish at room temperature for one hour. Preheat oven to 350° Fahrenheit. Sprinkle casserole with cheese and bake uncovered for 45 to 50 minutes, until mixture is puffed and cheese is golden brown. Slice and serve.

Blue cheese cole slaw

Prep time: 20 minutes

Cole slaw is a quintessential summer dish. Made with shredded cabbage and other vegetables, it goes well with burgers, hot dogs, and brats. This version, instead of featuring the classic dressing of mayonnaise, vinegar, and sugar, incorporates blue cheese to give the salad that special tangy flavor blue cheese lovers know and adore. The salad also gets creaminess from yogurt and crunch from such unusual additions as slivered almonds and apples.

Ingredients/Equipment:

8 oz. of white cabbage
1 stick celery
2 red tart apples, such as Gala or Jonathans

2 oz raisins

2 oz toasted slivered almonds

Ingredients/Equipment for the dressing:

5 oz plain yogurt

1 tbsp milk (optional)

2 oz crumbled blue cheese

1 tbsp chopped chives, fresh or dried

1 tbsp chopped parsley, fresh or dried

Salt and pepper to taste

Knife

Mixing bowl

Directions:

Shred cabbage as finely as possible and chop celery into small pieces. Cut the apples into small pieces and squeeze a little lemon juice over them to prevent browning. Mix ingredients in a bowl with the raisins and almonds. To prepare the dressing, mash the cheese with a fork and mix in the herbs and yogurt. Thin the dressing slightly with milk if desired. Salt and pepper to taste and toss the salad ingredients in the dressing.

The world's greatest macaroni and cheese

Prep time: 10 minutes

Cooking time: 45 minutes

Well, maybe not the greatest, but it is certainly in the top tier. This wonderful recipe features sharp cheddar and Parmesan cheeses, as well as cottage cheese and sour cream. The mixture of sharp and mild cheeses, as well as the tanginess of sour cream, create a rich and complex sauce that bears no resemblance to the box with the orange powder we all knew and loved as children. This is mac n' cheese for grown-ups, but kids will enjoy it too. It is simple enough to serve any night of the week, yet the sophistication of sour cream and Parmesan make it festive enough for a buffet supper.

Ingredients/Equipment:

1 8-oz package of elbow macaroni

8 oz shredded sharp cheddar cheese

12 oz cottage cheese

8 oz sour cream

⅓ cup grated Parmesan cheese

1 cup dry bread crumbs

¼ cup butter, melted

Salt and pepper to taste

Cooking pot

Colander

9x13 baking dish

Small mixing bowl

Directions:

1. Preheat oven to 375º Fahrenheit. Bring a large pot of lightly salted water to a boil, add macaroni and cook until tender. Drain.

2. In a 9 x 13 inch oven-proof baking dish, stir together cooked macaroni, all three cheeses, sour cream, and salt and pepper. In a small bowl, mix together breadcrumbs and melted butter. Sprinkle this mixture over the macaroni mixture.

3. Bake 30 to 35 minutes or until top is golden brown.

Scalloped potatoes with ham and havarti

Prep time: 20 minutes

Cooking time: 90 minutes

This recipe takes the old standby of scalloped potatoes and dresses it up with the mild creaminess of havarti. Ham and cream of mushroom soup also add flavor to this one-dish meal, but you could also use cream of celery or cheddar soup. Other additions include diced green pepper or parsley. This recipe serves six, so it makes a great weeknight dinner with a green salad and some bread.

Ingredients/Equipment:

5 or 6 medium baking potatoes, peeled and sliced

3 or 4 green onions or one small white onion, chopped

8 oz of ham, diced

1 can cream of mushroom or other creamy soup

½ cup milk

3 oz of havarti, diced

Salt and pepper to taste

Mixing bowl

2-quart baking dish

Knife

Directions:

1. Mix the soup with the milk until well-blended.

2. Using butter or a non-stick cooking spray, coat the bottom of a 2-quart baking dish.

3. Set aside one ounce of the diced cheese.

4. Layer potatoes, chopped onion, ham, and the rest of the cheese. Pour soup and milk mixture over the top and then top everything with the rest of the cheese.

5. Cover and bake at 350° for one hour. Remove cover and bake an additional 15-30 minutes until potatoes are tender and the top of the dish is golden brown.

Easy cream cheese Danish

Prep time: 10 minutes

Cooking time: 30 minutes

Use your homemade cream cheese to create this delicious Danish using refrigerated crescent dough. It bakes up in just 30 minutes, and since you do not have to mix the dough, you can easily make it for Sunday brunch and still have time to read the newspaper.

Ingredients/Equipment:

2 10 oz cans of refrigerated crescent dough

16 oz cream cheese, diced

¾ cup sugar

1 ½ tsps lemon juice

1 tsp vanilla extract

2 tsps sour cream

1 cup powdered sugar

1 tbsp milk

1 tbsp butter, softened

9x13 baking pan

Mixing bowl

Mixing spoon

Small bowl

Directions:

1. Preheat oven to 350° Fahrenheit. Lightly grease a 9x13 baking pan.

2. Line bottom of pan with one can of crescent rolls. Pinch all seams together to seal.

3. In a large bowl, mix together cream cheese, white sugar, lemon juice, vanilla, and sour cream. Spread filling on top of roll dough. Unroll second can of roll dough and place on top of filling.

4. Bake 20 to 30 minutes or until golden brown.

5. In a small bowl, mix together powdered sugar, milk, and butter. Drizzle icing over cooled Danish. Cut and serve.

Chapter Ten

Sharing the Bounty: Marketing Your Cheese

So you have started making cheese and are making really good cheese. Your family loves it, your friends love it, and you are having a great time. One morning, while standing in your newly constructed cheese cave, it hits you. *Hey! I could make money doing this!* Yes, you could. Kraft is not the only successful cheese maker in the country, and many local cheese makers started out just like you. However, before you run out and buy a herd of cows and 300 tomme molds, there are a great many factors to consider before trying to make and market your own cheese.

You Need a Plan

The greatest cheese in the world will not sell unless you have a solid plan for manufacturing, marketing, and distributing your wares. So grab a pad of paper and a pen, sit down, and start thinking up answers to the following questions.

How much time do I have to devote to making and selling cheese?

If you already have a 40-hour per week job, do you want to make cheese every night until midnight? Do you want to spend every weekend driving to differ-

ent farmers' markets? Do you want to stay awake until 3 a.m. packing boxes for mail-order customers? If you are just starting out, you probably will not be able to hire much help. If you have a particularly patient spouse or partner, you may have a total of two pairs of willing hands, but will that be enough? If you want this venture to be a success, you will need to devote a great deal of time and effort, not only to make the cheese, but to package and market it, not to mention the inevitable paperwork involved in a small business.

How much money will I need to invest?

Making cheese for sale means you will need more than one good cooking pot and a colander. At a minimum, you will need enough space and equipment to create a reasonable inventory. You will also need raw ingredients, wrapping paper, boxes, perhaps another refrigerator, a truck or van if you plan to haul cheese, some type of portable refrigeration if you plan to sell your cheese at a farmer's market, a stall or table for your wares, a canopy or banner, labels, shopping bags, and maybe a classy "Master Cheese Maker" apron. You can save some money by starting small, but there will still be significant expenses involved.

What about rules, regulations, and taxes?

In the United States, selling food is carefully regulated, and most of us would not want it any other way. Federal, state, and local regulations help ensure that our food is safe. If you want to sell cheese, or any other food product, you will have to learn and abide by these rules. You may have someone inspecting your kitchen or checking the temperature of your portable cooler. You may have to display a license or certificate to verify that your product is safe. You will have to carry liability insurance, just in case someone has an allergic reaction after eating your Brie. As a businessperson, you will also have to collect and pay any applicable taxes. Finally, you will need to keep meticulous records, both so you can see if you are making a profit and for tax time, as some of your equipment and supplies are deductible if you document them correctly.

What types of cheese should I make?

No one can start a cheese business and offer 100 different varieties right away. You will have to decide what will sell in your area and what you can make with the resources you have. If you are making and selling fresh goat's cheeses once a week at the local organic food store, you will need a completely different set of equipment and a different schedule than if you are making and selling 2-year-old cheddar. You may want to do some research and find out what types of cheeses are readily available in your area, and where a gap might be. That gap may be your best bet for creating a niche that your product can fill.

How do I market what I make?

Do you want to own a cheese shop? Do you want to sell online? Do you only want to sell at farmers' markets from May to September, or do you want your cheese in local gourmet shops year-round? Whatever your desire, you need to figure out how to get your cheese to the people who want it. That can take a great deal of trial and error, but if you identify your likely customers, you can come up with effective ways to let them know about your cheeses. You may also want to consider the competition. If you live in an area with 35 cheese makers who all make herbed goat cheese, perhaps you want to make cow's milk Colby instead.

All Questions Answered, Now What?

The legal steps

You have considered your options, and you realize that you want to make Brie-style cheese from organic milk. You have a source for the milk, and you have all the molds, equipment, and ripening space you need to make 60 cheeses a week. Now what?

First, find out what the laws are in your area. The United States Department of Agriculture (USDA) runs the Federal Food Safety and Inspection Service. The Federal Food and Drug Administration (FDA) also oversees food safety. Both organizations, as well as specific food inspection agencies in your state, can help you find out what you need to do to produce food that can be sold commercially. You will need to fill out an application to sell your cheeses, as well as submit to an inspection of your cheese-making facility. In addition to meeting federal guidelines, your state will probably have its own rules governing the handling and sale of food. Check with your state department of agriculture, food safety, or inspections to find out what you need to do to be compliant. In addition, there are both federal, and in many cases state, laws surrounding the issue of organic foods. If you wish to sell foods labeled "organic," be sure to familiarize yourself with these laws.

Depending on what state you sell your cheese in, you may or may not have to collect sales tax on the cheese you sell. If you are required to collect tax, you will need to contact your state's department of revenue and apply for a sales tax permit. You will then be required to pay the tax you collect on your sales to your state, usually on a quarterly basis. If sales tax is required, most markets will require you to produce your sales tax permit number before they allow you to sell at their venue. However, the responsibility for paying the appropriate sales tax still rests with you.

In addition to state and federal laws, there may be local laws that affect your business, whether they are health laws regarding how your kitchen needs to be set-up or zoning laws about selling foods from your home. Every area has different laws, so be sure to check your county or city laws regarding commercial production of foodstuffs.

As previously mentioned, it is also a good idea to have liability insurance to protect you in case a customer brings legal action against you. In addition, many farmers' markets and other venues will not allow you to sell your products unless you can prove you have liability insurance. For most small businesses, a $1-2 million liability policy is sufficient. These are not terribly expensive, usually only a few hundred dollars per year. Note, however, that if you produce cheese in your home, your homeowner's policy will not cover product liability; you need the specific business liability policy. Most major insurance companies offer this policy.

Make sure you keep accurate books. If you have a good head for math, keep your own spreadsheets of costs and sales. There are several excellent software packages, such as Quicken or QuickBooks, that can help you track what you spend and what you make. If you are not "math-gifted," see if you can find a self-employed bookkeeper to handle your books on a part-time basis. As noted, some of your expenses are tax-deductible if you authenticate them appropriately. You also need to know exactly how much it costs to produce and market your cheeses in order to know how to price them. You cannot do this without good records.

If you are serious about operating a small business, you will need to learn about the tax laws for your situation. As a business, you may be able to deduct costs including supplies, equipment, space for a home office, some travel, and even utilities. While there are many books and Web sites available to answer questions about taxes, your best bet is to find an accountant or tax preparer who specializes in small businesses. You want to maximize your deductions but still honor your obligations.

Branding yourself

There is also the question of logos and copyrights. If you just start out small, you probably do not need to design a logo or create a company name right away, but as your business grows, you may want to "brand" your products with a name and logo. You can register your company's name by going to Business.gov (**www.business.gov**) and following the links to the applications. If you have artistic talent, you can design your own logo, or most cities have freelance designers who can create logos for a reasonable price. Check your local phonebook or Craigslist.org for names. You can also have labels and packaging made for a reasonable price at various copy and printing businesses. When creating a name and logo, be sure that you are not using another company's trademarked brand. You can find out more about trademarks at the United States Patent and Trademark Office Web site (**www.uspto.gov**).

Most recipes cannot be copyrighted. However, as you create cheeses for sale, you may wish to register brand names or trademarks that are unique to your company and products. If your company grows beyond a local level, you should consult an attorney who specializes in trademarks and copyrights in order to protect your investment and your products.

Finding a market

Once the legalities are taken care of, you can start marketing your cheese. There are many possible avenues, some more complicated than others. The easiest and least expensive option is the local farmers' markets. Most farmers' markets are open to any qualified vendor, and the fee for participation is reasonable as well. Some markets require a flat rate for the whole season, but others will allow a vendor to pay for one session at a time. By showing up every Saturday for several weeks, offering free samples, and selling some product, you begin to create an identity for yourself and your product. If your cheese is a hit, word-of-mouth will soon bring more customers to your booth.

If you are a natural salesperson, you can market your cheese to local organic or gourmet stores. Pick a day and time when the manager is likely to be on duty but not particularly busy. Tuesday afternoon is often a good time to stop in and talk. Explain your product's selling points (natural ingredients, local producer, gourmet taste, etc.), leave a brochure or business card with your information, and offer to come in on a Saturday morning and provide free samples. While some chain stores do not have the flexibility to stock local products, many local markets welcome the added marketing opportunities and foot traffic a new product can provide. If you do get permission to offer samples, be courteous. Set up in a spot where you will not cause a traffic jam, and clean up after yourself when the tasting is over.

Local restaurants may provide another possible sales outlet for your cheese. As with stores, restaurants that specialize in gourmet offerings or fresh local produce are more likely to be receptive to your pitch than the drive-through burger joint.

Leave a sample of your product for the restaurant's manager or chef, if possible. They may be interested in purchasing cheese to serve their customers.

Finally, there are direct sales. In today's e-world, every type of product can be sold to customers almost anywhere. However, cheese, being a delicate and perishable product, can be difficult to sell online. If you do chose to use e-commerce, think through all the problems before launching your own website. For example, are there any laws you need to know about shipping cheese to another state or even another country? Will you need special insulated shipping containers? Will the cheese need to be transported in a refrigerated environment? How much will this add to your cost, and how much more will you have to charge your customers in order to make a profit? Finally, what do you do if someone orders 500 rounds of Brie, and you only have 30 in stock?

Creating a buzz

Selling the cheese is half the battle, and it can be easier if you know how to create a demand. Getting out there and sampling your cheese to potential customers is one of the easiest ways to get noticed, but there are other ways as well. Do not overlook any possibility to get your brand into the public consciousness. One good way to market yourself is to win an award for your cheese. Many state fairs and other festivals sponsor food contests. If they do not offer a cheese-making prize, perhaps there is a cooking category for the most creative use of cheese. Show up and cook with your product, and if you win, you have free publicity, not to mention bragging rights.

Do some research and find out about food publications and programs in your area, whether it is a newsletter, a cooking show on the local television station, or a weekly column in the local newspaper. Contact local food writers and critics and let them know about your product. If you can afford to run an ad, do so. If you can write an article (or find someone to do so) about your cheese, submit it. Most small publications of this kind need inexpensive articles, and they often have a genuine interest in promoting local foods and producers. If you are Internet savvy, consider creating a blog for your cheese-making operation. This is a great way to "meet" both customers and other cheese makers, exchange ideas, and publicize your operation.

Find out if there is a cheese-making organization in your area and join it. If no such organization exists, maybe you can start one. If there are only a few cheese makers in your area, create a broader organization of organic farmers, "slow food" advocates, gourmet gardeners, or whatever category appeals to you and fits your particular cheese-making operation. If there are wineries in your area, consider forming an alliance with these producers. A wine and cheese tasting, featuring all local products, is a great marketing tool.

Just do it!

If making cheese is really your passion, and you have worked out a plan, covered all the legal bases, and researched your market, go ahead and begin to produce cheese for sale. As noted, you do not have to produce 100 types at once, and you can control the amount of sales by picking and choosing your sales outlets. Start small, sell a few wheels at the local market, and see where it goes. Making and selling cheese can be a rewarding hobby, a second income, or a full-time business. It all depends on your willingness to invest time, money, and talent in creating and marketing the best cheese you have to offer.

Chapter Eleven

Getting Connected

Whether you are making cheese to enjoy at home or trying to create a business selling your wares, you need to know where to get the necessary ingredients and supplies. You may also want to connect with other cheese makers, just to see what else you have never tried. While there are probably hundreds of possible suppliers and organizations for you to investigate, this section gives you the most accessible suppliers and the best-known organizations. However, do some investigating on your own. Local suppliers and fellow cheese makers are great resources and easy to contact, with the added benefit of face-to-face interaction.

Milk

As previously discussed, quality milk is the number one necessity for creating good cheese. While some store-bought milk will work for some recipes, what if you need non-pasteurized milk or a reliable source of goat's or sheep's milk? What if you want certified organic milk? Your best bet is to start at the source.

The National Dairy Council (**www.nationaldairycouncil.org**) offers a directory of milk producers in each state at **www.nationaldairycouncil.org/AboutNDC/ DairyCouncilDirectory/Pages/DairyCouncilDirectory.aspx**.

This is an excellent first step in finding milk producers in your area because the directory links you with state dairy councils. Now, not every producer can sell milk directly to the public, but those who do will provide you with the freshest milk possible. There are also smaller organizations of producers who offer specific types of milk. These include the following:

The Wisconsin Sheep Dairy Association

www.sheepmilk.biz

Spooner Ag Research Station

W6646 Highway 70

Spooner, WI 54801

(800) 409-7953, ext. 2 (p)

The American Dairy Goat Association

www.adga.org

P.O. Box 865

Spindale, NC 28160

(828) 286-3801 (p)

(828) 287-0476 (f)

Northeast Organic Milk Producers Alliance

www.nodpa.com

30 Keets Rd.

Deerfield, MA 01342

(413) 772-0444 (p)

(866) 554-9483 (f)

Midwest Organic Dairy Producers Alliance

P.O. Box 1772

Madison, WI 53701

(608) 260-0900 (p/f)

Western Organic Dairy Producers Alliance

www.wodpa.org

Attn: Dr. Cindy Daley

College of Agriculture

California State University, Chico

400 West First Street

Chico, CA 95929-0310

(530) 898-5844 (p)

However, the easiest way to obtain good-quality milk is to investigate local organic and farmers' markets to find sources in your own area. Do not be afraid to ask for referrals or suggestions. Most producers love to talk about their operation, and they are always looking for new customers.

Cheese-making Supplies and Equipment

Unless you plan to create a cheese empire, you should start small when purchasing equipment. Good-quality cooking pots, colanders, cheese knives, and thermometers can be purchased at kitchen stores, department stores, and even discount stores. Your two most important pieces of equipment are your cooking pot and thermometer, so be sure to buy the best quality pieces you can afford. Too much or too little heat will ruin any type of cheese.

If you live in a large metropolitan area, you may have access to hobby stores or wine shops that sell brewing equipment. These outlets will carry some of the other items you need, including various sizes of cheese molds, skimmers, cheesecloth, and cultures and mold powders. If there are no such stores in your area, you may have to rely on mail order to fill your needs. There are hundreds of supply houses online. Here are some of the best-known. These companies carry a complete line of cheese-making products, which means you can get everything you need with one-stop shopping.

New England Cheesemaking Supply Company

www.cheesemaking.com

One of the best-known suppliers, their Web site also offers recipes and trouble-shooting tips, as well as links to other cheese makers and organizations.

54B Whately Road

South Deerfield, MA 01373

(413) 397-2012 (p)

(413) 628-4061 (f)

The Cheesemaker

www.thecheesemaker.com

A fairly small but quite complete online supply house, featuring books, cheese-making kits, additives and other supplies, and cheese presses, as well as information on cheese-making workshops offered by the site's proprietor, Steve Shapson.

c/o Cedarburg Home Brewing and Wine

W62 N590 Washington Ave.

Cedarburg, WI 53012

(414) 745-5483 (p)

Glengarry Cheesemaking and Dairy Supply Ltd.

www.glengarrycheesemaking.on.ca

Although this is a Canadian company, they have a New York office for U.S. shipments, so customs is not an issue.

P.O. Box 92

Massena, NY 13662

1-888-816-0903 (p)

Grape and Granary

www.thegrape.net

This company offers supplies for wine and beer brewing as well as cheese making.

915 Home Ave.

Akron, ON 44310

(800) 695-9870 (p)

Dairy Connection, Inc.

www.dairyconnection.com

This is a slightly smaller, less overwhelming company that caters to both the hobbyist and professional cheese maker. They have an excellent selection of rennet and cultures, as well as an extensive line of molds and forms to shape various cheeses.

501 Tasman St., Suite B

Madison, WI 53714

(608) 242-9030 (p)

(608) 242-9036 (f)

Wind Dance Vineyard and Cheese Making Supplies

http://winddancevineyard.com

This is another fairly small and accessible supplier. They have all the basics: molds, rennet, starter cultures, and presses. They also have a hotline for calls from cheese makers in trouble.

P.O. Box 257

Delano MN 55328

(612) 205-2420 (p)

Micro/Essential Laboratories

www.microessentiallab.com

This company offers a line of pH testing strips and meters.

P.O. Box 100824 |

4224 Avenue H |

Brooklyn, New York 11210

(718) 338.3618 (p) |

(718) 692.4491 (f)

Organizations for Cheese Makers

There are many large and small organizations for cheese makers. There are also websites and blogs where both hobbyist and professional cheese makers meet to share ideas. A complete list of these organizations would make a book in itself, but here are some of the best-known and most accessible:

American Cheese Society

www.cheesesociety.org

This is a national organization to promote American cheeses and cheese makers. They have an annual conference for cheese makers, as well as a yearly competition for the best American-made cheeses.

California Artisan Cheese Guild

www.cacheeseguild.org

This site celebrates the cheese makers of California.

Cheese Underground

http://cheeseunderground.blogspot.com

This blog features profiles of small-scale cheese makers from all over the United States.

Curd Nerds

http://curdnerds.com

This is a blog for cheese lovers and cheese makers, with links to suppliers, organizations, and articles about cheese.

New York State Farmstead and Artisan Cheese Makers Guild

www.nyfarmcheese.org

This is an organization for professional cheese makers both large and small in New York State.

The Pacific Northwest Cheese Project

http://pnwcheese.typepad.com

This organization is dedicated to West Coast cheese producers. It has a blog, along with an extensive directory of cheese makers from this area.

The Southern Cheesemakers Guild

www.southerncheese.com

This organization is for small-scale commercial cheese makers in the South.

The Vermont Cheese Council

www.vtcheese.com

This organization promotes and supports Vermont cheese makers.

Wisconsin Dairy Artisan Network

www.wisconsindairyartisan.com

This organization provides information to cheese makers in Wisconsin.

Final Thoughts

Congratulations! You now know just about everything you will ever need to know to make and enjoy fine cheeses. Whether this is the beginning of a fun hobby or a rewarding career, do not be afraid to use this book as your launching pad into glory. Remember the basics:

- Start small and simple.

- Use the freshest milk you can buy.

- Make sure you have the right ingredients and equipment.

- Clean cheese is happy cheese.

- Follow the directions exactly.

- Have patience; even the best cheese makers deal with an occasional flop.

- Have fun! This is not rocket science; it is cheesy science, and unlike most science projects, you can eat the results.

- If you decide to sell your wares, do your research and obey the rules before you sell the first wedge.

- Do not be afraid to ask for help. Cheese makers have a passion for their craft, and they like to share that passion.

Now go forth and get cheesy!

Glossary of Terms

Acidity: The measurement of sourness in a cheese recipe.

Affinage: A French term referring to the ripening and aging process of any cheese. This process can takes days, weeks, or months and can include such steps as soaking the cheese in brine, washing the rind, piercing the cheese to allow mold growth, turning the cheese to help it ripen, and placing it in a ripening or aging container at specific temperatures and levels of humidity.

Annatto: A coloring made from the seeds of a South American plant; annatto is added to many cheddar recipes to give the cheese the traditional yellow color.

Butter muslin: A finely woven cloth, similar to cheesecloth but with a tighter weave. It is often used to drain fresh cheeses, which have smaller curds than cooked cheeses.

Calcium chloride: This salt solution is added to many cheese recipes, especially where the milk being used has been pasteurized. Calcium chloride works with rennet to produce a firmer curd.

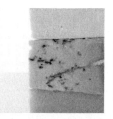

Cheesecloth: This thin cotton cloth is used to drain the curds in recipes for hard cheese. It is also sometimes used to line cheese molds.

Clean break: The point in cheese making where the curd cuts cleanly with a knife. A clean break is vital for nearly all ripened, washed-rind, blooming rind, or aged cheeses.

Cold water bath: The process of using a large pot filled with cold tap water and ice cubes. The cooking pot with the cheese or curds is put into this bath to cool the mixture quickly as needed.

Curd: The step in cheese making after the cheese has been cooked and/or treated with enzymes or rennet. Curd is the firm coagulated milk that results from this process, and it is the part of the milk that is made into cheese.

Curd knife: This is a long-bladed stainless steel knife with a rounded instead of pointed end. It is used to cut curds during the cheese-making process, not to cut the finished cheese.

Emulsifiers: Ingredients that bind together non-combative elements such as oil and water. Emulsifiers help make mixtures smooth and creamy, and they keep elements from separating.

Homogenized: Milk that has been processed so that the fat particles are emulsified and do not separate from the body of the milk.

Hot water bath: The act of putting the ingredients in a cooking pot into a larger pot filled with water and then applying heat. This is a similar principle as the double-boiler. Its purpose is to control heat more precisely and prevent scorching of milk and other ingredients.

Hygrometer: This instrument measures the humidity level of a container or ripening area. It is important when making many types of cheese, especially bacteria-and mold-ripened cheeses.

Instant-read thermometer: A common kitchen-use thermometer that when inserted into a mixture gives a temperature reading within ten seconds.

Lactose intolerant: A person who is sensitive to the lactose (a natural sugar) found in milk. People who are lactose intolerant have difficulty in breaking down this sugar, which cause them to suffer digestive distress.

Matting: The process of curds knitting together into a springy mass.

Mesophilic starter culture: A specific culture added to cheese recipes that cook at less than 102° Fahrenheit. This culture provides acidity and flavor to cheeses.

Mesophilic-m starter culture: A specific variety of mesophilic culture called for in some cheese recipes.

Mold: A form used to shape cheeses.

Non-homogenized: Milk that has not been homogenized. In non-homogenized milk, the cream will rise to the surface and must be skimmed off or mixed back into the body of the milk.

Pasta filata: A cheese that is heated and stretched in hot water to create a chewy texture. Mozzarella is a pasta filata cheese.

Paste: The body or inside of a cheese, as separate from the rind or the veins of mold.

Pasteurized: Milk that has been treated with heat or radiation to kill bacteria.

Penicillium candidum: A white mold that grows on the surface of specific cheese such as Brie or Camembert, which helps the paste of the cheese soften during ripening.

Penicillum roqueforti: A blue mold that produces the characteristic "veins" in such cheeses as Roquefort and Stilton. This mold also adds flavor and acidity to the cheese.

pH Balance: The balance of acid to alkaline components in any recipe.

Pressing: The act of expelling whey from cheese in order to knit the curd together.

Raw milk: Milk that has not been pasteurized.

Rennet: A blend of enzymes originally made from the stomach of young calves, kids, or lambs. Rennet is available in solid or tablet form, and a vegetable rennet is now available as well.

Rind: The outer covering or "skin" on a cheese.

Skimmer: This is a flat, long-handled tool, somewhat like a flat spoon, that is used to cut curd or to skim slices of curd from the larger mass.

Thermophilic starter culture: A specific culture added to cheese recipes that cook at more than 102° Fahrenheit. This culture provides acidity and flavor to cheeses.

Tomme mold: A commonly used round mold for cheese making. A tome mold is used to create the classic "wheel" shaped cheese.

Trier: This is a stainless steel instrument that is poked into a ripening cheese and removes a small sample of cheese from the core for tasting. A trier is especially useful when making cheddar or other cheeses that age for a long time and change taste as they age.

Ultra-pasteurized: Milk that has been exposed to an ultra high heat or radiation process. Such milk is shelf-stable (it does not spoil), but because all helpful bacteria have been killed during this process, it is not recommended for cheese making.

Washed-rind cheese: A natural rind cheese that is regularly wiped during the aging process with a cloth soaked in salt brine, ripening bacteria, or liquids such as wine, beer, or cider.

Whey: The liquid in milk that is expelled from the curd during the cheese-making process. Fresh whey can be used in other recipes, notably in making ricotta cheese. However, fresh whey must be used within two hours of its production during the cheese making process.

ℬibliography

Amrein-Boyes, Debra, 200 Easy Homemade Cheese Recipes, Robert Rose, Inc. Toronto, 2009.

Berger, Yves M., "Sheep's milk and its uses," Wisconsin Sheep Dairy Cooperative, <**www.sheepmilk.biz**> accessed November 23, 2009.

Carroll, Ricki, Home Cheese Making: Recipes for 75 Homemade Cheeses, Third edition, Storey Publishing, North Adams, 2002.

Cheese Club Archives, "Let's Bust Some Myths," **http://www.squidoo.com/ cheeseclub-archives**

Cheese Forum.org, "Cheese Making Equipment, Cheese Caves," **http://www. cheeseforum.org/Making/Cheese%20Caves.htm**

Cheese-France, "Chaource," **http://www.cheese-france.com/cheese/chaource. htm**

Cheesemaking.com, "Setting Up Your Own Cheese Cave," **www.cheesemaking. com/includes/modules/jWallace/OnLineNews/NewsFiles/Cave/Cave2.html**

Cookthink.com, "What is Monterey Jack Cheese?" **www.cookthink.com/refer-ence/95/What_is_Monterey_Jack_cheese?**

Corks and Curds.com, "Myths about Moldy Cheese," **http://corksandcurds. blogspot.com/2007/08/myths-about-moldy-cheese.html**

Dairy Farming Today.org, "Facts and Figures," **www.dairyfarmingtoday.org/ DairyFarmingToday/Learn-More/Facts-And-Figures/**

Dairy Sheep Association of North America, "Dairy/Milk," **www.dsana.org/dairy. html**

De Groot, Roy Andries, In Search of the Perfect Meal: A Collection of the Best Food Writings of Roy Andries De Groot, St. Martin Publishing, London, 1986.

Fallon, Peggy, Great Party Fondues, John Wiley & Sons, Inc., Hoboken, NJ, 2008.

Food Reference.com, "Feta Cheese," **www.foodreference.com/html/artfe-tacheese.html**

Forristal, Linda Joyce, "In the Kitchen with Mother Linda: Ultra-Pasteurized Milk," The Weston A. Price Foundation, <**www.westonaprice.org/motherlinda/ ultra-pasteurizedmilk.html**>, accessed November 27, 2009.

"Gogonzola," **www.gorgonzola.org/cheese**

Harris Jr., Barnett, and Springer, Frederick, "Dairy goat production guide," University of Florida Extension, <**http://edis.ifas.ufl.edu/ds134**>, accessed November 25, 2009.

"History of Limburger Cheese," **http://whatscookingamerica.net/History/Lim-burgerCheese.htm**

Johnson, Nathanael, "The Revolution will not be Pasteurized: Inside the Raw-milk Underground," Harper's Magazine, April 4, 2008, <**www.harpers.org/ar-chive/2008/04/0081992**> accessed November 27, 2009.

Kayal, Michelle, "Creating the Perfect Cheese Board," Richmond Times-Dispatch, December 23, 2009, **www2.timesdispatch.com/rtd/lifestyles/food_cooking/ article/F-CHES23_20091222-180203/313035/**

Lambert, Paula. Cheese, Glorious Cheese! More than 75 Tempting Recipes for Cheese Lovers Everywhere, Simon & Schuster, New York, NY, 2007.

Nair, Lindsey, "Of Grace and Gouda: Crozet Nuns Make Handmade Cheese," The Roanoke Times, November 15, 2009, <www.roanoke.com.extra.wb/226216> accessed November 25, 2009.

The Nibble.com, "Cheese Glossary," www.thenibble.com/reviews/main/cheese/cheese2/glossary8.asp

The Nibble.com, "The Difference Between Brie and Camembert," www.thenibble.com/REVIEWS/main/cheese/cheese2/whey/brie-camembert.asp

The Nibble.com, "Matching Cheese with Beer & Wine," www.thenibble.com/reviews/main/cheese/cheese2/cheese-and-beer2.asp

Practically Edible.com, "History Notes for Esrom Cheese," www.practicallyedible.com/edible.nsf/pages/esromcheese

Practically Edible.com, "Leerdammer Cheese," www.practicallyedible.com/edible.nsf/pages/leerdammercheese

Stilton Cheese.com, "History of Stilton," www.stiltoncheese.com/history_of_stilton

Smith, Tim, Making Artisan Cheese: 50 Fine Cheeses That You Can Make in Your Own Kitchen, Quaryside Publishing Group, Beverly, MA, 2005.

Victor Rodent Control "Myths and Half_Truths," www.victorpest.com/advice/rodents-101/myths

Wernick, Robert. "Roquefort," www.robertwernick.com/articles/Roquefort.shtml

Woman's Passions.com, "Cheese Myths: Let's Refute Rumors," www.womanspassions.com/articles/1453.html

Author Biography

Cynthia Martin is an author, college English instructor, and craftsperson. For fun, she cooks, cans, grows herbs, decorates cakes, crochets, and embroiders. For profit, she creates handcrafted jewelry, candles, and a line of natural bath and body products for sale through her company, Pretty Pig Products. In her spare time, she is an avid reader and antique hunter. She lives in Iowa with three cats and three ferrets.

Index

R

S

T

U

Ultra-pasteurized, 328, 34-36, 57, 65, 325

W

Washed-rind cheese, 105-106, 156, 215, 325

Whey, 329, 17, 24, 28, 40, 47, 49, 72, 75-76, 78, 85, 87-88, 91-96, 100-102, 104, 108, 110-112, 114, 117, 119, 122, 124-125, 128, 130-131, 133-134, 136, 139, 143, 146, 149, 151, 153, 155, 157-158, 161, 166, 172, 174, 176, 178, 184-185, 187, 189-190, 192, 200, 203, 205-206, 208, 211, 213, 220, 223, 226, 229, 232, 236, 242, 247, 249, 252-254, 257-258, 260-261, 263, 266, 269-270, 272, 274-275, 277-278, 284, 324-325

Y

Yogurt, 12, 29, 33, 35, 37, 59, 61-65, 68, 70, 86, 88, 196, 280, 300-301, 10